THE OLD-HOUSE RESCUE BOOK:

Buying and Renovating on a Budget

The Old-House Rescue Book:

Buying and Renovating on a Budget

Robert Kangas

Reston Publishing Company, Inc.
A Prentice-Hall Company
Reston, Virginia

Title page art provided by
David Hodges of
Just Your Type
Philadelphia, Pennsylvania

Library of Congress Cataloging in Publication Data

Kangas, Robert.
   The old-house rescue book.

   Includes index.
   1. Dwellings – Remodeling – Handbooks,
manuals, etc. 2. House buying – Handbooks,
manuals, etc.
I. Title.
TH4816.K36   643.7   81-17841
ISBN 0-8359-5214-2   AACR2
ISBN 0-8359-5213-4   pbk.

10   9   8   7   6   5   4   3   2   1

Printed in the United States of America

To

MOTHER AND FATHER

Contents

Introduction

10   PLASTER, PAINT, AND WALLPAPER PROJECTS   139

11   MASONRY PROJECTS   159

12   PLUMBING PROJECTS   181

Introduction

This book was written to help people who want to renovate old houses with their own hands.

Buying an old house in rundown condition and fixing it with your own labor may be the only way to avoid the inflated prices of new construction. Renovation may be a way to bring back and enjoy a style and quality of living that has escaped most of us. Renovating can become a consuming passion when a person painstakingly restores and rebuilds a building for personal and historical reasons.

Whatever leads you to want to renovate an old house with your own hands, you will need some basic tools. This book is one of those tools. It contains formulas, checklists, procedures, and resources for most situations that you are likely to encounter.

This is also an idea book. It will help you find a house for the least money, and will show you how to recycle old materials and use new materials in unusual ways. All of the methods have been tested, and they work. You will save money with them, and they can suggest other ideas that you can use in your special situation.

The focus is on simplicity at all times. You will be able to think of more complicated projects than the ones described, but the basic projects here can get you started—and it's been my experience that the hardest thing in renovation is to get started.

The whole idea behind renovating on a budget is to buy an old house that is basically sound and hasn't been modernized. You then repair or replace the basic systems. You uncover and restore the walls, floors, and woodwork that wait under many layers of paint, wallpaper, and linoleum, and you recycle old fixtures, adapt inexpensive new ones, and use a minimum of new construction to fit the house for your needs.

This use of as much of the original house as possible is what makes the method so economical. For that reason, this book will take you away from materials like paneling and drop ceilings, which cover up, and bring you to methods and materials that will uncover and reveal what is already there.

Because buying a house with the potential for being inexpensively renovated is so important, the book opens with that process. Tools and materials are discussed next, with the emphasis on simplicity and economy. Happily, the few classic tools and materials you will need are inexpensive and durable.

The largest chapter in the book is devoted to basic systems. The life-support lines of your house are described so that you can plan, repair, and replace them. These systems will involve the most complicated and costly work that you will do on your house. I hope to show you that basic house systems are less complicated and more forgiving than those on your car. In many cases you can install a new system by following the path of the old. You simply buy and replace what was once there. This imitation approach works well for the novice renovator and is a way to teach yourself plumbing and heating skills. I will describe the standard parts so that you can order what you need to repair or replace each system.

Fixtures are discussed with an eye to recycling and adapting. There may be many fixtures worth repairing in your old house, and you will be able to find or buy usable ones from other sources. In many cases, the quality and design of the fixtures you repair and adapt will be better than those of new ones.

Painting and finishing complete the text portion of the book. The methods and materials described here are the basics for inexpensive but professional finishing touches.

Following the discussion of the projects is a brief glossary of words and terms that are used in the book but are not defined fully in the text because that would slow up the discussion of the procedures. These words are defined conversationally, as if you were talking to a builder or a fellow renovator. Renovators need to know some of the professional jargon of the building industry, but they also need to know how these words affect them directly and how they relate to the procedures in this book.

At the very end of the book are a few pages of construction and renovation lore. This is information that didn't quite fit into any of the text or projects and is too basic to be a part of the glossary. The hints and tricks here are borrowed from experienced renovators and will help you to handle some special situations that may arise.

⤙ACKNOWLEDGMENTS

I would like to thank Hanley Bodek and Margaret Sigler for their invaluable assistance. I also appreciate the help of the University of Pennsylvania's Department of Architecture, which allowed me to use line drawings that begin some of the chapters. The photograph of the house that appears at the beginning of each chapter was provided with the kind permission of Carol and Sidney Williams, and I am grateful for their immeasurable help. The photograph was taken by Lee Carlson.

1

DEVON

WINSTON ROAD

WINSTON COURT

FIELD AVENUE

SITE PLAN

0   50   100   150   200

1

Buying and Inspecting a Property

Real estate people say that the three things to consider when shopping for a home are: location, location, and location. For our purposes, we can amend that saying to location, location, and condition.

You want to think of location in two ways. First, is the property well placed in terms of transportation, work, schools, shopping, and other amenities? Second, and this is where the renovator differs from the regular buyer, how does location fit into your long-range plans for fixing up and living in the house?

Occasionally a rundown house can be found in a neighborhood of well-kept homes. Perhaps the property suffered a fire or a long succession of careless renters, or it has been vacant for years while an estate was settled. More commonly, houses ripe for renovation will be part of whole neighborhoods that have become dilapidated or abandoned.

This is where your search becomes tricky. Obviously, you don't want to invest your time and money in a neighborhood that is still on the way down. Ask the real estate agent about the history of the area, what happened to make the area decline, and what is being done to restore the area.

You can tell a lot about an area by making several tours in your car and on foot. Look for signs of renovation. Check such things as the mix of private residences and apartment buildings. An area with an abundance of rental units can be difficult to bring back once it is run down. Too many rental units in a neighborhood can create problems with parking, street noise, and the neglect of the buildings by tenants and absentee landlords.

Positive signs are new construction, owner-occupied buildings, and the basic soundness of the housing stock. A neighborhood of single-family houses is often a good bet for restoration because the residents will tend to have the same ideals and aspirations for each other's houses and the area in general.

In almost every city where renovation activity is going on, the lines are pretty clear. Certain sections become attractive and are renovated; then the action jumps across town or expands to adjacent areas. Study community newspapers, classified real estate ads, and a city map to identify renovation activity. Talk to people who are already renovating for their opinions on neighborhoods and the path of progress.

People and places to check for information include contractors who do renovations, real estate offices in and around the neighborhoods, banks and savings-and-loan associations, city hall (some cities have earmarked certain sections for renewal and will be glad to advise you on their plans), neighborhood associations, and planning and zoning commissions.

Location is as important in renovation as it is in conventional real estate. You must research carefully and completely with your eye to the future. Areas can change quickly, and you may be surprised that a quiet little street of three years ago is now a traffic-clogged nightmare because the city decided to promote commercial and night-life business two blocks away.

One more thought on location—the best values in property are likely to be on the fringe areas of your chosen neighborhood. As things become more risky and speculative, the price drops. If you wish to buy a bargain property, you can take a more intelligent risk if you arm yourself with some of the research mentioned above. The reward for guessing where the next hot neighborhood will be is a prime property for a bargain price.

Some neighborhoods become so fashionable as to rule out the bargain hunter. Shells with nothing in them but floors and walls can be priced at what a new house costs and more. Some historically or architecturally distinguished neighborhoods may have limits on the kind and quality of renovation that can be done. All of these factors can drive the cost of housing beyond your reach.

CONDITION

Once you have narrowed your search to specific neighborhoods, inspect as many properties as you can. Don't limit yourself to the offerings of one agent. By seeing the range of houses available, you can be more sure of what is a fair value. Make notes after each inspection tour, and review them before going out to see other houses. You will quickly get a feel for the market in your area, and when it comes time to make a deal, you can bargain from some firm knowledge and not emotion.

The most important aspect of a house that you plan to renovate inexpensively is the physical layout. You do not want to do much in the way of moving walls, stairs, or other major elements of the house. You will have plenty on your hands without altering the floorplan. If you feel that you cannot live with the way the house is set up, you should forget that property and move on.

Next in importance is the actual condition of the house. This can range from a shell, which is a roof, walls, floors and little else, to a handy man's special, which is a house with all systems intact but with worn out or obsolete fixtures, inadequate wiring and plumbing, and an ancient heating plant.

Buying and inspecting property is fraught with emotion. It's an activity most people don't do very often, and caution and common sense escape them at times. I would advise going back two or three times to a property that interests you. Between your inspections, consult this book and the projects in it to decide what you can and cannot do to the house.

INSPECTION CHECKLIST

It is very easy to miss things (even things as obvious as radiators, windows, and doors) in the heat of inspecting a property. Your imagination renovates each room as you pass through. You need a checklist for the important items—the ones that can save or cost you big money.

Exterior

Roof. Check the design. A flat, tarred roof is easy to repair on your own. Sloped roofs of slate, copper, or shingles are more difficult and expensive to work on. Steeply pitched roofs on three-story or higher buildings are extremely difficult to work on and may require a professional contractor for repair or replacement.

Windows. Count how many need to be replaced and would need security hardware. Inspect the frames for rot by probing with a knife. Sound frames can be reglazed with new glass and putty by an amateur. Rotted or broken frames must be replaced with new wood or metal windows, and replacement of windows is a job for a contractor or skilled amateur.

Brickwork. Check for settlement by looking for jagged cracks near windows and doors. Detect bowing of the walls by sighting down the building, leaning out of the highest window. There are cures for minor masonry problems, but major structural flaws should disqualify the house or have the advice of a structural engineer. Inspect the mortar joints. If the mortar is more than ⅛ inch below the surface, the house may need pointing, which is tedious labor but it can be done by the amateur. A white deposit on masonry is efflorescence, which can be removed by washing down with an acid solution.

Although both of these buildings are in rough condition inside, they are basically sound. This shot shows how straight the walls have remained.

Gutters and Eaves. Evaluate carefully. Since this is high-ladder work, you may not want to do any of it yourself. A few problems like painting and small patching are okay, but think twice about any three-story or higher building with complicated and deteriorated trim.

Frame Houses. Inspect the lines of the house to detect any sagging or out-of-square condition. Sight along the roof ridge (from the upper story of an adjacent building) and the four corners. Note the type and condition of the exterior skin. Determine if the skin would have to be painted, repaired, or replaced.

Interior

Roof Leakage. Check for water damage (usually appearing as brown spots on plaster or wallpaper) on the highest ceiling. Peeling wallpaper or stained attic beams also signal leaks. Once a leak is stopped, water damage can usually be repaired by scraping, spackling, and repainting.

Settlement. Look again at doors and windows. Large cracks in plaster and tears in wallpaper indicate excessive settlement. Sometimes windows and doorways will be knocked out of square by settlement. Sticky doors and windows may also indicate this problem. Check floors by getting down on your hands and knees and sighting along their length. Excessive humps and waves may point to structural problems that you would be better off avoiding. Sometimes things will settle so badly that the whole interior has a caved-in look. Walls, windows, doors, stairs all seem to be on a lean. You *must* avoid situations like this; you could go crazy and broke trying to

get everything back into line. The most settlement you should accept in any house is one or two problems that you feel you can cure. Rebuilding three square feet of brickwork will give you plenty of work.

Hidden Damage. Check in the basement for evidence of termite or dry rot damage. Probe beams with a penknife, and don't accept softness that extends more than ¼ inch in depth. Note any sagging, replaced, or jacked-up beams, which might indicate problems below the surface. Replacing structural lumber is expensive and requires expertise and a crew of workers.

Foundation. Make a final check on settlement problems by looking at the basement. Large cracks, bowed walls, and excessive deterioration of the masonry are big problems. Dampness or water in the basement is often a drainage problem. There are good procedures for this if you are willing to work at it.

Stairs. Check for basic soundness. You can replace individual treads and tighten up loose bannisters, but you should avoid total-loss staircases because they are tricky and expensive to rebuild.

Floors. Do some detective work here. Pry up old rugs, linoleum, etc., and see what the real floor is. You may find hardwood in good condition. Hard and soft wood floors that are sound but need sanding are fine, but avoid houses with floors that are burnt, rotted, or excessively patched. New sub and finish flooring is expensive and requires much time to install correctly.

<u>A Badly Deteriorated Upper Floor.</u> Water from an open window and a leaky roof has rotted a section of flooring away. This house would require new flooring and perhaps one or two new joists. The price would have to be low to justify buying this building.

<u>A Shell with a Sagging Window.</u> The window is sagging because the brickwork around it is deteriorated. The window would have to be rebuilt and a new unit installed. The rest of the house is pretty much in square. If you could deal with the window problem, this might be a good shell to work on.

A Bad Risk for Renovation. This house has structural problems. The upper windows are starting to lean outwards. There are settlement cracks under windows. The metal star to the left of the front door tells that the front of the building is bowing outward and an attempt was made to stop it. Part of the cornice is rotted.

Side View of the Same House. A poor stucco job and deteriorated roof have combined to let the weather in to attack the structure. Many bricks are gone, and most are eaten away or undermined. A professional would have a bad time with this house. The interior has a caved-in look, and most of the floors are rotten.

Walls and Ceilings. Aside from large settlement cracks, don't worry about walls and ceilings too much. Note how many rooms have plaster intact, how many need large patching, and how many should be demolished and redone with drywall. Walls and ceilings are easily worked on, and most people have good results with their own labor.

This shell has had only one layer of wallpaper for its whole life, and even this is coming off by itself. The plaster underneath is in good condition. The window frame is rough but restorable. In all, it is a very good bet for simple and inexpensive renovation.

Woodwork. Make a note of how much woodwork is intact, including doors, cabinets, baseboards, and moldings around doors and windows. Unless wood has been burned or chopped, it can be restored with paint remover and patience. Original woodwork that has been removed or heavily damaged must be replaced by new wood or salvaged woodwork. Finding or reproducing woodwork to match is tedious and frustrating, so you may want to install simple strips of new wood in some rooms.

Kitchens and Bathrooms. This is where a house that checks out well in all other areas can fall short. Are the fixtures outmoded, broken, or missing altogether? You can spend a lot of money in a short time on bathrooms and kitchens. A good sign is that fixtures are in a workable layout, which saves you money. You can replace elements one at a time without disturbing the whole system. Also check to see if the kitchen and bath are ganged, that is, do the two areas share the same water supply and drainage system? This arrangement saves you money if you have to replace broken pipes.

Basic Systems

Heating Plant. First, is there one? Determine whether it is working or not. If in doubt, assume the worst. Is it coal, gas, or oil? The only acceptable furnaces are gas or oil (or in rare cases, a coal furnace converted to oil). If the furnace is oil and in doubtful condition, check the oil tank to make sure it exists, and see what condition it's in. If the tank seems intact, that's a hopeful sign. Gas furnaces that have been kept dry are often functional despite neglect.

Ducts and Radiators. Inspect the hot air ducts or hot water pipes that carry heat to the house. Again, these can

The roof in the foreground is covered with pebbles. This was done to help preserve the roof below. Before you can fix or replace this roof, you must shovel these pebbles onto the ground and haul them away. This is an example of the kind of surprise that may be waiting for you when you buy a shell. See if you can get on the roof of a house before buying it, or check it out from a neighboring house.

Back View of a Good House for Renovation. The windows would have to be replaced, but the brickwork is in excellent condition. The joints look like they have been pointed in the last ten years. The roof has a very gentle slope, which makes it easy to work on.

give a clue to the condition of the furnace. If they are in good shape, you will have saved hundreds of dollars right there. Follow the ducts and pipes as well as you can through the rest of the house. Do the ducts terminate in registers? Do the pipes connect with radiators? If so, the worst thing you will have to do is replace the furnace to get the heat on. If the ducts become twisted husks of rusty steel somewhere between the first and second floor or half the radiators are cracked or missing, you have a considerable expense facing you.

Drainage System. In a shell, the cast-iron sewage pipes are likely to be broken, rusted through, or perhaps gone entirely. Inspect the situation as closely as possible; the condition of the exposed pipes in the basement is all you can go by. If the pipes still have useful life (strong, unflaky walls) left in them, you will have saved several thousand dollars.

Plumbing System. This consists of the hot- and cold-water supply pipes. Trace the system from the water meter in the basement to the kitchen and bathrooms. Note the hot-water heater (if there is one). In shells, you can assume that it's worthless. The best situation is fairly new water pipes of copper or brass (scrape them with a penknife to check). These pipes can be salvaged. Less good is iron or steel pipe (it has noticeable threaded fittings), which tends to close up with minerals over the years and can rust into uselessness when not in use. If the house has lead pipes, you know that it's a real antique, probably with pull-chain waterclosets. Unless the system is of copper or brass, forget what's there and think in terms of replacing it all with new copper tubing.

Electrical. If the house isn't being used right up to the time you inspect it, don't trust the wiring unless it's been replaced in the last five years. In a property that is livable, go into the basement and find out the size of the fuse box or circuit-breaker box. Anything less than 100 amps means inadequate wiring. When you inspect a shell just assume that you will replace the wiring.

Porches, Sheds, Walks, and Trees. Finally, you should inspect the condition of any porches or sheds attached to the building. Will you use them, repair them, or tear them down? Inspect the public sidewalk for buckling or deep cracks. You are responsible for keeping your sidewalk in good repair. Are there any trees that threaten your building or other buildings? Removing a large tree from a tight space can be troublesome and expensive.

✎ NONTRADITIONAL WAYS OF BUYING PROPERTY

There are at least two methods of purchasing a house to renovate other than working through a real estate agent. All counties run sheriff's sales of real estate that is in arrears in taxes. Check newspapers for announcements, and ask to be put on the county or city list for advance notice of these sales. The sales in large cities are usually run every month.

The sale is generally run as an auction. A minimum price is set, and bidding starts from there. It goes quickly and professionally, as in any well-run auction. You should sit in on a few auctions to get a feel for how it goes. The sheriff often specifies that you must have 10 percent of your successful bid in cash

An Example of Unexpected Expenses. This backyard has five ailanthus trees growing in it. Two of them are close to the foundation. The cost of removing them would have to be figured into the renovation. These could be felled pretty easily, but in a smaller backyard with bigger trees, they might cause problems. Also, check the foundation in the basement to see if any growth has buckled or damaged the walls.

View of a Backyard Filled with Rubble and Debris to a Depth of Two Feet. Cleaning this mess out should be figured into the renovation. The price of the building could probably be negotiated downward on the basis of this debris.

or certified check at the time of the sale. The balance is payable in 30 days. Obviously you must have cash in hand to get a property at auction, but there are some great bargains to be had. Solid brick or stone homes in good locations can go from $1500 to $5000. Often you will be bidding against professional real estate people who do some renovation work on the side.

Commercial properties as well as residential come up for auction. They often command higher prices, but by anyone's standards, they are bargains. One entrepreneur bought a huge grain elevator at a tax sale and is turning it into a residence.

There are a few drawbacks to buying at auction. Some sales specify that the title to the property is conveyed to the buyer "subject to the right of redemption." This means that the original owner has a year (or some other period) to pay his taxes and penalties and refund to you what you paid (plus interest) to get the property back. In this situation, the prudent buyer would wait a year before doing any work on the chance that the first owner wanted to exercise his redemption right.

These tax sale properties can be hard to inspect. Some may be occupied right up to the sale; some may be abandoned and boarded up for years. Additional worries include the possibility that the property may have liens, judgments, and unpaid bills owing on it. Some sheriff's sales convey a title which is free of any of these obligations, while other sales do not.

If a property being sold at a tax sale appeals to you and you think you can get it for a good price, the services of a real estate lawyer to clear up these other matters would be a good investment. In spite of all the difficulties involved, properties are sold every month to professionals and amateurs for bargain prices.

A second alternative is to investigate whether the city in which you plan to live has a program to encourage renovation. The best of these programs is the urban homesteading law, which a few cities like Baltimore and Philadelphia have passed. Under this program cities make city-owned houses available to renovators. The title is usually conveyed for one dollar. The city requires you to renovate the house up to a standard, which they specify in the law. Further, they ask you to live in the house for a period (usually seven years) before you rent it or sell it.

One of the nice things about this program is that the selection of properties is done for you. The city has identified certain neighborhoods and blocks that are ripe for renovation and has acquired the vacant properties. The program also provides for low-interest loans, grants, and technical advice to qualified applicants.

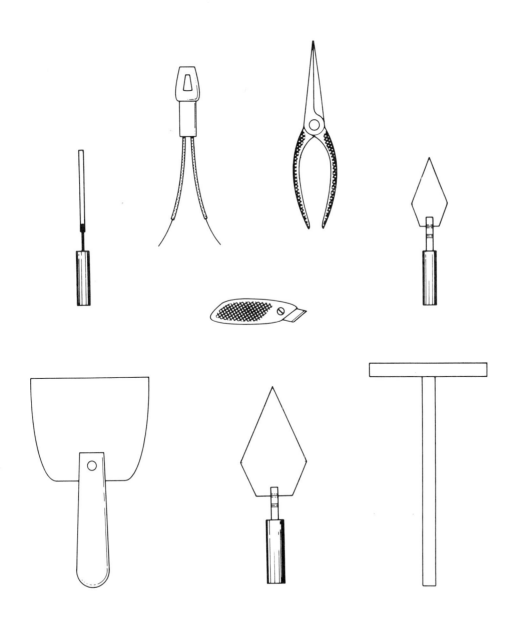

2

Tools

If you do most of your renovation work yourself, you will be saving piles of money. Invest some of that money right now in the correct tools of the right quality, and you will save time and frustration. You don't have to buy all of the necessary tools at one time, but it is wasteful of your time and patience to start a specific job without assembling all of the tools that you will need for that day's work.

You don't need the most expensive tools with fancy finishes or cherrywood handles to ensure quality or get the job done. Look for tools that are designed to perform well and that don't waste money on appearance. The descriptions below will help you to choose the basic tools you will need.

I save money by buying my tools at a chain discount store that has a large do-it-yourself department. I ensure quality by closely inspecting each tool with its purpose in mind. I also keep in mind that most tools were designed to do one thing well, so I steer clear of multipurpose miracle tools that promise too much.

⤙ EVERYDAY TOOLS

Demolition and Salvage. The most useful tool is a wrecking bar. It should be at least two feet long with a prying blade on one end and a big claw on the other for pulling nails and getting leverage.

Drywall. Only three tools are needed here beyond a hammer.

1. A razorblade utility knife, used for scoring and cutting drywall sheets. Buy one that has a large steel handle that's comfortable in your palm.

17

2. A taping knife with a flexible 6-inch-wide blade, used for applying joint compound to nail holes and pressing joint tape along corners and seams.

3. A T-stick, which you can make by nailing two 2 x 4s together in the shape of a "T". The leg of the T should be several inches longer than ceiling height, the cross piece should be 4 feet long. This stick is a valuable extra set of hands when installing drywall overhead. To use it, just have a helper maneuver it from the ground while you hold the other end of the drywall from a ladder. Once the T is jammed in place, it will hold while the helper hands you hammer and nails.

Electrical

1. A 98¢ neon circuit tester is a good safety item to make sure that a line is dead before you work on it.

2. Several sizes of flat-bladed insulated screwdrivers.

3. A penknife for stripping insulation.

4. A pair of standard pliers.

5. A pair of needle-nose pliers for twisting wires into loops for fastening to terminals. Get the kind of needle-nose that has built-in wire cutters.

Masonry

1. A medium size (8 x 5 inches) trowel for most jobs.

2. A tuckpointing trowel (¼ x 6 inches) for repairing mortar joints.

3. A small pointing trowel (5 x 2½ inches) for repairing stone joints and laying brick in tight places.

4. A mortar hawk, which is a sheet of metal with a post for your hand so that a supply of mortar can be held while on a ladder or in other awkward places.

5. For mixing mortar you need a square-bladed shovel and a mortar pan or wheelbarrow. A wheelbarrow is recommended because it is useful for other jobs as well.

6. A brick-cutting chisel with a blade about 4–5 inches wide for cutting and fitting bricks and blocks.

Measuring

1. A good quality metal tape measure about 16 feet by 1 inch with a locking device for the blade and a clip for your belt.

2. A metal yardstick and a 6x6-inch metal square are useful for making accurate cut lines.

Painting

1. For interior work, you need a wood or aluminum step ladder large enough to let you paint the highest ceiling.

2. A large (8 x 12 feet or larger) dropcloth. Canvas is best, paper is okay but fragile, and thin plastic is the worst. You can use old sheets or blankets and get good protection, too.

3. For latex paints, use a roller with a handle that will accept a 6-foot extension pole. A roller pan and a 2-inch brush for cutting in corners and details is all you need.

4. For oil-based paint and finishes, you will need brushes ranging from 1 to 6

inches wide and plenty of masking tape to make clean edges.

Note: Most people simply won't clean roller covers, pad painting devices, or brushes. Buy disposable roller covers and cheap nylon brushes to get around this aspect of human nature.

If you are going to be painting a whole house, I would buy a case of disposable roller covers (twenty-four 9-inch roller covers) and ten each of 1- and 2-inch nylon brushes. You will have enough equipment to take advantage of any free labor that happens along, and you can let the brushes freeze up with paint when you are done with them.

Buy quality natural-bristle brushes only for critical detail painting of woodwork and cabinetry, and be prepared to clean and store them properly so that they last.

You may see small pad painting devices and be tempted to use them. They can be excellent for cutting in work, but be sure to keep them very clean. Even small bits of dried or caked paint can spoil the smooth action of these pad painters.

Plumbing

1. Most jobs can be handled with a combination tubing cutter and reamer for copper tubing up to a 1-inch diameter.

2. A hacksaw for odd sizes of pipe and PVC tubing.

3. A 6-inch adjustable wrench and two 14-inch pipe wrenches for fittings.

4. An inexpensive propane torch with a medium-flame fitting (½ inch in diameter) for soldering pipes.

5. Steel wool for cleaning tubing.

Refinishing

1. A razorblade scraper with a 4-inch replaceable blade and a 1-foot cushioned handle. With this you can strip wallpaper, remove softened paint from baseboards and doors, and clean windows of paint splatter.

2. A putty knife with a 1½–2-inch wide blade for tight places and grooves.

3. A wire brush with a 12-inch handle is invaluable for cleaning off grime, rust, peeling paint, and for getting softened paint out of turnings, cornices, and designs.

Note: The only piece of power equipment you must have is a power finish sander. These sanders are inexpensive and readily available at most discount stores. Buy an orbital-type sander for fastest cutting action. The pad size should be about 3½ x 7 inches and the motor rated at ⅙ hp or better. The finish sander will do a good job of resurfacing baseboards, drywall, and old plaster walls. The finish sander will prepare stripped wood for paint or urethane. On drywall or plaster, the finish sander will smooth joints, holes filled with spackle, repaired cracks, etc.

If you have a lot of refinishing to do, you might want to buy a portable belt sander. These are heavy-duty machines that can resurface floor areas and can quickly remove old paint and varnish.

Buy a belt sander with a 3-inch-wide belt and a dust-bag attachment. The motor should be rated at about 1 hp. With this machine you can resurface wood, plaster, stone, marble, glass, and metal.

These machines are expensive but are the ultimate for quick and efficient refinishing.

One more power tool that can speed stripping is an electric heat gun. You move the gun over the surface to be stripped, and the heat from an electric coil blisters the paint or wallpaper. You then scrape the blistered material off with a putty knife or razorblade scraper.

Expect to pay about what a good drill costs for a good quality heat gun. The gun can more than pay for itself if you have a lot of stripping to do; however, you will probably have to go over detail areas with a chemical stripper even after the bulk of the finish is off.

Safety

1. Most important is a good pair of safety goggles to protect your eyes. Get the kind that are a true goggle, not just glasses with little side shields. Wear them any time material is in the air—when sawing, drilling, pulling nails, tearing down plaster.

2. Buy a dust respirator to protect your lungs. There are permanent models with replaceable filters, but I prefer the inexpensive disposable kind you buy in boxes of 12 or so. Wear the respirator when sanding any kind of drywall or plaster and when resurfacing with the belt sander. It's also a good idea to use one when working with any kind of insulation material.

3. Invest in a good set of leather gloves with 4-inch canvas cuffs. These will protect your hands when handling lumber, using the wrecking bar or cutting and fitting fiberglass insulation.

4. If you will be doing a good deal of heavy work (especially demolition of walls, etc.), buy a pair of 6-inch-high steel-toe work boots. They are worth the extra few dollars for the protection that they give to your feet.

Security

1. For installing locks, you need a variable size (up to 3 inches in diameter) hole drill which chucks into your ⅜-inch drill.

2. For security hardware such as steel grates, fire escapes, etc., you will need a brace and auger bit for boring deep holes in wood.

3. For setting bolts and for anchoring in masonry, buy a carbide-tipped ½-inch masonry drill bit about 6 inches long with a ⅜-inch shaft.

Woodworking

1. For most work, you can get away with a 16-ounce claw hammer. Get one with a fiberglass handle and rubber grip so that you can work for long periods without fatigue.

2. A set of drill bits from ¹⁄₁₆ to ¼ inch will handle most of your screws and pilot holes.

3. Three basic screwdrivers are required—a large and a small flat-blade and one medium Phillips head. Since you need only three, buy the highest quality screwdrivers that you can find with long square shanks and padded handles. If you need other odd-size screwdrivers, you can buy a cheap set for occasional use.

4. In power tools, buy a power circular saw with a 7¼-inch blade. This is the

single most useful power tool there is. Make sure that it has a depth-of-cut adjustment and an angle adjustment that allows you to make bevels and angles. Since you will be using this tool a lot, you should select it with extra care. Heft the saw in the store, and check its balance and maneuverability in your hands. One advantage of the cheap plastic-housed circular saws is that the saw is lighter than the metal ones and may be easier for you to handle.

5. The second most useful power tool is the variable speed reversible drill with a ⅜-inch chuck. Just about every major manufacturer makes a drill with these specifications. As with the circular saw, you should buy the drill that fits your hands the best. Check the trigger action for smoothness, and see if the reversing switch is located conveniently and designed so that it doesn't change the direction unexpectedly. Plastic-housed, double-insulated drills, like circular saws, offer lightness, economy, and electrical safety.

6. One other power tool that is close to mandatory is the sabre saw. These little saws handle like a drill or circular saw but can cut like a portable jigsaw. You can buy blades for this saw that allow you to cut just about any material you could use in a renovation. The great virtue of the sabre saw is that you can cut scroll work and irregular shapes with ease starting from a small hole. The sabre saw makes fitting soft tile and electrical boxes easy. The thing to look for when shopping for a sabre saw is the action of the blade. An orbital action is superior to straight reciprocating action, and you will have

to pay a premium for it. Other than this major feature, you should evaluate a sabre saw like a drill or circular saw—for fit, weight, and economy.

⤳ ACCESSORIES

Circular Saw Blades. These come in great variety for just about every sawing job.

1. Combination—good for most situations cutting with and against the grain of the wood.
2. Rip—for fast cutting with the grain.
3. Crosscut—for extra precise cuts across the grain.
4. There are also special blades for plywood, sheet metal, plastics, and flooring (where occasional hidden nails may be hit).

Drill Bits

1. For your electric drill, you should buy "high speed" (rather than "carbon") twist drills. High-speed denotes quality.
2. Use carbide-tipped drills for masonry and ceramics.
3. For drilling large holes (½ inch or more) in soft wood, use a ⅜-inch shank auger bit with the square end cut off. This modified auger bit can then be used in your electric drill if you drill at low speeds and moderate pressure.

Hacksaw Blades and Sabre Saw Blades. Available with varying amounts of teeth per inch. Use a fine-toothed blade for thin stock and a coarse-toothed one for thick stock.

Sandpaper. Use aluminum- or silicon-oxide sandpaper in power sanders. It stays sharper and lasts longer than flint papers, which are fine for hand work. Most renovation jobs can be handled with the standard coarse, medium, and fine grades, although extra fine may be required for delicate work on moldings and details.

Sawhorse. When doing a large amount of cutting, drilling, sanding, etc., a pair of sawhorses make the work easier. You can make your own by buying a set of specially made metal brackets and cutting 2 x 4s for the legs and crosspieces. The horses should be about 20 inches high. If you don't mind bending down to work, a pair of metal or plastic milk crates work well too. If you contemplate doing a large amount of cabinetry and fine work, a vise bench is a good investment. These new benches can hold just about any shape securely.

↜ SPECIAL TOOLS

These are tools that are not absolutely necessary but can speed work, increase accuracy, or make for a smoother finished job.

Countersink Drill Bits. These drill a hole that allows the screwhead to sit below the surface for fine work. Get a set that will accommodate all the flatheaded screws you plan to use.

Crosscut Hand Saw. Most of your work can be handled by the power circular saw, but a crosscut hand saw is useful when there is no power or the job is small and you don't want to bother setting up the power saw.

Hand Stapler. These are very useful for installing insulation, vapor barriers, carpet, etc. Buy a pistol-grip stapler that fits your hand well—some staplers can pinch you no matter how you hold them.

Levels. These are useful for building stairs, cabinets, brick walls, etc. Get an aluminum frame model 18–48 inches long and a small plastic model 3–5 inches long with hooks for hanging on a line.

Lock-Grip Pliers. Often called vise grips, these large-jaw pliers have a locking mechanism that allows you to hold the work without applying constant pressure. They are helpful in certain plumbing and drilling jobs.

Mini-Hacksaw. This is a handle for holding a standard hacksaw blade from one end. It is handy for getting at small spaces, cutting drywall for wall outlets, etc. Because the blade is supported from only one end it is very easy to damage or bend the blade. You can hold a plain hacksaw blade with gloves or cloth and get the same effect.

MultiPliers. (Also known as Channel Locks.) These work like a tool that combines the features of an adjustable wrench and a large pair of pliers. They are useful for plumbing.

Nail Set. This simple tool drives the heads of nails below the surface of the wood. It is absolutely necessary for fine work when you want to putty over the hole before sanding and finishing. It is also useful for setting nails below the surface in old hardwood flooring before sanding. Buy one with a square head so that it won't roll away when you put it down.

Sledgehammer. A sledge with a 10-pound head should be adequate for most jobs. You can quickly break up concrete, brick walls, set posts, etc.

Tin Snips. These are good for cutting sheet metal, roll roofing, and asphalt shingles. Avoid snips with stamped handles, and buy a sturdy pair with cast handles and machined cutting surfaces.

⤸ EVERYDAY HARDWARE

Brads. These are very thin nails similar to finishing nails and useful for fine work such as picture frames and small cabinets.

Common Nails. These are the nails for framework and rough woodworking. They have flat heads and pyramid-shaped points and are available from 1 to 6 inches in length. You should have an assortment of them on hand from 1½ to 3½ inches in ½-inch steps. Shop where you can buy your nails by the pound to get the best price.

Electrical Cable Staples. Even though they are called staples, these fasteners are driven with a hammer. Use them to fasten plastic and steel-covered electrical cable to framing. The standard size is ½ inch wide by 1 inch long.

Finishing Nails. These are used to fasten molding and trim and in any fine work where you wish to set the head of the nail below the surface. They are commonly available from 1 to 4 inches in length. Keep at least three sizes on hand—1½, 2, and 3 inches for general work.

Masonry Nails. As the name implies, these nails can be driven into mortar and soft brick. They are very hard and will break before they bend. Available in roughly the same sizes as common nails, they come in two varieties: cut or flat nails, and round with spiral grooves in the shank.

Roofing Nails. These are very sharp, large-headed nails that have been galvanized to prevent rusting. Common sizes range from ½ to 3½ inches. These are very useful nails not only for roofing but for drywall sheets, decking, fencing—anywhere that a large-headed, rust-resistant nail is required. Some roofing nails are made of copper or aluminum for long-lasting rust resistance.

Special-Purpose Nails. When extra holding power is required of a nail, as in repairing squeaky floors or using unseasoned lumber, there are several possibilities. Cement-coated, hot-dipped, and ring nails all have better than average holding power. The ultimate nail for holding power is called a *spiral nail* or *drive screw*. This nail twists as you drive it and gets a tremendous grip on the wood.

Bolts. Sometimes you will have to use bolts for security hardware or for joining two large wood joists. Two kinds of bolts are generally used. Carriage bolts have a square shank at one end to keep them from turning when they are tightened. Machine bolts have a square head, which is held by a wrench while the nut is tightened. Bolts can be expensive if bought singly. If you want to save money, buy them by the bag or box.

Flat-Head Screws. Most of the time you will use flat-head wood screws, which will make a flush surface when driven into a countersunk hole. They range in size from less than ½ to 3½ inches long. Select a screw length ¼–½ inch less than the total thickness of the material to be joined. As with bolts, buy screws by the box to save money.

Masonry Anchors. These are useful for fastening brackets, lighting fixtures and the like to concrete or brick. Drill a ½-inch hole in the masonry with a carbide-tipped drill, insert a ½-inch lead anchor (also known as a cincher), drive with a setting tool, and fasten the fixture with a screw or bolt. Anchors are sold with the proper setting tool and screws or bolts.

Sheet-Metal Screws. For most light-duty jobs, a round-headed screw about 1 inch long will serve. Drill or punch a hole in the metal slightly smaller than the diameter of the screw. The screw will tap its own threads in the metal as you drive it.

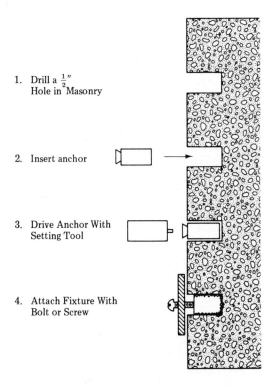

1. Drill a $\frac{1}{2}''$ Hole in Masonry

2. Insert anchor

3. Drive Anchor With Setting Tool

4. Attach Fixture With Bolt or Screw

Anchoring in Masonry.

Washers. Use flat metal washers to prevent the nut on the end of a bolt from chewing into the wood.

⤷ DOOR AND SECURITY HARDWARE

Hinges. The most used hinge is the *butt hinge*. It has a removable pin so that you can remove a door without unscrewing it. The butt hinge is available in various sizes and finishes. Brass plated and bright steel are the most common finishes. For doors, a 3½ x 3½-inch hinge is about right, and for most cabinets a 2 x 2-inch hinge will do.

For utility work such as gates and basement doors, a *strap hinge* is best.

This hinge is screwed to the surface of the door and frame (not the edge as with a butt). When there is not enough room on the door frame to install a strap hinge, a *T hinge* is used.

Locks. For ease of installation, good security, and low cost, there are only three kinds of locks you need to know about.

1. **Deadbolt**—This lock provides the best security for the price. When locked, a solid bolt drops down into a cast slot, which is anchored into the doorframe. The deadbolt is available with a single cylinder for solid doors or a double cylinder for doors with glass panes. Deadbolts resist prying

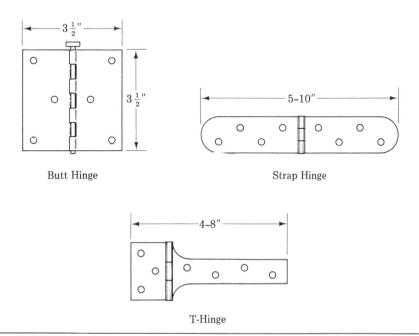

Butt Hinge

Strap Hinge

T-Hinge

Basic Styles of Hinges.

and tampering, and you should have at least one on each exterior door in your house.

2. **Nightlatch or Slamlock**—This is useful when combined with the dead-bolt lock. It has a beveled bolt that automatically engages with a slot when the door is closed. The bolt can be pushed out of the slot from the outside with a piece of spring steel, which is why it should never be used alone unless security is not a problem.

3. **Police Lock**—For the ultimate in low-cost security, the police lock is the best choice. It consists of a keyed cylinder, cast door mechanism, and a 4-foot steel bar and floor socket. When locked, the bar prevents anyone from forcing the door. The more force applied, the more the bar digs into the floor. When the key is used, the door mechanism releases the bar, which is then free to travel up a guide and allows normal entry.

All three locks should be installed using the manufacturer's instructions and templates. The only special tool required is a hole drill for installing the cylinder.

Security Bars. In some situations, you may want extra security for first-floor windows. A variety of window bars are available. Metalworking shops can make up custom bars from steel rod, heavy gauge screening, and flat stock. One low-cost option is available. Check with local salvage yards for old iron or steel fencing. With patience and a hack-saw, you can cut the fence into window guards and use masonry anchors or bolts through the window frame to secure them.

⤷ SPECIAL-PURPOSE HARDWARE

Jacking Post. This is a combination tool-hardware device. It can be used as a tool for lifting heavy weights (a porch rafter for instance) while repairs are made, or it can be set in place, adjusted and left permanently (as a cure for a sagging joist in the basement perhaps).

Mending Plates. Made of flat steel with countersunk screw holes, these plates are used for repairing window frames and reinforcing weak joints. The common shapes are L, T, and flat oblong.

Metal Framing Fasteners and Anchors. These are similar to mending plates but are heavy duty and used for new construction. These fasteners are nailed into framing members and eliminate the need for toenailing and other tricky procedures. Truss fasteners, post anchors, beam fasteners, joist hangers, and stud angles are commonly available. These kinds of connectors are also used in electrical installation and eliminate the need to frame out switchboxes and outlets. Just ask at the electrical supply house for electric boxes with drywall nailing legs. Buy your fasteners by the box to save money.

3

Building Materials

The job of renovating your house will call for many different materials. The ones described below are standard materials available at most building supply houses. I have selected materials that offer the best value for the money and are easy to work with. There are many other excellent materials and products that your taste and budget may allow.

⤳ WOOD PRODUCTS

Board Lumber

The two basic kinds of board lumber you are likely to need are 1 x 12-inch white pine (utility grade) and stair tread. White pine of this size is very versatile and can be used for baseboards, molding, trim, fencing, cabinet and storage-unit construction, and many other jobs.

Ten-foot lengths of 1 x 12 seem to be the most versatile size to have around as stock lumber. Pick out your own pieces, and buy boards that are dry and warp free. Allow a 10 percent wastage with this wood for rough ends and unwanted knots, but save your small pieces for little projects.

White pine board is also available in 1 x 6-inch and 1 x 8-inch sizes. These are useful for door and window framing. You may pay a premium for these sizes at the lumber yard, so you might want to buy only 1 x 12-inch white pine and use your circular saw to cut the widths that you need as they come up.

You can look at 1 x 12 white pine as a good stock size of board lumber to have around. You can cut it into strips as narrow as 1 x 1 inch with your circular saw. It can be carved, sanded, and routed into ornamental shapes. It can be painted, stained, oiled and waxed, coated with urethane, or left natural.

Stair tread is the other basic board lumber you are likely to need. Tread is sold in 8- or 10-foot lengths and comes as wide as 11 inches and as narrow as 8 inches. If you have to build or replace stairs, don't try to substitute another material for stair tread. Stair tread is specially cut and milled for this purpose; it resists flexing and has a rounded nosing for safety. All you have to do is cut the proper length for your job.

These stairs are made of old joists and new stair tread. Almost all of the lumber in an old house can be recycled, with the exception of the wood lath behind old plaster.

One other size of board lumber is useful and versatile—1 x 2-inch furring strips. Furring strips come in various lengths; 6, 8, and 10 feet are the common ones. Furring is utility lumber and is mostly used for hidden applications. Use rough furring strips attached to a masonry wall as a nailing surface for drywall. You can use smooth furring strips in rough cabinetry, as simple framing, and (in certain cases) molding and trim. Rough furring strips are often sold by the bundle at a low price.

Allow a 20 percent wastage when buying this way.

Dimensional Lumber

This is the lumber that you will use for structural framing. The common 2 x 4 is an example of dimensional lumber. Most of your work can be handled with 2 x 4s. They are available from 6 to 20 feet in length. Unless they are to be exposed and finished, buy the utility grade, and select the pieces yourself. Look for pieces that are straight and dry, and don't be too concerned with knots.

Except for special projects, the only other sizes of dimensional lumber that you are likely to need are 2 x 12-inch for joists and stair carriages and 4 x 4-inch square posts for fence supports and joist supports. These pieces of lumber are available from 6 to 20 feet in length, and it is important that they be free of knots and splits that can affect their strength.

Remember that dimensional lumber and board lumber are named and sized for their fresh-cut sizes. The pieces will be slightly smaller when dry. A 2 x 4 is not really 2 inches by 4 inches; it is actually 1½ inches by 3½ inches.

Dowels

These are round pieces of wood of various diameters; ¼, ½, ¾, and 1 inch are the common sizes. Dowels are useful for making bathroom towel racks, clothes closet rods, screw plugs, etc.

Molding

The most useful and popular molding is called *quarter round*. It looks as if it was part of a dowel that was cut in fours. Its major use is for covering the gap between the baseboard and floor. Buy molding in ten-foot lengths. There are other styles of wood molding available. Ask to see a molding chart or sample board at the lumber yard to get an idea of what your supplier has.

SHEET MATERIALS

Sheet materials include plywood, chipboard, drywall (also called gypsum board or sheetrock), various wood and wood-like panels, glass, and certain plastics.

Chipboard

This is an extremely versatile material. You can make cabinets, room partitions, speaker enclosures, shelves, floor coverings, and a hundred other things from it. It is low in cost, has good fire resistance, is easy to cut, and takes a variety of finishes. Chipboard is now replacing plywood as a sheathing material in new frame construction because of its cost benefit.

The material is made from sawdust and wood flakes bonded with pressure and glue into 4 x 8-foot sheets. Its major drawbacks are a poor bending strength and vulnerability to moisture (although with an exterior glue and a proper finish even this last is not a big problem). Available in thicknesses of ¼, ⅜, ½, ⅝, and ¾ inch.

When cutting chipboard, use a sharp blade because the material is very hard and dense. (You might want to try a carbide-tipped blade for long life.) Keep the blade clean of any resin or glue residue by rubbing it with a rag soaked in kerosene or paint thinner.

Drywall

This material has eliminated the need for complicated and costly conventional plaster over lath for interior walls and ceilings. It comes in 4 x 8-foot sheets in ⅜-, ½-, and ⅝-inch thicknesses. It is applied with galvanized roofing nails or special drywall nails to framing members. Drywall can also be applied to existing damaged plaster walls using extra long roofing nails that reach through the two layers to the original framing.

Use ⅜-inch for double-thickness construction and for applying over old plaster. Use ½-inch and ⅝-inch for new single-layer construction over furring strips or framing.

For high-moisture areas like kitchens and baths, use a special moisture-resistant ½-inch drywall. This drywall makes a good base for epoxy paints, plastic laminates, and ceramic tile.

There is also a special ½-inch drywall that is treated to resist extreme fire and heat. It is known as "fire resistant" or "fire code" drywall. It is often used in two layers for party walls, hallways, stairs, and other areas where superior fire resistance is desired.

Glass

The two major choices here are single strength (³⁄₃₂ inch thick) and double strength (⅛ inch thick). Use double-strength glass for transoms and window panes over 2 x 2 feet. Check with your supplier to find out if he will cut the glass at no charge. It may be worth paying to have your glass specially cut for irregular shapes needed for ornate windows.

Plywood

Plywood is a good choice for jobs where strength is required (building a platform on the floor or closing up a doorway). It is losing out to cheaper materials in general construction because of its cost. It is available in interior and exterior grades, one or two sides smooth, and in thicknesses of ¼, ½, ¾, ⅞, 1, and 1¼ inches. Like most sheet materials, the standard dimensions of plywood are 4 x 8 feet.

⤳ MASONRY MATERIALS

Brick

Buy common face brick for all-purpose work. Brick can be used to build fireplaces and chimneys, repair walls, and make steps. It can also be laid in a bed of sand to make a walkway or patio.

Concrete

This is a basic material used for making sidewalks, floors, steps, patios, and for making repairs. For small jobs, buy premixed concrete in 45- or 90-pound bags. Use gravel mix for deep repairs and sand mix for thin slabs and small cast items.

For bigger projects, order your concrete delivered from a truck or bring it home from a supplier who has a concrete carting system to lend. Ready-mixed concrete should conform to ASTM specification C94. Simply ask for C94 concrete for your general projects. Concrete is measured in cubic yards. To estimate your needs, multiply the length of your project in feet times the width in feet times its thickness in *inches*. Then divide the result by 324. This gives the cubic yards needed.

$$\frac{L' \times W' \times T''}{324} = \text{Cubic Yards Needed}$$

Concrete Block

These are available hollow or solid in the standard size 8 x 8 x 16 inches and have the same basic uses as brick. Block lays faster than brick and is a good choice for large projects.

Mortar

This is used to lay brick and block and for repairing the joints in existing masonry. It is available premixed in 50-pound bags, as mortar cement (to which you add sand) in 70-pound bags, and as a home mixture made from portland cement, hydrated lime, and sand.

Quarry Tile

This is a very hard and impervious earthenware tile, supplied in 6-inch squares, which is useful for floors, countertops, hearths, and other areas where great durability is desired. Set quarry tile with tile adhesive or mortar depending on the subfloor or surface, and fill the gaps between the tiles with a cement material called *grout*.

Terra-cotta Flue Tile

This comes in square and round shapes of many diameters and in 2-foot-long pieces. Order the size that will fit inside the existing flue with a ½-inch clearance. Flue tile is used to line old chimneys to make them smoke and fire tight. The pieces are lowered by rope into the old flue and are stacked one on top of the other.

4

First Steps

⤸ EXTERIOR FIX-UP

One of the first things you should do to a property after you take possession is to make a good inspection of the exterior and pick out problem areas to attack. Concentrate on the exterior first because you want to correct basic things like poor security, roof leaks, and bad drainage before they can deteriorate further and ruin any work on the inside.

Roof

Inspect for leaks and damage. If you have a flat, tarred roof in need of repairs, you can do the job yourself with a combination of roof cement and roof coating. Roof cement is available in 1- and 5-gallon cans and is an asphalt-plastic compound with mineral fibers. It is extremely sticky and can even be applied to a wet roof. Use a triangular trowel to spread the material over cracks and holes in the roof. Pay special attention to corners, chimneys, pipes, and any place where there are joints or where two different materials meet. Clean your tools and hands of roof cement with paint thinner. (Turpentine and benzine work well, too, but are more expensive than paint thinner.)

After patching holes and cracks with roof cement, apply one or two layers of roof coating. Available in 5-gallon cans, this material is about the consistency of honey. Apply over a dry roof on a warm day with an old broom or a special flat roof brush which you can get at the roofing supply store. Pour some coating and then spread it with the brush over a small area. Work about 12 square feet at a time. Repeat the process until the whole roof is covered.

Work from the high side of the roof to the low side to take advantage of gravity when spreading the coating. If you got on the roof through a hatchway, be sure to work so that you can apply the last bit of coating from inside the hatch. If you use a ladder, be sure to leave a pathway clear to it which you can coat just before you leave the roof.

Coating soaks into the roofing felt and asphalt below it and keeps it from drying out and cracking. The combination of coating and roof cement will provide protection for about five years. Coating-and-cement is an easy way to protect and seal a flat roof. The treatment can be repeated several times and will increase the life of an asphalt-and-felt flat roof.

For roofs in really bad shape, you can rent a roofing kettle to melt solid asphalt. If you give your roofing supplier the square footage of your roof, he can give you the proper amount of material and can also recommend a place to rent the kettle to melt the asphalt.

Break up the solid asphalt with a sledge and axe. Drop the chunks into the kettle and light the burner. Keep adding chunks as the asphalt melts.

When the asphalt is molten, draw 5-gallon cans of it and carry them to the roof. Pour the hot asphalt and spread it with a broom or roofing brush. The procedure is the same as with roof coating.

This treatment is called *hot mopping,* and it does an excellent job of sealing an old built-up roof. You will need a helper to draw the buckets of asphalt and give them to you on the roof.

I have had good results with a solo procedure for fixing flat roofs. The effect is much like hot mopping, but it is easier and only takes one person.

Measure the roof area to be treated. Buy one 5-gallon can of roof cement for each 60 square feet of roof area. Buy an oblong flat roof trowel about 5 x 12 inches. Make sure that the trowel has smooth, *not toothed* edges.

On the roof, get down on your hands and knees (knee pads are recommended) and use the oblong trowel to apply a single smooth coat of roof cement to the whole area. The coating should be ⅛–¼ inch thick. Use the trowel in broad strokes to smooth the coating out and blend edges together.

Best results are obtained if the job is done when the outdoor temperature is about 75 degrees; the coating will be at the right consistency for spreading. After the coating is applied, hotter days will bond and set it to the old roof.

Repairs to metal roofs are seldom needed. If you have the good fortune to have a copper roof, you can expect very few problems. Repairs to copper are made by soldering. Study soldering skills (see the plumbing how-to), and use a propane torch, copper plates, flux, and wire solder to make any repairs.

Tin roofs are more vulnerable to deterioration. Repair any cracks or holes with roof cement. Tin roofs can be painted with a thick, red lead paint called "red roof." This paint fills in small cracks and seams. Use at least two coats, and try to paint on a cool, cloudy day to avoid drying the paint too quickly. (Flat tin roofs can be treated with roof coating in the same manner as built-up roofs. Use a stiff paint brush to coat the metal ridges and seams.)

If you have cracked or broken *slates* in your roof you can make repairs by using a nail cutter. Buy a nail cutter from your roofing supplier. This inexpensive tool lets you get under a broken slate and free it.

Slip the long end of the cutter under the broken slate. Fish around until one of the slots in the cutter hooks around a nail. Strike the bottom of the cutter with a hammer to cut the nail. Repeat this procedure with the cutter until you have freed the slate.

After removing the damaged slate, take a 2 x 12-inch strip of copper or aluminum and nail it over the joint formed by the slates below the damaged one. Use copper nails for copper strip and aluminum nails for aluminum strip. Put two dabs of roof cement next to the metal strip in the space where the new slate will go. Take the new slate and slip it into position. Bend the bottom of the metal strip over the bottom edge of the new slate to hold it in position, and cut off any excess strip.

To replace a torn or damaged *asphalt shingle,* cut the shingle out with a utility knife or tin snips. Use a small (1-foot) wrecking bar or claw hammer to pull out nails and bits of old shingle.

Pull back the overlap from neighboring shingles. Cover the area with roofing cement, including the overlap from neighboring shingles. Place the new shingle in the roofing cement, and secure it in place with about six roofing nails. Dab roofing cement over the new nailheads and let the neighboring shingles fall back into place.

Gutters

Check for leaves and debris in the gutters that might cause water to back up and enter the house. Clean and check the gutters for integrity of joints and proper fit with the downspouts (the pipes that carry water from the gutter to the ground). Patch small holes with dabs of roofing cement.

If the gutter and downspout work is rusty but sound, you should paint with any one of several special paints for this purpose. The least expensive paint is the same red lead roofing paint that retailers call *red roof.* Another option is a metal primer that contains zinc chromate. After the gutters are primed, they may be painted with an oil-based color coat.

On the ground, check to make sure that the water is being conducted away from the house. Make sure the drains are not blocked by leaves or gravel and that downspouts are turned correctly to spill water away from the house and not into a basement window or along the foundation.

Windows

Replace broken panes of glass and deteriorated glazing; repair weak frames with T and L mending plates and check wooden sills for damage. If the frames and sills need paint, buy the best exterior paint (oil or latex based) that you can afford and apply it immediately to halt any more damage from weather. Worn wooden sills can be covered with metal sill covers. Check with your roofing supplier for preformed sill covers that attach with nails or screws. Caulk the places where new sill covers meet brick and wood with latex or rubber caulk to prevent water entry to the material below.

Security Bars. Decide if first-floor windows need the protection of security bars and install them *before* you start any work inside. Purchase bars through a custom metal shop, salvage yard, or a local classified-ad publication; or you can cut your own from lengths of steel fence. (See the how-to on security bars.)

Basement Windows. One often neglected area of home security is basement windows. Can they be locked, and do they offer sufficient resistance to force? If not, add small metal gratings or bars as you would for full-size windows. One low-cost option for basement security is to remove the existing window and demolish the frame until you have a plain masonry opening. Then take standard 8-inch hollow concrete blocks and lay them with mortar in the opening. The block is laid with the holes exposed so that some light and ventilation can pass through. On the basement side of the block, you can build a frame in the opening with 2 x 4s and rehang the old window.

Doors

Check doors for security purposes. Are all exterior doors of solid wood or metal? They *should* be for best security. All exterior doors should have at least three hinges. Replace doors, and tighten and add hinges as necessary. Install at least one deadbolt lock to all exterior doors.

Brick Repairs

Survey the building and note the need to remove efflorescence (a white alkaline deposit, which should be removed immediately with a solution of muriatic acid and water), replace bricks, crumbling mortar, etc. While serious repairs demand quick action, small problems can be let go for a few years. The idea behind the first survey is to catch and repair items that can grow worse quickly.

To remove efflorescence, mix 1 part muriatic acid to 9 parts water. Use a stiff brush to wash the wall down with the acid solution. Wear goggles and rubber gloves to protect yourself. Rinse the acid solution from the wall with pure water from a hose. Spray water across the wall for 20 minutes to remove any excess acid. (See the how-to on masonry and brick pointing for other repairs.)

Carpentry Repairs

Repair or replace unsafe steps, porch floorboards, railings, etc. There is no need to do fancy work at this time; just correct any safety problems that you may have.

INTERIOR FIX-UP

Demolition and Cleaning

After the exterior has been sealed and made secure, you can concentrate on the inside. Survey the house and decide if you will need to hire a container to haul away trash, old plaster, etc. The amount of junk that can come out of an old house is staggering. You will want to get rid of old wallpaper, linoleum, rugs, and the like. Your trash problem is further compounded if you demolish plaster walls and get rid of old bathtubs, sinks, and appliances. The situation can get really desperate if the basement is full of debris and you also throw out the old duct work, a water heater, and a furnace.

Most municipal trash services simply won't touch the kind of material that comes out of a house under renovation. The best you can do is throw out a bit at a time packaged so that the trash men can handle it. I have gotten rid of old plaster by packing it in liquor boxes and putting 8 or 10 of them out each trash day. Wallpaper and linoleum can be put out in sturdy trash bags. Thin pieces of wood, like lath and old molding, can be put out by bundling it with twine into a size that can be handled by one man.

Old appliances and fixtures are a problem. Check with your sanitation department to see if appliances may be put out on the street. Some cities will send a special truck around to pick up ranges and refrigerators. *You must remove the door from any refrigerator (or similar appliance) that you put out on the street to ensure that no young child can be suffocated by being trapped inside.*

One of the best ways to have appliances and fixtures hauled away for free is to offer the whole house of them to a second-hand dealer who specializes in these items. If you have a few pieces that the dealer wants, he will often take everything off your hands and sell what he can't use for scrap. If you can't make a deal like this and the city won't pick up the appliances and fixtures, you will have to borrow or rent a truck to haul them to a dump or landfill.

The most efficient way to deal with the trash problem is to rent a container. These containers are the size of a car, with walls about 5 feet high. The container company drops one off in a parking space in front of your house and you fill it with trash, scrap, etc. In a week or two, the truck comes around again and hauls the container away to be dumped at some landfill.

Containers are sized in cubic yards. Typical sizes are 6, 12, 24, and 40 yards. A 6-yard container is suitable for cleaning out surface debris only from a small house. A 12-yard container will handle the surface debris of a large house and perhaps the plaster and lath from one room that you demolish. Containers from 24 to 40 yards are needed for whole-house interior gutting, demolition of sheds and porches, backyard excavation, basement excavation, and the disposal of appliances, heating systems, and portions of the building's structure.

If you rent a container, it is in your interest to use it efficiently. Make sure that all materials you dump are fully compressed so that they take up the minimum space. Lay long lengths of lumber next to each other neatly and build up the container in orderly layers. Some renovators use unwanted doors to build up the sides of the container so that more material can be piled in. Container companies frown on this practice for economic and safety reasons, and you may have better uses for old doors than this. If you have a fireplace or wood-burning stove, you can save and store scrap wood, lath, and other wood products for burning and save the container for trash of absolutely no value.

Large items like furnaces have to be broken into small pieces in order to haul them away. Use a sledgehammer to break up a cast-iron boiler into manageable pieces. Take ducts apart with a hacksaw, tin snips, and an ax. Compress sheet metal and fold it into small pieces. Unwanted steel pipes can be dismantled with a hacksaw. Saw the pipe into 8-foot lengths to be put into the container.

Sturdy cardboard liquor boxes are invaluable for hauling trash. They are available for free by going to the liquor store on the day that they receive stock. Not only can liquor boxes be used to put material out for trash collection, but they are also the safest way of carrying loose material, like plaster rubble, up and down stairs.

Cleaning out a house is a big job, and it can run into money if you use a truck or a container. In spite of this, don't put the job off. Having everything that you intend to replace out of the house will make planning and executing renovations much easier. As renovations progress, you will accumulate plenty of new trash that will cut into space for work and storage of new materials.

You can even make some money while cleaning out your house. Many times you will find that you cannot use some fixture or material that is in serviceable shape. This is the time to use the local classified-ad publication. You can list old bathtubs, sinks, stoves, and marble and slate mantels, and the chances are good that someone will want the item. You may receive only a token payment for the item, but at least you didn't have to pay to have it hauled away, and someone else is getting the use of it.

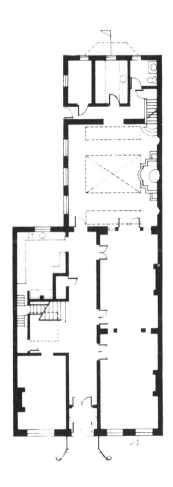

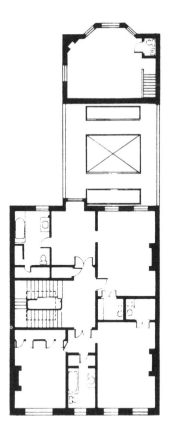

5

Basic Systems

After the house is cleaned out and sealed, you can plan basic systems. Basic systems include heating equipment and insulation, plumbing systems (drainage lines and hot- and cold-water supply pipes), electrical systems, and gas-supply lines.

Deal with basic systems first after the clean-out because they are likely to require some demolition, and their location dictates where certain other features must be placed later in the renovation.

⌁ HEATING

The technology for solar heat is beyond the scope of this book, and wood and coal heat are usually too cumbersome for urban and suburban use. So, for our purposes, there are really only three feasible heating fuels: natural gas, oil, and electricity. Electricity is much too ex-

pensive a heating fuel at this time, especially for older houses that are poorly insulated and weatherstripped. The choices narrow down to gas and oil.

If gas heat is available in your area, it should be strongly considered. It is a very clean and convenient fuel that doesn't require storage tanks or deliveries (except in rural areas). Equipment that burns gas has a long life and requires little maintenance.

In areas where gas service is not available, oil is the other choice. It requires a 200-gallon (or larger) storage tank in addition to the furnace. Oil-burning equipment is efficient and reliable but does tend to need more maintenance than gas equipment.

Hot-Water System

There are gas- and oil-fired versions of this system. Flame heats water which is then allowed to circulate through pipes

43

connected to radiators in the upper part of the house. Water circulates naturally by convection or is forced through the system by a pump called a *circulator*. A circulator pump is usually required for efficient operation in a large house. The hot-water system is a closed system, with the cooler water returning to the furnace to be reheated. If your house has radiators, this is the system you should use.

Hot-Air System

This system is available in oil- and gas-fired versions. Flame heats air, which is distributed through metal ducts to the upper parts of the house. Some old systems use large ducts with no blower attached, allowing convection to do the moving of the air. Modern systems use blowers to distribute air quickly through the house.

One drawback to the hot-air system is that the air is super heated at the furnace and tends to dry out. This dry air can cause the humidity level of the house to drop. Continued low humidity can bring discomfort to residents and can even cause furniture to become unglued, as it shrinks by giving up its moisture. One solution is to install a humidifier at the furnace to restore moisture or to buy portable humidifiers for the living spaces.

Planning the Heating System

The choice you make will depend on what already exists in the house you buy. The ideal system would be a gas-fired, hot-water system. Least ideal would be an oil-fired, hot-air system.

If the house has radiators, it is worth restoring the hot-water system. If it has ducts, it is generally not worth the expense to change to hot water. If you have to start from scratch, hot air will be cheaper to install than hot water.

If you need to replace the existing furnace, you can find out what size you need by finding the rating plate on the old furnace. Find the "input BTU per hour" and the "output BTU per hour" and record these numbers. Use these numbers when ordering a new furnace from a plumbing supply store, catalog, or heating contractor. These numbers are your best measure of furnace performance. Regardless of differences in individual design between furnaces, any unit with the same BTU rating will perform well in place of the old one.

When you order a replacement furnace, get a package deal. This means your furnace will come with a circulator or blower, control box and thermostat transformer, pressure and temperature gauge (for hot-water systems), the proper flue connector, and the correct safety equipment along with instructions for installation and operation.

Call different suppliers with your BTU specifications, and get their prices for complete packages. By ordering a package, you get a lower price than for separate components and you make sure everything matches so that all you or your heating contractor has to do is hook the new unit to the existing system. The only other component you need to buy is a thermostat.

Furnaces are heavy and cumbersome, so see if you can get delivery thrown in with the price of the package. If you pick the furnace up yourself, make

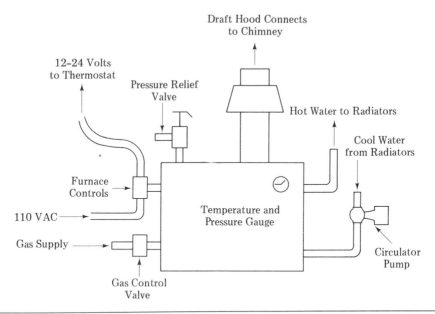

12–24 Volts
to Thermostat

Pressure Relief
Valve

Draft Hood Connects
to Chimney

Hot Water to Radiators

Cool Water
from Radiators

Furnace
Controls

110 VAC

Gas Supply

Temperature and
Pressure Gauge

Circulator
Pump

Gas Control
Valve

Components of a Gas-Fired Furnace.

sure that you have a truck and two helpers to muscle the unit around.

If you do all of the work on your heating system yourself, be sure to check every component carefully. If you buy a package furnace, you can be certain that it is properly matched and functional; however, you must inspect every inch of piping and all the radiators in a hot-water system plus all the gas and oil supply lines that will feed the furnace. Be wary of old oil tanks, and check them carefully for leaks, cracks, and sediment. Most duct systems are trouble-free, but you might want to clean them with a vacuum cleaner from all the register openings before connecting a new furnace package.

Make sure that the existing flue is sound and gas tight. Be prepared to do some mortaring around the base of the

chimney; furnace fumes seem to degrade mortar quickly. Line defective flues with terra-cotta liners, as described in the how-to section, to make them gas and smoke tight. Be sure to use the manufacturer's recommended flue connector, and follow the manufacturer's instructions for testing the furnace's draw once it has been installed.

In some communities a permit is required to replace heating equipment, and a safety inspection is made to ensure proper operation. This inspection is often made by urban gas companies. If you do the work yourself, you should obtain all the information and permits before you order replacement heating equipment.

In general, if the ducts (or pipes and radiators) are sound and you replace the original heating plant with a new package furnace, your heating system will be operational. The only other component involved is a thermostat. There are two options. A standard heating thermostat is a switch that responds to the house temperature and shuts off or turns on the furnace as required to maintain a constant temperature. A clock thermostat consists of two thermostats coupled by a 24-hour clock. This thermostat allows you to control the furnace for energy savings by selecting between a high temperature setting and a low temperature setting. The clock is set to run the furnace on the high setting when people are home and awake; the clock switches to the low setting at times when people are away or asleep. This clock function is worth having because using a high/low setting can save you 20 percent or more on your energy bills.

A standard or clock thermostat is mounted on an interior wall at shoulder height and is connected to the furnace control equipment by two small-gauge wires. You may use the existing wires behind an old thermostat if you are content to use the old location for a new thermostat. If you wish to place a new thermostat in a new room or on a different wall, you must run new two-conductor cable between the thermostat and the furnace control equipment. High-fidelity speaker wire is ideal for hooking up a thermostat.

⤸ INSULATION

Insulation should be considered a basic system because it is the primary way that you control your heating costs. Insulation is a type of investment, and so it has a payback period in which it returns its cost and thereafter provides a dividend. Until America secures cheap and plentiful energy, insulation payback and dividends will continue to be considerable and will become more attractive with each passing year.

If you insulate the area above your topmost ceiling with 6½ inches of fiberglass insulation, you will save the cost of the material with the first heating season. Every year after, the insulation will save you its cost. There is no excuse for not installing some kind of insulation in your house.

The single most effective place to put insulation is above the topmost ceiling of your house. It is like putting a lid on a pot. A blanket of insulation keeps the heat from rising quickly through your house and out the roof.

The best all-around insulation is *fiberglass*. It is inexpensive, easily worked, has good fire resistance, and is readily available. It comes in 3½- and 6½-inch thicknesses and in 15- and 23-inch widths. You can buy it unfaced or with one side kraft paper (a brown paper-bag-like material) or with one side foil (aluminum foil bonded to kraft paper). The paper and foil facings are useful for new installations where a vapor barrier is needed. The unfaced insulation is good for adding to existing insulation or where no vapor barrier is needed.

The facing or vapor barrier should always face toward the living space. The purpose of a vapor barrier is to turn back moisture from the living space and prevent it from soaking the insulation and reducing its effectiveness. A vapor barrier also assists in making the living space feel more comfortable because, at any given temperature, the higher the humidity, the warmer people will feel.

You will see R numbers used to describe insulation. The higher the R number, the more resistance to transfer of heat. With fiberglass, the thicker the material the higher the R number. For ceilings, a minimum of 6½ inches or R-19 is recommended, and for walls, a minimum of 3½ inches or R-11 is recommended—

the more insulation the better. Some new houses are constructed with 6½-inch insulation in the walls and 13 inches in the ceilings, and they perform beautifully in saving energy.

In an old house it may be impractical to do much more than put 6½-inch fiberglass between the ceiling joists. Obviously, you don't want to tear down good walls to install insulation; however, if you do demolish even one interior

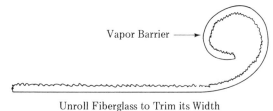

Unroll Fiberglass to Trim its Width

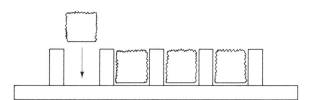

Insulation Should Fit Snuggly Between Rafters
Above Ceiling — vapor Barrier Facing the
Living Space

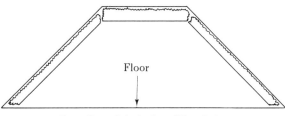

For a Heated Attic, Install Insulation
Between the Side and Top Rafters

Installing Fiberglass Ceiling Insulation.

wall that faces an exterior surface, you should insulate it when you reface it. Every bit of insulation helps, especially when you are working with low-cost fiberglass.

Some contractors are offering a service that claims to insulate existing walls in old buildings. The two major insulating materials used are *blown-in cellulose* (a plant fiber) and *foamed-in urethane* (a chemical product that expands and hardens in place). The cost and performance of these services is questionable because of the extreme difficulty of filling wall cavities completely through small drilled holes; and the hidden nature of the work makes it difficult for the homeowner to check its quality. In some old masonry homes, plaster is applied directly to brick and stone, and there is no cavity present in which to blow or foam in insulation.

You can save energy with fiberglass insulation in other ways besides insulating walls and ceilings. Insulate ducts and heating pipes when they pass through an unheated space. If you have an unheated garage or basement through which ducts or heating pipes pass, wrap them in 3½-inch insulation to keep heat loss low. Save money on your hot-water bills by wrapping any exposed sections of hot-water pipe in 3½-inch insulation. (See the how-to on pipe wrapping.)

You can increase the efficiency of hot-water radiators by stuffing a pad of insulation wrapped in reflective foil between the wall and the radiator. This pad reflects more heat out into the room and keeps the radiator from heating the section of the wall that faces the outside. (See the how-to on radiator pads.)

Storm Windows

After installing insulation in all the logical places, the next most cost-effective, energy-saving step you can take is to install storm windows. Like fiberglass, storm windows retard the passage of heat from inside to outside by trapping air. Savings from storm windows can vary, but you can expect them to save their cost within several years and pay dividends for many more years before requiring replacement.

The most available and least cumbersome storm windows are the combination storm-and-screen units. These windows are often called *triple-track* or *self-storing* units. The window is mounted on the outside casing and left in place permanently. Window and screen panels run up and down in tracks so that seasonal changeover is accomplished by simply pulling the screen or glass into place from inside the house.

When buying storm windows, be aware that units with overlapping corners are stronger than units that have mitered corners. Also, a baked-enamel or a vinyl-clad finish will last longer than the plain aluminum or "mill" finish, which has a tendency to oxidize and pit if not painted. Check the operation of the glass and screen panels and their latches on a sample unit at your supplier's showroom. Remember that you are looking for a tight window that will insulate by trapping air.

Storm-window companies are in one of the most competitive retail businesses. Get several bids for your order to compare prices—especially if you purchase installation service along with the windows. You may be able to get a better price by buying windows and installation in January, February, and March, which are slow months in the business.

If you want to install storm windows yourself, you must measure each window to be covered. There are two ways to measure. You can measure so that the storm window covers the window frame and sits even with the exterior wall. In this case, you would measure the inside width and height of the exterior window frame. Add 2 inches to each measurement to account for the storm-window mounting flange.

You can also measure so that the storm window sits within the window frame, slightly below the surface of the wall. For this, measure the height from the bottom of the lower sash to the top of the upper sash. Get the width by measuring only the total width of the window sash.

To install, simply screw the units to the window frame. Most windows come predrilled to make this easy. Position the window so that the vent holes or slots in the mounting flange are at the bottom. Use a helper to hold the window from inside the house as you install the screws and check to make sure that the window is square in the frame.

After the window has been screwed in place, caulk any gaps between the mounting flange and the window frame with a good quality latex or rubber caulk. Take care not to plug the small vents in the bottom of the unit with caulk; they are needed to let water vapor escape.

Low-cost storm windows can be constructed that will last *one season*. Take a length of 1 x 12 white pine and saw it into 1½-inch-wide strips. Stretch clear plastic sheeting (use a sturdy thickness to resist tearing by the wind—3 mil or thicker) over the window, and attach it with the pine strips and 2-inch galvanized roofing nails or 2½-inch finishing nails.

There are commercial kits for making temporary storms that use aluminum or plastic strips. They are great for emergencies or for fast installation. Temporary storms are only a holding action until you can install permanent units.

One great thing about storm windows is that they preserve and protect the older windows that came with the house. Using storm windows can allow you to save the original windows. Make sure that the old windows are repaired with mending plates, cracked glass is replaced, and everything is glazed and painted before you install permanent storm windows. With the protection of the outer storm windows, even rough original windows can be used.

Replacement Windows

Some houses have windows and frames that are too far gone or missing altogether. Order replacement windows with single- or double-glass panes; these replacement windows screw or nail into the old opening and can be installed from inside the building.

Replacement windows come in wood, vinyl, and aluminum. If you buy vinyl or aluminum units, check to make sure that the frames are packed with insulation material. The vinyl and aluminum units are low maintenance and eliminate constant painting.

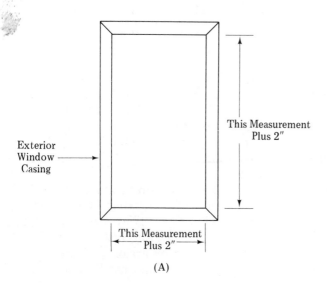

Exterior
Window
Casing

This Measurement
Plus 2″

This Measurement
Plus 2″

(A)

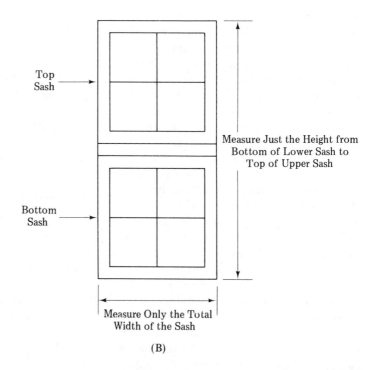

Top
Sash

Bottom
Sash

Measure Just the Height from
Bottom of Lower Sash to
Top of Upper Sash

Measure Only the Total
Width of the Sash

(B)

Use (A) if You Wish the Storm Window to
Sit Even with the Exterior Wall

Use (B) if You Wish the Storm Window to
Sit Recessed a Bit from the Wall

Measuring for Storm Windows.

The double-glazed units consist of two panels of glass separated by an air space. If the frames are well insulated and the sashes are well sealed, they can be used without storm windows.

You may still want to install storm windows for greater efficiency with double-glazed windows, and you should definitely do so if you use single-glazed replacement units.

Like storm windows, replacement units are sold and installed by many companies, so you should get several bids for your job. Since they can be installed from inside the house, it makes sense to do the work yourself and save some money.

If the original window frame and pulleys are in good shape but the sashes are rotted or broken, you can order new wooden sashes from a lumber or mill yard. The new sashes will come complete with glass, and you can install them in the old frame. (See the how-to on window pulleys and weights for details on installing the sashes.) You will need to paint the new wood and then install storm windows to complete the installation.

PLUMBING SYSTEM

Next on the checklist is the plumbing and drainage system. Here you may run into problems, since many communities forbid anyone but a licensed plumber from doing work. Read your local building code for information on plumbing requirements.

I will describe how to make repairs for the benefit of those who can do so and for the information of those who must contract the work so that they can deal intelligently with the contractor.

One way to get around the high cost of having a plumber do the work is to make it as easy as possible for him to function. If you need new hot- and cold-water lines, you can clear a path for the plumber by cutting the holes, removing the fixtures, etc., that slow him up. This way you pay the plumber for his skill in laying and joining pipe, not for his carpentry and demolition skills. Discuss this plan with the plumber when he comes to the house to make an estimate.

Money can also be saved if you find a plumber who will let you install your own fixtures. Again, the idea is to pay the plumber for skills that only he can practice. There are beautifully designed water heaters, sinks, faucets, toilets, showers, and bathtubs available that come complete with clear instructions. If you can get the plumber to bring the pipes up to the location of the fixture and stop, you can install the fixture yourself and save hundreds of dollars.

Most craftsmen are sensitive to a person who is trying to redo an entire house, and you shouldn't have any problem finding a sympathetic plumber who is willing to go along with either or both of the above proposals. For those people who want to go it completely alone, be prepared to study and practice some plumbing skills before attacking your house. (See the plumbing projects for details of the skills required.)

A Typical Water-Supply System

Here is an overview of a typical water-supply system to give you an idea of what is involved:

Water enters the house and passes through a water meter which measures the flow for billing purposes. Just before

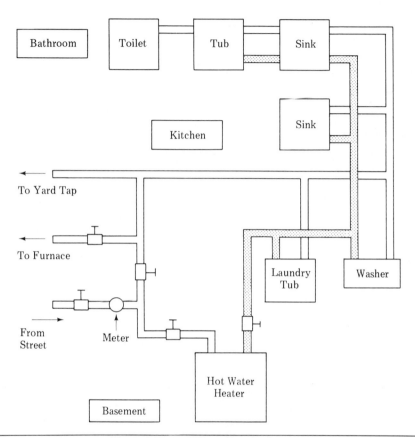

Typical Home Water Supply System.

or just after the water meter, there is a valve which is the main shut-off. This controls the supply of water to the whole house. After this valve, the system splits into two parts—the hot system and the cold system. There are usually shut-off valves installed at the beginning of each system so that one or both can be isolated.

The hot system consists of a pipe leading to a hot-water heater (gas or electric, or sometimes part of an oil furnace) and a pipe leading away from the heater. The feed pipe supplies cold water

to the bottom of the heater; the other pipe draws hot water from the top of the tank and feeds this water to the rest of the house.

As hot water is drawn out of taps upstairs, an equal amount of cold water is drawn into the heater to be warmed. Following the pipe as it leads away from the hot-water heater would take us to places of use like the washing machine, laundry tub, dishwasher, kitchen sink, bathroom sink, and tub or shower.

Going back to the main shut-off valve to trace the cold system, we would see that the cold system bypasses the heater and then supplies the same areas and fixtures as the hot system, plus a few others (that don't require hot water) like the hose tap in the backyard, toilet tanks, and the boiler in a hot-water-heating furnace.

Fittings and Fixtures for a Water-Supply System

Water Meter. If yours is damaged or missing, call the water department, and they will install one and charge it to your next bill. It's important to have a meter in good working order so that you pay only for the water you use.

Main Valve. It may be large and forbidding, but it is no different from a bathroom tap in function. It should com-pletely shut off the flow of water so that work can be done to the rest of the system.

Pipe. Soon after the main valve or meter, the pipe should become ½- or ¾-inch copper for the rest of the system. The ½-inch size is suitable for one- or two-story houses with one bath and one kitchen. The ¾-inch copper is best for three-story houses with apartments or extra bathrooms. There should be valves at the beginning of the hot and cold piping so that each system can be isolated. Fittings for copper pipe are soldered (also called *sweating*). Any threaded fitting must first have an adaptor sweated on to the pipe. Copper pipe is available in both rigid and flexible forms. Buy rigid pipe for most applications, and use sweated-on fittings to make turns and connections. Use short runs of flexible

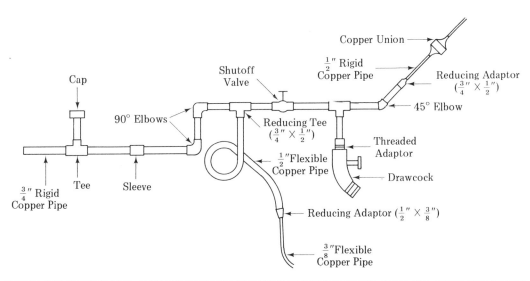

Fittings and Connections for Copper Pipe.

pipe to bring your water supply close to a fixture in a tight location—flexible pipe can take up any slack created by bad planning or poor measuring and cutting.

Sweat fittings for copper pipe include:

Elbows for making 90-degree turns.
Tees for making branch connections.
Sleeves for connecting two pieces of straight pipe.
Valves for controlling the supply of water.
Drawcocks with hose fittings for washing machines and garden hoses.
Caps for closing off a run of pipe.
45-degree elbows for gentle turns.
Adaptors that connect two different sizes of pipe (½ to ¾ inch for example).
Various adaptors with a sweat fitting on one end for copper pipe and a threaded fitting on the other for water meters, valves, and other accessories.

Hot-Water System

Hot-water Heater. Pipes leading to and from the heater should have shut-off valves sweated on so that the heater can be isolated from the system for repair and replacement. Threaded fittings called *unions* occur just before the pipes enter the heater so that the heater can be disconnected with a wrench. The unions are sweated to copper pipe and then screwed together to form a water-tight seal. (Unions are ordered by the type and size of pipe used. Most heaters are connected with ½- or ¾-inch copper unions.)

The heater itself will be gas or electric. Gas requires a flue connected to a chimney and a gas-supply line of black steel pipe. Heaters have different capacities and recovery rates. A four-person house with dishwasher and clothes washer will need a 50-gallon fast recovery heater or an 80-gallon slow recovery heater.

Fixtures. After the hot-water heater, the ½- or ¾-inch pipe leads to the various appliances and fixtures. In a ¾-inch system the pipe reduces to ½-inch branch lines that go to the "wet" areas of the house. In the basement, the branch line terminates in a faucet above the wash tub and in a hose tap for connection to the hot hose from the washing machine. In the kitchen, the branch line will terminate in a kitchen faucet and will supply a dishwasher either through a faucet fitting or directly in the case of a built-in unit. In the bathroom the branch line will supply a faucet in a tub or shower and a faucet on the bathroom sink.

Cold-Water System

The cold system bypasses the water heater and supplies the washtub and washing machine in the same way as the hot system. In addition, a branch line may run to the hot-water furnace, with a valve just before joining the furnace, for making up lost water. This furnace valve is normally closed and is only opened during bleeding of radiators (see how-to). Another branch line will often run to a drawcock located on the outside of the building for a garden hose.

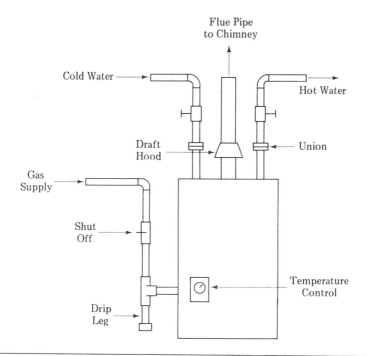

Components of a Gas-Fired Water Heater.

Fixtures. The cold system goes everywhere the hot system goes and supplies every fixture in the same way. The only difference in the kitchen is that there is no cold branch line to the dishwasher. In the bathroom, in addition to the cold line that connects to the sink and the tub, there is also one that supplies the toilet tank. Cold water from a ½-inch pipe feeds the toilet tank through a ⅜-inch reducer and a special toilet-supply fitting.

⤶ DRAINAGE SYSTEM

In old houses, the waste-water drainage system will invariably consist of vertical cast-iron pipe, with horizontal steel or lead pipe connecting basins and tubs to the main vertical stack.

Inspect the main vertical stack carefully to determine if it is worth saving. Holes and cracks can be patched, but pipe that has become thin and scaly will probably have to be replaced. Branch lines of steel or lead are often leaky or clogged with debris. These branch lines are fairly easy to replace using copper tubing, and they should be for best performance of the system.

If the cast-iron stack must be replaced you have two options: new cast-iron or plastic pipe. The installation of new cast iron is a job for a professional plumber. The cutting, fitting, and lead caulking of cast-iron pipe is a skill best left to a pro.

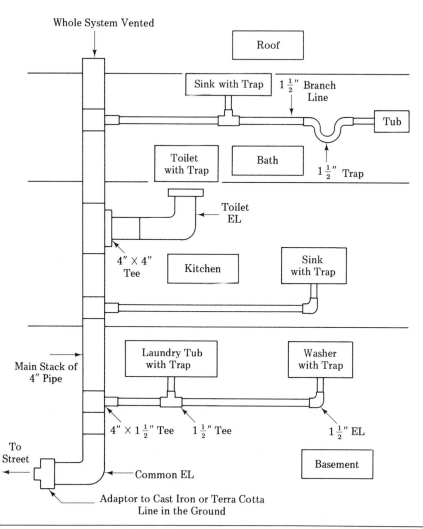

Typical Home Drainage System.

If your community permits the use of Polyvinyl Chloride (PVC) drain pipe and allows the amateur to install it, you are in luck. (Some community codes may not sanction the use of PVC because it can give off toxic gas when it is involved in a fire.) PVC pipe is easy to handle, cut, and install. PVC is also much cheaper than cast iron. Even if you decide to let a professional replace your drainage system, PVC will save you money over cast iron.

Patching Cast-iron Pipe

If the line is cracked, use a metal-plastic putty compound formulated especially for cast-iron cracks (available at the plumbing store). Another option is to use an epoxy putty. Epoxy putties come in two cans and are mixed together before applying to the crack. They harden to make a very durable, waterproof seal. Regardless of the material you select, use a putty knife to push patching compound into the crack. Make sure the crack is clean and dry before applying any material, and keep water out of the line for at least 48 hours.

If there are holes in the line, use cast-iron mending plates, which come in different sizes for different diameter pipe. Order as many plates as there are holes, and get a container of plumber's putty. Take a handful of plumber's putty and knead it in your hand until it is pliable. Place the putty on the concave side of the mending plate, and press it evenly over the entire concave surface. Press the plate over the area to be patched, and secure it with the U-bolt and nuts provided with the plate. Water can be run in the line immediately.

Clearing a Line

If the line is clogged with debris, rent a rotary drain cleaner. This tool is a motorized drum with a steel cable inside. The cable has a sharp cutting head and, as the drum turns, the cable spins and the head bores through the blockage. Use gloves to protect your hands as you feed the cable down the line. You must run water down the line as you work to wash away the blockage as it is broken up by the cutting head. Use a garden hose to introduce water into the line if no working fixtures are connected.

You can use a drain-cleaning company to do this work for you. Get several prices for the job, and find out about any guarantees they may offer. Neither you nor a company will be able to clear a drain that has collapsed underground. No reputable company will charge you full price if this turns out to be the case.

Less serious blockages can often be handled with a manual *snake*—a long piece of spring steel which can run down a line and around gentle corners. Buy a snake about 1 inch wide for main drains and ½ or ¼ inch for branch lines.

Replacing Branch Lines

Old clogged horizontal branch lines of steel or lead should be replaced. Take up floorboards and expose the run of pipe. Cut or disassemble the pipe with a hacksaw or wrench and remove the old material. Carefully loosen the fitting that taps into the cast-iron stack. You may have to use the propane torch to heat the fitting, then tap it with a hammer, and finally use a pipe wrench with an extension handle to remove the fitting. You can make an extension handle by getting a 4-foot length of 2-inch steel pipe; it will fit over the end of the pipe wrench for extra leverage. Preserve the fitting you remove from the cast-iron stack and use it when you order new pipe and fittings. The plumbing store can use the old fitting to give you the proper adaptor to connect copper pipe to cast iron.

Replace the branch lines with copper pipe and fittings. The most common diameter for copper drain pipe is 1½ inches. You will have to get a large-flame fitting (1-inch diameter) for your propane torch to sweat these large fittings and pipes successfully. When you order pipe and fittings, show the old fitting that went into the cast iron and ask for one that will take 1½-inch copper on one side and cast-iron threads on the other.

As you are laying the new copper lines in the floor, check to make sure that the whole run is on a gentle angle toward the cast-iron stack. It should be because you are simply following the path of the old pipe. If the run is not pitched correctly, you will have to notch some joists or shim others up to get a continuous slope. The proper slope for horizontal branch drain lines is ⅛ inch per foot.

Make sure that you sweat a piece of copper tube and the cast-iron adaptor together and screw the assembly into the main stack with pipe compound before you complete soldering the rest of the run. This order of work prevents the heat of the torch from destroying the seal between the adaptor and the cast-iron stack.

At the fixture end of the run, you will have to know what size drain trap and tube you will be using before you sweat on the proper size adaptor. (See the how-to on drains and traps for details.)

PVC

If you have to replace the entire sewage system and your community allows amateurs to work with PVC pipe, you can do it very easily.

PVC pipe and fittings are available in every size and configuration that cast-iron pipes come in. To replace a whole system, simply draw a diagram of the existing cast-iron system, note how much of what size pipe and fittings is involved, and order everything in PVC. Measure and count the fittings in the old stack before you demolish it. Some retailers sell complete PVC waste kits with everything you need to handle one bath and one kitchen.

All that you need to install PVC is a hacksaw, sandpaper, and a can of PVC cement. Joints are made by marking cuts with a pencil, cutting with a hacksaw, roughing up the pipe ends with sandpaper, wiping the pipe and fitting with cement, and putting the two pieces together. The joint should be undisturbed for 20 minutes. Water can be run through the completed line in 24 hours.

Working with PVC is very much like working with copper tubing and fittings except that, instead of sweating the joints with solder, you apply a cement that reacts chemically with the PVC and bonds it. Do not use any cement that becomes dirty, changes color or consistency, or is old.

Traps

After the main sewage stack and branch lines are repaired or replaced, fixtures are connected to the system with traps. Traps are tubes which are bent so as to trap a plug of water which then seals off the tube from any gas in the sewage system. Toilets come with built-in traps, but it is necessary to install a separate trap for every basin, sink, tub, and shower in the system.

Traps are generally made of brass with chrome plating. These brass traps screw together with nuts and rubber washers. Other traps (usually for hidden applications such as under a shower base) are made of PVC or galvanized steel.

With sinks and basins, traps fit into pieces of tubing called tailpieces which extend below the fixture outlet. Water flows into the trap and down a tube which mates through an adaptor to the 1½-inch branch drain lines.

With old-fashioned claw-footed bathtubs, a waste-water kit of brass is installed which ties the main drain and overflow outlet together and sends the water to a point below the floor. Either a galvanized trap with adaptors to 1½-inch copper or a 1½-inch PVC trap with proper adaptors is used there.

For modern built-in bathtubs and showers, use a galvanized or PVC floor trap tied into the drain tailpiece with an adaptor.

PVC traps are put together with cement and can accept chrome-plated brass tube on one side and 1½-inch PVC pipe on the other.

Galvanized traps are used in steel-pipe branch lines and can be used in 1½-inch copper branch lines with the proper adaptors. Use pipe joint compound when mating the fittings on galvanized traps.

Chrome-plated brass traps for sinks and basins are available for connecting them to drain lines in the wall or the floor. Wall traps are P traps and floor

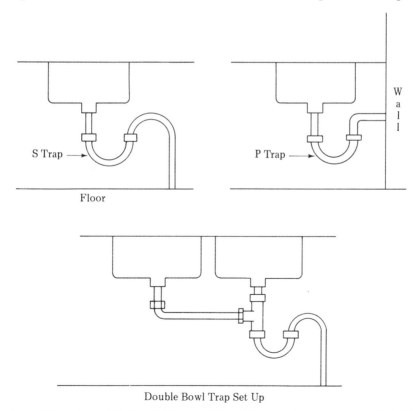

S Trap

Floor

P Trap

Wall

Double Bowl Trap Set Up

Trap Styles for Kitchen and Bathroom Sinks.

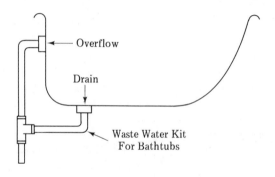

Overflow

Drain

Waste Water Kit
For Bathtubs

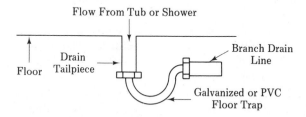

Flow From Tub or Shower

Floor

Drain
Tailpiece

Branch Drain
Line

Galvanized or PVC
Floor Trap

How a Bathtub Is Tied into the Drainage System.

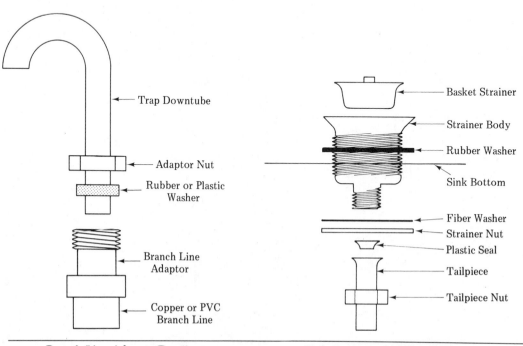

Trap Downtube

Adaptor Nut

Rubber or Plastic
Washer

Branch Line
Adaptor

Copper or PVC
Branch Line

Basket Strainer

Strainer Body

Rubber Washer

Sink Bottom

Fiber Washer

Strainer Nut

Plastic Seal

Tailpiece

Tailpiece Nut

Branch Line Adaptor Details.   **Sink Outlet and Tailpiece Details.**

traps are S traps. Chrome-plated brass traps are also available for servicing double-bowl sinks. Tubing and fittings are supplied which tie the two sink outlets together and send the water through a single trap and out into the floor or wall.

⌁ PIPE AND FITTINGS

When buying pipe, it is important to have the proper size for the flow requirements of the fixture or appliance. When repairing or replacing pipe, follow the sizes that were there before. For new work, get the advice of the plumbing supply people for the length of the run and the input of the appliance or fixture.

In general, for modern hot- and cold-water supply you can use ½-inch copper tubing, which is standard for new work in small houses, or ¾-inch with ½-inch branches, which is suitable for large houses and multiple baths and kitchens.

Rigid copper tubing comes in 10- and 20-foot lengths. Flexible copper tubing may be ordered in smaller lengths. Use rigid tubing for economy, and make turns and adjustments with fittings. Use flexible tubing for short runs near the fixture where you want to take up slack between the branch line and the fixture inlet.

Steel pipe is useful for gas-supply lines and a hot-water heating system. Steel pipe is available in a galvanized or black finish. Because steel pipe is connected with threaded fittings, you must use pipe-joint compound or thread tape to seal the connections against leaks.

You will have to order your steel pipe precut and prethreaded to save the bother of buying or renting a steel-pipe cutter and threader. Remember that fittings add a few inches to a pipe's length but that threads and fittings together are less than the sum of their separate lengths. Most of the time, if you have a rough idea of how long your straight

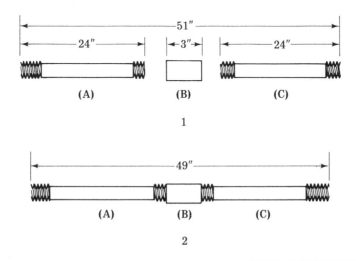

Threaded Pipe Grows Slightly Smaller When Joined.

runs will be, the plumbing house can give you precut sizes that will just about measure up. Any slack can be taken up with threaded pieces called *nipples*. Nipples come in sizes ranging from close (a close nipple would be just enough to connect two fittings) to 12 inches in ½-inch steps. Anything longer than 12 inches would be considered a pipe.

Fittings for steel pipe are roughly similar to copper fittings. There are Tees, elbows, sleeves, unions, caps, valves (with steel pipe, valves are of two kinds—water valves and gas valves), and various adaptors to step up or step down the size of pipe.

Unions are particularly valuable in the fitting of steel pipe. Because of the requirements of threading, you may find that the only way to repair or replace a given run of pipe is to use a union instead of a sleeve. Unions allow you to work on a single run of pipe without disassembling the other pipes it may be connected to.

One other steel fitting is known as a *flexible appliance connector*. This is a specially formed brass tube that screws onto steel pipe at one end and connects to a gas appliance at the other. These connectors are flexible and can take constant vibration and allow the appliance to be moved occasionally for cleaning or repair. Buy only the length you actually need as they are expensive, and any excess length might get bent or caught behind the appliance.

Steel Pipe and the Heating System

If you have a hot-water heating system, chances are that it uses steel pipe to distribute water to cast-iron radiators. (The only other option would be copper pipe to modern baseboard radiators.) At the radiator there are two unusual valves. One is the radiator shut-off, which isolates an individual radiator from the heating system. This valve does not permit you to disconnect the radiator for repairs; it only checks the flow of warm water into the unit. For repairs you have to drain the whole system.

The shut-off valve looks like a "T" placed on its side with a handle on top. To install the valve twist the valve onto the pipe coming out of the floor (using pipe compound or tape), and tighten with a wrench until it faces the radiator. Mate the valve with the beveled fitting coming out of the radiator, and tighten the nut that is integral with the radiator fitting. No joint compound is needed for this beveled fitting.

The other valve on a radiator is a small fixture called a *bleed*. It is operated by a radiator key (buy several at the plumbing store). This valve is opened to let any trapped air out of the radiator when filling the system or during operation (some air in the system will be liberated by heat).

Replace a broken bleed valve with an adjustable wrench, and use pipe compound on the threads. If the valve is broken off, it will be necessary to buy a special tool called a *stud extractor/thread chaser* at the plumbing store to remove the stump and retap the hole.

GAS-SUPPLY SYSTEM

A gas meter, supplied and serviced by the gas company, takes gas from a branch line off the main and introduces it into the house. There is usually a main

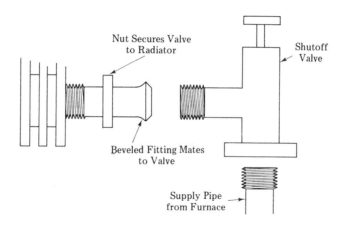

Nut Secures Valve to Radiator

Shutoff Valve

Beveled Fitting Mates to Valve

Supply Pipe from Furnace

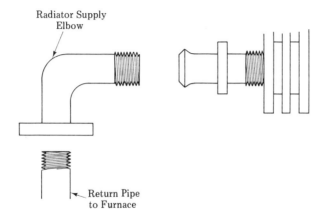

Radiator Supply Elbow

Return Pipe to Furnace

How a Radiator Is Connected To Heating Pipes.

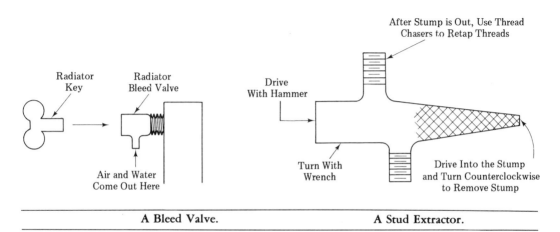

Radiator Key

Radiator Bleed Valve

Air and Water Come Out Here

Drive With Hammer

After Stump is Out, Use Thread Chasers to Retap Threads

Turn With Wrench

Drive Into the Stump and Turn Counterclockwise to Remove Stump

A Bleed Valve.   **A Stud Extractor.**

shut-off valve integral with the meter. From the meter, gas is distributed to various parts of the house in black steel pipes.

A pipe runs to the gas furnace through a shut-off valve and into the furnace control equipment. Another pipe runs to a gas-fired water heater through a shut-off valve and into the heater control equipment. A gas-fired clothes dryer also has its own pipe and shut-off valve delivering gas to its integral control equipment. All equipment using gas in a basement or utility room has an external shut-off valve on the pipe supplying it so that the flow can be cut for servicing and replacement. Each pipe also has a drip leg (which looks like a "T" lying on its side) that allows moisture on and in the pipe to drip straight toward the ground instead of into the sensitive safety controls of the equipment.

Upstairs, gas is supplied to the kitchen stove. The steel pipe terminates in a shut-off valve, which is connected to a flexible appliance connector that runs into the stove.

Meter. This is the responsibility of the gas company. If you call to have one installed, the rest of your system should be ready to be connected. Simply bring the main pipe near the place where the meter will be, and the installer from the gas company will tie it in.

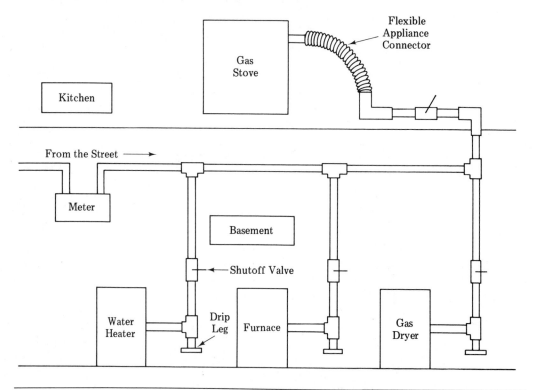

Typical Home Gas Supply System.

Pipe and Fittings. For a gas system, the only choice is black-finish steel pipe and fittings. Galvanized pipe and fittings are not acceptable because the zinc can flake off and clog small gas orifices in your equipment. Shut-off valves should be made of brass and can have a long handle or a short turning post. Use the long-handle valves on a furnace, water heater, clothes dryer, and any appliance that may need to be quickly shut down. You can use the smaller turn-post valves on gas stoves and appliances that will need infrequent service.

Install gas pipe and fittings with thread tape or thread compound that specifically resists gas leakage—check the label of your product for this. Each joint in a gas system must be pressure tested with a detergent solution to check for leaks. (See the how-to on steel pipe.)

⤙ ELECTRICAL SYSTEM

With the electrical system you may run into the same difficulties as with plumbing. Some communities will not allow the amateur to wire his own house, while some communities will allow the home-owner to do everything but the fuse or breaker box.

If you check and find that the law won't allow you to do the work yourself, you may be able to save some money by employing the same strategy as with plumbing. See if you can clear the way for the electrician to work. Also avoid having the electrician install extensive built-in lighting. About the only place you need a wall switch and overhead lighting is in the kitchen and bathroom. Anywhere else, you can have the electri-cian install an outlet near the door, and you can use floor and table lamps for room lighting.

By restricting built-in lighting and opting for a simple system of outlets, you can supply your own plug-in fixtures. If you have enough outlets of the proper capacity, you can run room air conditioners, dishwashers, stoves, washers and dryers, intercoms, time switches, and a host of other appliances on a plug-in basis. If you do opt for outlets instead of built-in lighting, you should have at least three duplex outlets for each room.

Floor and table lamps can be purchased inexpensively on the used market and rewired very easily. They can even be found on the street on trash day and can be recycled with rewiring and a new shade. Floor lamps and table lamps have the virtue of being more in harmony with an old house than modern built-in or overhead lighting.

Overview of a Typical Wiring System

Power is supplied by the electric company by three wires that connect high on your house to the sevice entrance cable. Your wiring responsibility starts with this thick, three-wire cable. It is mounted to the house with masonry anchors and clips. The top of the cable connects to the electric company's wires through an insulated entrance head, and the bottom of it leads to a meter socket. The meter socket is installed either in the basement or outside at eye level. The electric company's meter is plugged into this socket and measures the power you draw for billing purposes.

After the meter, the cable runs to the service panel—a large steel box in the basement or utility room that contains fuses or circuit breakers and which splits up the power to the various branch circuits. Fuses and circuit breakers are safety devices that sense when a circuit has malfunctioned or is overloaded and is in danger of overheating. Fuses are one-time devices and must be replaced when they blow. Breakers are permanent devices that trip when overheated but can be reset after the problem has been corrected. Breakers are the obvious choice for a modern and efficient wiring system.

From the service panel, small-gauge (usually 12-gauge), three-wire cables run off to various sections of the house to supply power to outlets, switches, appliances, etc.

One more wire runs from the service panel. This is a single wire that is usually connected to the water pipe. This is a neutral (or ground) wire used to provide a secure ground for the system.

Each separate circuit is protected by a fuse or circuit breaker so that one branch doesn't affect the other. The service panel contains a main shut-off switch, which cuts power to all the individual circuits. Shut-off for the individual circuits is accomplished by removing individual fuses or throwing individual circuit breakers to "off."

Before You Begin

You will run the risk of electrical shock and fire if proper working methods and installation are not followed. Unless you are highly motivated to learn the proper way to work, you are better off leaving this part of the renovation to a professional.

If you decide you want to do the work yourself, check with the local building authority and find out if you are allowed to install wiring. If so, they will probably tell you that a wiring permit is needed and that an inspection will be necessary before the work is approved. You should also buy a copy of the National Electric Code, which gives the regulations and correct installation methods and materials.

For those who will leave replacement of the electrical system to a professional, I will provide some information about planning the system and how it is installed so that you will be able to work intelligently with the electrician.

Planning the Electrical System

The minimum service for homes of up to 3000 square feet is 100-ampere. This will provide for lighting, refrigerator, electric range, and electric water heater. You should also be able to handle an electric dryer and room air conditioners with 100-amp service.

If you want central air conditioning and electric heat, you will have to go to 150- or 200-amp service. The extra capacity of these services will also give you a healthy reserve for the future, even if you don't plan on central air conditioning or electric heat.

For 100-amp service, the size of the copper entrance cable will be either #3 (100-amp) or #2 (115-amp). In either case, the conductors should be insulated in flexible plastic cable or flexible metal armor for ease of installation. The cable is fastened to the building with metal clamps and masonry anchors. The cable should be fastened every 4 feet along its length. For additional protection, the cable can be encased in metal coping or conduit from ground level up to 10 feet.

The meter socket is a standard item, but you will have to specify if it's going to be installed indoors or outdoors so that the proper unit and fittings can be ordered. The socket is fastened to the wall with masonry anchors. An outdoor meter is recommended because the electric company can take readings without disturbing the residents.

The service panel is ordered by its capacity—100 amps in this case. Get one set up for breakers, as they are superior in every way to fuses. In addition to buying one 20-amp* breaker for each branch circuit, you have to get the proper clamps and fittings for inserting cable into the service panel. You will need one large clamp for the service cable coming from the meter socket and smaller clamps for branch cables and ground cable coming out of the panel.

For the grounding wire, use a #4 copper ground wire and connect it with a pipe clamp to the water pipe where it enters the house. If you have to connect it to the house side of the water meter, use a jumper cable to bridge the water meter and provide a secure ground. Attach the jumper wire with pipe clamps to the street side of the meter and the house side of the meter.

For branch circuits use #12 copper plastic-insulated cable. Plastic cable is easy to work with and #12 conductor is adequate to handle up to 20-amp circuits. Use 2-wire grounded cable which consists of 2 insulated wires, one white

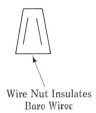

Wire Nut Insulates
Bare Wires

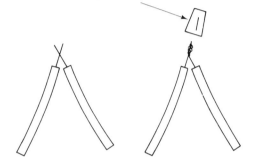

Twist a Wire Nut
Over the Wires

Twist Bare Wires Around
Each Other

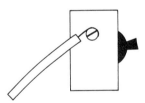

Screw-on Device Tightens
the Wire in on Itself

Form the Wire Into a
Clockwise Loop With
Needlenose Pliers

Electrical Connection Basics.

---

* If you install 20-amp branch circuits instead of the more common 15-amp, you give yourself a healthy reserve capacity for the future. With 20 amps, you can add more lighting and appliances to the system as years go by.

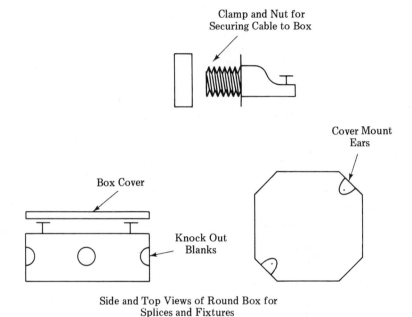

Clamp and Nut for
Securing Cable to Box

Cover Mount
Ears

Box Cover

Knock Out
Blanks

Side and Top Views of Round Box for
Splices and Fixtures

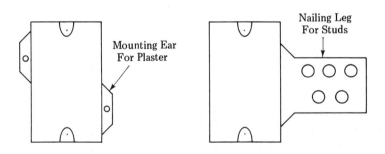

Mounting Ear
For Plaster

Nailing Leg
For Studs

Top View of Two Styles of
Oblong Boxes for Switches and Outlets

Basic Electrical Boxes.

and one black, and a bare copper wire. This cable provides an extra measure of safety over 2-conductor ungrounded cable because it allows you to use grounded outlets and fixtures. A grounded outlet has two slots for plug blades and a U-shaped hole for the ground blade of the plug. This system provides a continuous ground for any appliance connected to it, guarding against shock in the event any metal parts become live with electricity.

Connect the cable to the outlet by attaching the black wire to the brass terminal, the white wire to the silver terminal, and the bare wire to the green ground terminal.

Most branch circuits can be handled with #12 cable and 20-amp circuit breakers. There are some heavy-duty circuits that require different treatment. Electric cooking ranges, electric water heaters, and all-electric clothes dryers require special cable and breakers for their circuits.

Heavy-duty circuits generally consist of a 50-amp circuit breaker protecting a 240-volt line of #6 copper cable. Most heavy-duty circuits use 240 volts (instead of 120 volts) because power can be delivered more efficiently at the higher voltage.

Planning Circuits

You should provide for at least two separate circuits per floor for outlets and lighting. This plan will prevent plunging a whole floor into darkness if one circuit malfunctions. Good electrical planning will include one outlet and lighting circuit for every 500 square feet of floor space.

There should be a separate circuit for each bathroom. Each kitchen should have two 20-amp circuits for refrigerator, kitchen appliances, and freezer. These kitchen circuits should be only for heavy-draw kitchen equipment, not lighting. If the kitchen has an electric range, there should be a heavy-duty 240-volt circuit just for the range. A dishwasher and garbage disposal should be serviced by one separate circuit.

Good electrical practice also indicates that a laundry room should have a separate circuit for the washer and dryer; if the dryer is an all-electric unit, there should be a separate 240-volt heavy-duty circuit for it. A furnace should have its own circuit, and a workshop should also have a separate circuit for power tools. An electric water heater should have its own heavy-duty 240-volt circuit, and it is also a good idea to have a separate circuit for outdoor security lighting and a separate circuit for common hallway lighting.

Planning electrical service requires that you analyze your electrical needs and try to plan now for the future. Will you be adding living space in a few years, converting a closet into a darkroom, or setting up a workshop with power tools? Putting in extra electrical capacity is always cheaper now than later.

Things You Can Do for Yourself

Even if you decide to let a professional do the wiring for you, there are many simple electrical projects that you can handle yourself. Replacing switches and outlets and rewiring lamps are all simple, straightforward projects. Other simple projects are installing time switches, doorbells, intercoms, and outdoor security lighting.

As you do a few of these projects your confidence will improve. Remember to observe these basic electrical safety rules:

Always cut power to the circuit you are working on. Throw the breaker to "off," or remove the fuse entirely. Double-check by using a neon tester before handling wires. An extra

measure of safety is to cut power to the whole house before working.

Never connect a white wire to a black wire (except when wiring some special-purpose switch configurations). Connect the black wire to the brass-colored terminal on all devices. Connect the white wire to the silver-colored terminal on all devices. Connect the bare wire to the green terminal on all devices.

Laying Things Out

When planning and laying out basic systems, a good way to avoid complicated snaking of wires and burying of pipes is to provide a utility channel. When you are doing a total restoration of plaster, it is often practical to chop a 2-foot-wide channel in a central wall from the basement to the top floor. Pipes and wires can run inside this channel. You can frame the channel about one foot out from the wall with 2x4s and cover with white pine or chipboard. Use screws to attach the sheathing so that you can open the channel up from time to time as needed. After the channel is completed, you can use wood molding and patching plaster to mate the channel edges with the surrounding plaster.

From the central channel you can run wires and pipes under the floor by taking up the boards and notching or drilling the joists to take pipes and wires. The floorboards can be replaced over the utilities and secured with screws.

One advantage of this system is that utilities are easily accessible for repair or modification both in the channel and under the floorboards. You won't be able to take up floorboards under hardwood floors without marring the design. In this case, you might consider running branch utilities off the central core by putting them behind baseboards, which can be removed and the studs behind them notched or drilled.

Another approach is to make use of any old ducts that may exist in the house. Some houses were converted to radiator heat from duct heat, and the old ducts are usually intact. This is especially useful for wiring. To take advantage of straight ducts, just drop a rope from the duct opening to the basement and tie the wire to the bottom of the rope. Pull the rope slowly back up through the duct and the wire will come up too. For ducts with gentle curves, use a flat wire snake about ¼ inch by 30 feet. Run the snake down the duct, attach the wire, and pull up.

You can make use of the channel that may exist for the vertical sewage stack. Uncover the stack and run water supply pipes alongside the sewage stack. This works well with water-supply pipes because the vertical stack goes just about everywhere that you need to run water lines.

There is nothing to prevent you from running pipes completely exposed. Many old houses have exposed heating and gas pipes, and exposed pipes and ducts are a part of the design of many modern interiors as well. If your decor can stand exposed pipes, just run them from the basement to the top floor. All you have to do is cut holes in each floor. Pipes should stand out from the wall by about 6 inches.

⤷ VENTING SYSTEMS

There is one other basic system that you should know about. Forced-air venting systems are often required to exchange

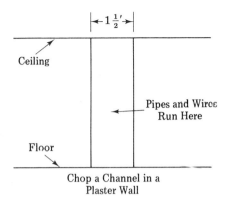

Chop a Channel in a
Plaster Wall

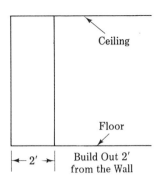

Build Out 2'
from the Wall

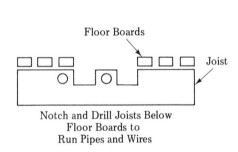

Notch and Drill Joists Below
Floor Boards to
Run Pipes and Wires

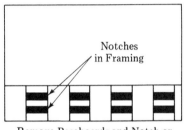

Remove Baseboards and Notch or
Drill Framing to Run
Pipes and Wires

Methods for Running Utilities.

the air in bathrooms and kitchens. Moisture and cooking fumes can build up in these areas and must be removed to avoid damaging plaster and paint. Most local building codes specify that each room of a house must have at least one window to the outside. If you partition a new kitchen, bathroom, or laundry room in your house, it may be impossible or impractical to provide that minimum window requirement. In this case a forced-air venting system is the answer.

Venting systems consist of a wall or ceiling fan and a short run of duct to the outside. The duct is usually equipped with a one-way flap so that outside air

cannot enter the room through the vent. Exhaust fans are rated by their ability to move cubic feet of air-per-minute (CFM). A kitchen fan should be able to move at least 2 CFM for each square foot of floor area. A bathroom fan should move at least 1 CFM for each square foot of floor area. A fan in an enclosed laundry room should move about 1½ CFM for each square foot of floor area.

Most situations can be handled with a through-the-wall type of ventilator fan with built-in duct work. These units are complete kits that only require creating an opening through an exterior wall and connection to a power source. They often come with expandable duct sleeves that adjust to the thickness of the wall. Ceiling fans require more complicated installation and separate ductwork, but they are generally more quiet than wall-mounted units.

Most ventilators come with built-in, pull-chain switches for manual operation of the fan. All ventilators can be wired to turn on and off with a light switch, which guarantees that they will run when the room is being used. There are also spring-wound 30- or 60-minute time switches available that are installed in a wall-switch box for automatic control of ventilators for extended periods.

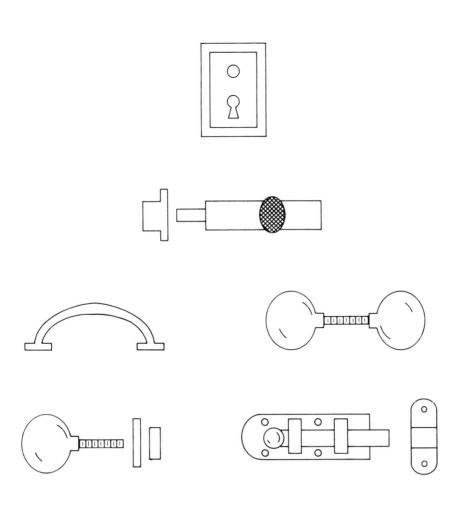

6

Fixtures

You can spend a good deal of money on fixtures for your home unless you keep an eye out for bargains and opportunities for recycling. Here are a few suggestions on budget fixtures for the various rooms of your house.

⌐ BATHROOM

Unless the toilet is in perfect shape, replace it. A new toilet is not expensive, and it is worth every penny to have a quiet, reliable toilet. The least expensive toilet will be a reverse-trap tank toilet in white vitreous china. This is a proven design and is efficient and easy to maintain. It can operate on any water pressure (important in old houses with small water mains), because the flush comes from water stored in the tank.

Toilet seats are interchangeable for all toilets with standard-size bowls. The least expensive seat is enameled, molded wood. It will last about 10 years. The next step up is solid high-impact plastic. These seats are worth the extra cost as they will not fade and are very durable.

Try to find a cast-iron pedestal sink. They are available through secondhand shops, salvage yards, and the classified-ad paper. These sinks look great in old houses, and they save you money and time because they don't require a cabinet as more modern sinks do. You can replace the old-fashioned faucets with conversion kits available at the plumbing store. Measure the distance between the centers of the two faucet holes in the sink. Take the measurements to the store and ask to be shown the various faucet options. Be sure to convert to a mixing type of faucet unless you like to fill the bowl from the individual hot and cold faucets every time you want warm water. Replace the old drain outlet with

This sink is installed without a cabinet to save money and space. It is mounted on hangers fastened to the wall. Because of its chromed supply sets and a chromed S trap, the installation looks clean and neat with its exposed parts. Note the hexagonal quarry tile flooring.

A Recycled Pedestal Sink. This sink was found in a shell and new fittings were added. The porcelain is still in good condition, but when it wears out it can be refinished. This sink will probably last 100 years.

a new unit that incorporates a pop-up mechanism instead of the old rubber-plug-and-chain arrangement. The new drain outlet will mate to a new brass-and-chrome trap for connecting the sink to a branch drain line.

These old sinks should last forever. The cast-iron construction makes them hard to chip because it provides a firmer base than pressed steel. When the porcelain gets worn, you can have it re-coated by a commercial company that does the job in your home, or you can paint the sink yourself with a two-unit epoxy paint.

If you decide to buy a new sink, you should choose cast iron or solid porcelain in preference to the cheaper enameled pressed-steel sinks. There are composition-product or cultured marble sinks available that perform well, but all but the most expensive ones are manufactured in styles that need separate cabinetry, so the total cost goes rather high.

A cast-iron claw-footed bathtub is worth restoring. It was made to stand alone on the floor, so it saves you the bother and expense of a built-in tub. Buy a simple mixing nozzle from the plumbing store and a new brass waste-water kit, and you're in business. Like the pedestal sink, these tubs should last indefinitely. If the tub won't clean up with scouring cleanser, you can have the porcelain redone or paint it with epoxy. Kits are available for converting these tubs into stand-up showers. Also investigate the possibility of hooking a hand-held telephone style shower into the water supply to make washing hair an easier task.

The simplest and cheapest shower is going to be a plastic-composition shower stall which you can buy at discount department stores, plumbing supply stores, and home-improvement stores. It consists of a square molded base which connects to a drain and three plastic sides that clip or screw together. This shower can be put up and connected in a few hours. These units are cleanly designed, and if you put them against a wall they can look as if they were built in. Most of the units come complete with drain, tailpiece, and drain cover, mixing faucet and shower head, and all fittings. All you have to do is supply ½-inch copper tubing to connect the unit to hot- and cold-water pipes.

For toilet paper and towels in the bathroom, construct holders out of scrap white pine and doweling. Make simple shelves out of white pine and use metal brackets to mount them on the wall.

Instead of a conventional medicine cabinet, buy an interesting old mirror and hang it on the wall over the sink. Underneath it put a few shelves to hold shaving equipment, soap, toothbrushes, etc. Store the rest of the bathroom supplies in a separate free-standing cabinet or on more shelves elsewhere in the bathroom. If you use a free-standing tub and sink for your bathroom, it is more attractive to use this style for cabinets, mirrors, and towel and paper holders rather than modern built-in units.

↜KITCHEN

The best choice for the kitchen sink is stainless steel. It is inexpensive, won't chip or deteriorate, and will last a lifetime. Stainless-steel kitchen sinks come in single- and double-bowl styles. A dou-

A simple towel rack made of 2 x 4 and dowel.

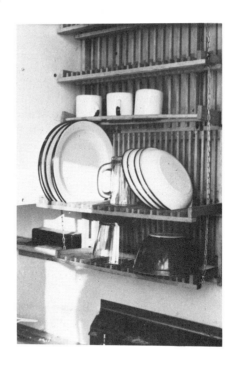

An Interesting Solution to a Space Problem. There wasn't room in this kitchen for a conventional drain board, so the renovator suspended a wooden rack above the sink to allow dishes to drain directly. When trying to avoid cabinetry in the kitchen, think about hanging things from the walls or ceiling.

ble-bowl sink is a worthwhile extra-cost option. Two bowls allow you more preparation and clean-up space.

Buy strainers and tailpieces that are matched to the sink. The only other item you need is a single-lever faucet. A single-lever faucet is ideal because it is simple and trouble free. Single-lever faucets can be totally rebuilt in half an hour with an inexpensive kit. A brand-name, single-lever faucet should last for 20 years or more with periodic rebuilding of the moving parts.

At the bare minimum you will need a cabinet to mount your sink in and a storage system for pots, pans, and kitchen utensils. There are floor- and wall-mounted prefabricated cabinets available, but it is difficult to find them in the materials and styles suitable to old houses at a reasonable cost.

One option is to build your own cabinets with 2 x 4s and chipboard. Surface them with a rugged material such as quarry tile. The standard height for cabinets that must match ranges and stoves is 36 inches. (See the how-to projects for details on building and surfacing cabinets.)

Save money by avoiding wall-hung and built-in cabinets for pots and utensils and hang these items by nailing 2 x 4s or 1 x 12 white pine to the wall and driving hooks into the wood for the pot handles. You can stain the wood or sand and bleach it for a natural look.

You can save money and make a virtue of the open look by following the design of a professional kitchen. In a professional kitchen everything is in sight—most things hang or are on open shelves. You can eliminate the need for five conventional cabinets by hanging a 4 x 5-foot section of ornate iron fence from the ceiling and hanging all your pots from it with S hooks.

Used stoves and refrigerators can save you money and in many cases are

Two Examples of Iron Fence that Can Be Recycled. The piece leaning against the fence is going to be hung from the ceiling in a kitchen as a rack for pots and utensils.

built better than new units. Look for them in the classified ads. Gas stoves are superior to electric ranges because you can control the burner heat more precisely.

Porcelain and steel gas stoves from the 1920s and 30s are fairly abundant in secondhand stores and on the private market. These old stoves can be cleaned up easily and will still provide years of service. The one drawback is that they don't have pilot lights or automatic oven thermostats. You must buy an oven thermometer and light the burners by hand. The very lack of these sensitive controls is what makes the stoves so durable—there is very little to break.

↘ ELECTRICAL

The key to saving money on electrical fixtures is to adapt and recycle. Rewire old floor lamps and old metal and porcelain fixtures that you come across in your renovation.

Shop for electrical parts at a place where you can browse through the selection. Often you can construct something out of a few odd parts. Check out the variety of threaded lamp parts that interchange and fit with each other. Lamps can be constructed out of almost anything; overturned clay pots, a cluster of Y sockets fitted together, or a stainless steel bowl with a hole drilled in it.

For utility lighting, use a bare bulb in a porcelain socket that can be screwed to any surface. These sockets come plain or with a pull-chain switch.

For outside lighting, avoid fancy decorative fixtures that may not withstand the elements well. Use outdoor floodlight bulbs mounted in porcelain and metal holders with swivel necks for adjusting the direction of light.

Find industrial electrical supply houses and scan their catalogs for inexpensive, well-designed fixtures that you can adapt to your own uses.

↘ CABINETS AND DOOR HARDWARE

To harmonize with the look of an old house, you should choose classic styles of door and cabinet hardware. These classics are also cheaper and often easier to install than modern styles.

For doors, use glass or plain white porcelain doorknobs. Use simple brass backing plates for the knobs. Brass knobs are available and look very good, but the plating can quickly wear off unless you go for solid brass.

For cabinets use plain porcelain or wood knobs. These are sold with brass or black bolts that go through a single hole in the door. There are also solid brass or black-finish handles for sliding doors or windows that mount with screws. Any of these products are good for simplicity and durability.

To hold cabinet and closet doors in place, use magnetic catches. They are inexpensive, simple to install, and don't wear out because they have no moving parts.

For bathroom doors, use a simple brass or steel surface-mount sliding bolt for one-way locking. For a neater look, you can install a device called a *mortise bolt,* which is concealed in the edge of the door.

You may have to go to a large hardware store that specializes in door hardware to find these items. Look in the Yellow Pages listing for hardware stores, and see if there is a store that specializes in decorative or architectural hardware.

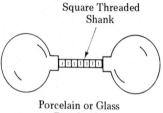

Square Threaded
Shank

Porcelain or Glass
Doorknob

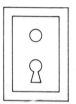

Brass Backing Plate
for Knobs

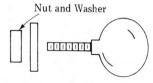

Nut and Washer

Porcelain or Wood
Cabinet Knob

Brass Handle for
Doors or Windows

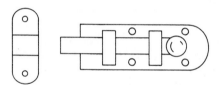

Sliding Bolt
Surface Mount

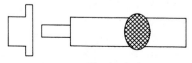

Mortise Bolt
Hidden Mount

Magnetic Catch and Plate for
Cabinet and Closet Doors

Hardware for Doors and Cabinets.

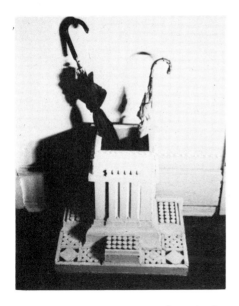

A Cornice Piece that Was Found on the Street During Demolition of a Building. It makes an unusual umbrella stand.

A Quarry Tile Countertop on a Chipboard Cabinet. Notice how the edges are bound with strips of white pine.

Two Views of a Sink-and-Cabinet Unit Constructed of Recycled Doors and White Pine. The old and new materials combine well. The countertop is laminated butcher block, which is available precut for single- or double-bowl sinks.

7

Working on
the Living Space

After you have planned and placed your home's basic systems, you have accomplished the difficult work. Renewing and replacing the vital parts of a house takes time, money, and skill. Putting the rooms of an old house in order is less expensive and more fun. Don't be tempted to renovate rooms before you tackle the basic systems, however. If you do you will have to undo and redo a lot of work. Leaky roofs have a way of staining new paint jobs; wires, pipes, and ducts find a way to rip up woodwork and hardwood flooring.

Waiting for the basic systems to be renovated has another benefit. You are forced to wait a bit before tearing into the rooms, and you can start your work more rationally.

If you live with the way the house is for a while, you may come to appreciate it more. By waiting, the temptation to rip everything out and start over is quelled a bit.

If you remember, I advised you to find and buy a house that was set up in a way that pleases you. This is true even of shells. The idea is to save as much of the original house as you can.

Saving, recycling, and restoring beat total remodeling in several important areas. By saving and restoring you gain the following advantages:

You save money and preserve workmanship that you can't buy anymore.

The materials in old houses are top quality. You probably can't buy material as good.

Restoring an old house's original features makes a unified and harmonious renovation.

A carefully restored house has greater market value than a half-new, half-old remodeled house. This market value advantage can range up to 20–30 percent.

Detail of a Restored Staircase. Everything here is original. There had been a fire, but the wood was not badly burned, and it could be restored.

Window Opposite Staircase. This window was in the same fire, but with careful stripping and refinishing, the details came back. Notice the insulation wrapped around the hot-water pipe at right.

Everything in this picture is new except the stair rail, balusters, and baseboard. There is a new plaster wall, new stairs, and new floorboards. The old materials combine well with the new construction. The new materials are simple and natural and emphasize the restored items.

One approach to security is to make shutters for windows. The hinges used here are special shutter hinges, but "T" hinges could be used as well. Notice the industrial style light fixture above the shutters.

Consider the problems that drastic changes can cause:

Extensive demolition or changing the shape of rooms generally requires a building permit and architectural drawings.

Tearing something out involves demolition, mess, disposal, new material costs, labor, and clean-up.

Tearing something out may also have a wave effect and cause damage or changes that will take two or three other jobs to put right.

All of this is by way of saying: Stop and consider before rushing into something. Remember that restoring merely involves stripping, repairing, and refinishing, but tearing out involves all that and much more. Consider the clashing effect that some modern materials can have when placed in an old house next to original work. You must use care and judgment when selecting hardware, fixtures, paint, and finishes for an old home.

There are times when starting from scratch is the best way. There may be parts of an old house that are so rotten, outmoded, and unnecessary that they must be replaced. But save as much as you can. You might want to try some unusual ideas in order to avoid tearing out. I have installed new drywall sheets directly over damaged plaster walls and ceilings. I experimented and found out where the studs were below the old plaster. I fastened the new sheets with extra long nails right through the old plaster and into the old studs. The resulting wall was thicker and more soundproof than before, and there was very little mess to contend with.

Most people demand absolute newness for bathrooms and kitchens. Go with your instincts here, but consider the effect you can achieve with free-standing fixtures, classic materials, recycled cabinets, and simple design in hardware and finishes.

When you start planning your interior renovation, you should expose yourself to the best in design. Read magazines and books, and attend lectures and courses on the subject. Visit restored homes done by amateurs, experts, and museums. Decide what you like and why. Get pamphlets and reports by historical commissions and neighborhood associations on paints, hardware, craftsmen, lumberyards, and other resources that can be helpful to you.

⤷ LIVING WHILE YOU WORK

One way to get started on your renovation and to guarantee that you keep going is to move into your house as soon as possible. This has several advantages. For one thing, you save the money that you would be spending on another living space. For another, you get an intimate feel for your house which may affect your plans for restoring it. And again, living with the renovation process forces you to get started on each new project and keep going until it is completed.

You can move into your house as soon as it is cleaned out, sealed from the elements, and made secure. If you time your purchase of a home correctly, you can work through the warm months without having to fix the heating system. This can buy you the time to make enough repairs to let you move in and get organized before you start thinking about a major expense like replacing the heating plant.

If you do want to move in as soon as possible, I recommend that you renovate a space for living somewhere on the highest floor. Being on the highest floor keeps you somewhat removed from the dust and mess of any renovations happening on the other floors. As a minimum, you would have to have electric service, water, and a toilet to get started. Move in only what you need to live. Leave most of your furniture and personal belongings in storage so that they won't get dirty from construction dust.

⤸ A RENOVATION TIMETABLE

A rough timetable of events in a renovation that you can use as a guide for your own work follows on page 90.

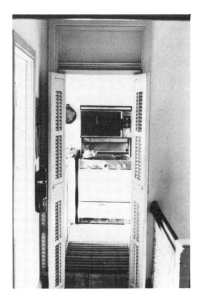

These long window shutters have been recycled into doors for a kitchen where they contribute to the sense of light and space.

A Quiet Corner in a House under Renovation. This room needed nothing more than to have the wallpaper and woodwork stripped and refinished. The renovator did this room first and moved some furniture in. By so doing, he has a place to rest and relax while finishing some of the more difficult parts of the house. Doing one small part of the house inspires you to complete the rest and provides valuable experience that gives you confidence to tackle other jobs.

1. Fumigate an infested shell.

2. Seal exterior of house, roof, windows, gutters. Remove efflorescence from bricks, and repair damaged siding.

3. Install security hardware and materials.

4. Repair walks, steps, and porches. Trim threatening trees and growth.

5. Clean out the house; dispose of trash and floor coverings; strip wallpaper; and demolish old plaster. Throw out or sell unusable fixtures and appliances.

6. Repair interior safety problems—steps, floors, doors.

7. Deal with basic systems—electricity, water, gas, drainage, heating, hot-water heater.

8. First opportunity to move in. Renovate a *small* living space, and create a crude kitchen and bath.

9. Continue with basic systems. Plan and install fixtures, more wiring, insulation, and storm windows.

10. Basic systems completed. Start renovating living space. Patch plaster, strip woodwork, install drywall, frame partitions, and replace doors and hardware.

11. Plan and install basic cabinets and fixtures in the kitchen and bath. Install sinks, toilets, tubs and showers. Any built-in or overhead lighting is installed. Built-in closets and storage units are constructed.

12. Sanding and finishing—drywall, plaster, woodwork, cabinetry, floor sanding.

13. Painting and finishing—walls and ceilings painted, woodwork and floors finished, cabinets painted, fixtures refinished.

14. New tile and floor coverings, also countertops.

15. Second opportunity to move in.

16. Improve basic systems—outdoor lighting, time switches, doorbell-intercom, more insulation, storm windows.

17. Improve exterior—point bricks, new steps, make fence, paint trim, brick walkways, etc.

↘ GUTTING AND FINISHING

If you are determined to change the interior of your house completely and start all over again, there is one low-cost option. You can demolish all the interior walls and ceilings down to the brick and joists. You can leave the brick walls bare and install new drywall over the ceiling joists. Use salvaged framing wood to partition new kitchens and bathrooms. Use drywall to cover the framing. The rest of the space is left open. The floors are sanded and finished or are covered with new hardwood, tile, or chipboard. Use new white pine to make baseboards and window casings and to bind the places where drywall and bare brick meet. The brick is cleaned by sandblasting or an acid bath and left exposed as part of the design.

The resulting space is a contemporary open plan that is very adaptable to a number of designs. One option is to let each area be defined by rugs and furnishings and not to partition anything except bathrooms. Another way to go is to use partitions of 2x4s and drywall to change the floorplan of the space. What was originally one large room is now free to be partitioned into two or more intimate rooms. Modular units can be easily installed in the newly created raw space. Skylights, metal stair units, and completely prefabricated kitchen and bathroom units are all possibilities for a totally contemporary lifestyle within a gutted older building.

The demolition must be carefully planned. Hire containers to put lath and plaster in. Tear the walls down with a wrecking bar. Use the crooked end to pull lath and plaster off the framing and joists in large hunks. The demolition itself goes suprisingly fast, but the cleaning up takes time. Use a wheelbarrow

and cardboard boxes to haul plaster to the container. For upper floors, build a plywood chute out of a window to direct plaster and lath into the container. Save any framing wood that you come across.

When you clean everything out, work on the bare brick walls. They will be dirty so wash them down with a strong solution of trisodium phosphate (available at paint stores). Use a flat scrub brush on a handle, and keep washing down until the color of the wall lightens and evens out. You can rent a sandblaster to clean the walls, but it makes an unholy mess. Any especially tough stains can be removed with muriatic acid (available at masonry dealers).

Front View of a Building Just About Completed. The cornice has been painted, and all that remains to be done is to remove the efflorescence from the bricks with a solution of muriatic acid. The only brickwork that had to be done to this front was to replace three bricks above the door.

Detail Showing the Classic 6-panes-over-6-panes Window. This and other classic styles are available from lumber and mill yards if you can't restore existing windows. The 6-over-6 window is available in wood or aluminum frame models.

When the wall is clean go over it carefully and point any bad joints with mortar so that they are sealed. If you don't want to clean and point the wall and you want a lighter, more finished effect than bare brick, you can paint the bricks with an oil-based paint. Use a brush, and thin the first coat with paint thinner so that it spreads easily over the rough surface. Brush the second coat on full strength.

Cover the ceiling joists with drywall. Use a ladder and a T stick to install. Insulate with fiberglass between the joists before covering with drywall if the ceiling is just below a roof or uninsulated space.

Use salvaged framing members to create bathrooms and kitchens. Cover the frame with drywall or use chipboard (which allows you to use less framing lumber). Bind the places where brick, drywall, and window come together by using strips of white pine. Cut 6-inch strips of white pine for new baseboards. Drive masonry nails through the wood into the mortar joints to secure the baseboards.

Refinish the floors or cover them with a new material. For economy you can use 1 x 6 roofing boards or 1-foot squares of chipboard. (See the how-to for details on flooring.)

Leave radiators, drain pipes, water pipes, and gas pipes exposed. Run electrical wires inside a wooden channel or inside metal conduit. Use industrial-style metal outlet boxes for electrical outlets. Secure fixtures to the brick walls with masonry anchors.

<u>Two Views of Security Bars Made of Salvaged Iron Fencing.</u> The window on the right is protected by two lengths of fence butted end to end.

This homemade skylight is built of scrap wood and a piece of plexiglass. Where the wood and glass butt, the roof is covered with roof cement. Security is provided by ½-inch concrete reinforcing rods, which can be bought cheaply by the bundle at steel supply houses. Prefabricated skylights are also available with aluminum mounting lips that are screwed into the roof and covered with roof cement.

A Small Porch Made of Scrap Wood. Notice the gutter boxes and downspouts for draining the roofs. Between the downspouts is PVC drainpipe, which the renovator elected to run outside the building to save space inside.

One drawback to this open plan is that you lose a small insulating factor when you tear out plaster and lath walls. Exposed brick can be cold. Combat this by pointing every gap in the wall, caulking window frames inside and out, and insulating behind every new drywall ceiling and wall that you make. Also see the how-to on insulating pipes and improving the efficiency of radiators.

__Many old buildings have top floors that are shorter than the lower floors.__ This invites deck building. The deck shown rests on concrete blocks that sit directly on the roof. Four-inch-by-four-inch beams sit on the blocks and support the decking. After the deck was built, roof cement was applied around all the blocks to prevent water leakage.

8

Painting and Finishing

The most important thing to remember about painting is that the surface to be painted must be prepared. It's strange how an otherwise careful craftsperson will go a little crazy when it comes to painting. It must be the promise of quick results, the thought that when paint is on things will look so much better, that infects people.

Try to take painting slowly and rationally. The painted surface will look only as good and be as durable as the care you take in preparing the surface.

Surface preparation in renovation includes: chemical stripping, sanding, washing, wire-brushing, scraping, and priming. When painting wood, you must remove thick old accumulations of paint with chemical stripper and then sand. You must scrape old wallpaper and flaking paint off walls and ceilings, patch holes, and sand smooth. You should wirebrush rust and scale off metal, and

thoroughly wash with detergent and water. When painting surfaces with only one or two coats of old paint, scrape and sand off any loose and flaking paint and wash with detergent and water.

Taking the extra time to prepare the surface will make the painting go more smoothly and the job will look better and last longer than if you slap a coat of paint on hoping to cover everything up.

⤵ WALLS

After the plaster or drywall has been prepared by sanding, you can paint with a latex paint. Latex paint is perfect for interior walls and ceilings because it is inexpensive, relatively odorless, quick drying, and cleans up easily with water. The best way to apply it is with a roller and a 2-inch brush.

Before painting with a roller, use the narrow brush on all the corners and all the places where the wall abuts a fixture, a window frame, a doorframe, and the baseboards. Cutting in all the difficult and tight places where a roller can't go lets you really fly when you do use the roller.

Use a 9-inch-wide roller to fill in the spaces between the cut-in lines. If you are painting over naked plaster or drywall you will probably have to use two coats of paint. Cut in the corners and tight places for the second coat and roll the rest.

⤳ WOODWORK

When the woodwork has been prepared down to bare wood or sound old paint, use a primer before the final color coat. The primer provides a good surface for the final coat to bite on and it is slightly resilient so that an occasional bump or nick won't cause the final coat of paint to chip off. It costs you no more to use a primer. If you put a color coat on bare wood you would have to use two coats to get an even finish. With a primer, one coat should cover. The most versatile primer for wood is a latex-based product that will prime wood for oil or latex paints.

There are many kinds of finish paint for woodwork but for a glossy, easy-to-clean surface, select an oil-based paint. Apply it with a brush and use masking tape or a paint guard to keep from over-painting onto walls or floor. You can use an old slat from venetian blinds to make your own paint guard. Carry a rag with you as you go along to wipe up spills, drips, and splatters. Oil-based paint cleans up with paint thinner. Use a little thinner on a rag to dab hands clean, and soak brushes in soup cans of thinner to keep them soft during breaks. Buy inexpensive paint thinner in gallon jugs or cans for economy.

This is what can happen to corners if you don't use wall repair tape before painting. Corners are stress points and can open up after repair unless you take special precautions.

If you want to keep a brush soft and ready for more painting of the same color in a few days, you can wrap it in a plastic bag and stick it in the freezer. Thaw the brush for half an hour before painting again. Use paint thinner and brush cleaner to prepare brushes for long-term storage.

You can also paint woodwork with water-based semigloss latex paint. Semigloss imitates the shine of oil-based paint and can be cleaned and scrubbed just like oil-based paint; but semigloss also has the advantage of drying quickly and cleaning with soap and water as does latex wall paint. Use a primer and one color coat of semigloss just as if you were using oil-based paint.

For any natural woodwork that you have stripped and cleaned, you can finish with clear urethane varnish. Urethane varnish will darken the color of the wood slightly, and so you should strip and bleach the wood one shade lighter than you want it to be when urethaned.

Three coats of urethane varnish is the standard for a shiny durable finish on wood. The urethane coats should be applied within 48 hours of each other. If more time elapses between coats, rough up the surface with steel wool or fine sandpaper to provide a good bite for the new urethane. No priming is necessary with urethane; the first coat sinks into and seals the wood, and then the top two coats provide the glossy low maintenance finish. Urethane cleans up with paint thinner.

Two other finishes are possible for wood. Raw wood can be stained with an oil-based or latex-based stain. Of the two types of stain, the oil-based penetrating stain is the more durable. The stain is carried to a depth of ⅛-¼ inch into the wood by the solvents in the stain. Latex stains tend to lay much more on the surface of the wood and are more vulnerable to weathering and mechanical damage.

Related to stains are clear and colored wood preservatives. Clear preservatives are powerful solvents that can sink into wood and increase its resistance to rot, insects, and water damage. There are several brands of clear preservatives available on the market. Any of them will do a good job if applied liberally to raw wood. You should check the label of your product to make sure that the surface can be painted or otherwise finished after it is treated with preservative.

One of the oldest of the colored wood preservatives is *creosote oil*. It is a coal-tar derivative, and it is very economical to produce. Creosote preserves telephone poles, railroad ties, and pier pilings. It colors the wood a dark brown that will mellow over the years. Creosote is very effective against insects and ground moisture. You can use it for fence posts, landscaping timber, and rough fencing boards. Creosote is used for exterior purposes only, because of its strong smell. Once wood is treated with creosote it cannot be painted or stained with any other material.

Oil-based stains, preservatives, and creosote can be applied with a brush. You should use rubber gloves or coat your hands with petroleum jelly to protect yourself. All of these products should be applied in two or three coats. Latex-based stains clean up with water and pose no threat to your skin.

⤸ FLOORS

For hardwood or natural wood floors that have been sanded, use a clear urethane floor varnish. Three coats are necessary for a glossy and low-maintenance finish. Cut in around the baseboards with a small brush and then fill in the large area with a brush just a little smaller than the can opening. Large areas can also be coated with a thick-nap paint roller—just pour urethane into a clean roller pan and feed the roller frequently with urethane as you work. A roller with an extension handle makes coating floors easy.

Floors and stairs can also be painted. Look for floor and deck enamel blended with urethane. You might want to select a dark color that won't show the dirt and wear quickly. Use two coats, and cut in the corners before filling with a large brush or roller. A floor that has been cleaned and well-prepared should look good for many years with the new deck paints that are available.

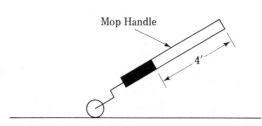

Mop Handle

4'

Rolling Floors with Urethane or Deck Paint.

⤸ METAL

Fences should be wire-brushed to remove rust and then cleaned with detergent and water. Use a rust-inhibitive (fish-oil base) primer over bare metal and then cover with a color coat of oil-based paint. You may want to use spray cans on ornate fences, but they are uneconomical for really big jobs. If the fence is ornate you will make better progress with a small fat brush than a big flat one.

Gutters and downspouts of galvanized steel can be painted with a special red lead or zinc oxide primer developed for them and then covered with an oil-based color coat. You may want to use a latex exterior house paint on gutters, but read the label or ask the store personnel about the paint's durability on metal.

Paint a metal roof with a red lead primer paint (red roof). This paint is thick and can fill in small cracks and seams. Use two coats of primer for a simple low-maintenance finish. Use one coat of primer and one color coat of an oil-based paint if color is important, but remember that roofs take a tremendous beating and even the best exterior paints will fade.

⤸ EXTERIOR WOODWORK

After all the exterior trim, window and doorframe and porch woodwork has been prepared, you can paint with a primer and one color coat. Clear urethane is not recommended for exterior wood—it cannot stand the ultraviolet rays of the sun. Use a top-quality oil-based or latex-based exterior paint. You get what you pay for in paint, and it makes sense to apply the best you can afford on the exterior so that you won't have to do it every five years. Both oil- and latex-based exterior paints look good and are durable; however, oil-based paint will look glossier and may stay cleaner (especially in sooty urban locations) than latex.

Use a small fat sash brush for painting window frames and door frames. Use a large flat brush for straight runs of trim and porch posts.

CHIPBOARD

Chipboard takes a good finish when it is primed and then painted with oil-based paint. When you use chipboard for kitchen or bathroom cabinets you might want a more durable epoxy-based paint. Chipboard can also be finished with clear urethane varnish. It darkens and looks like cork. The chipboard will soak up the first two coats of urethane, so be prepared to use three or more coats to get a shiny surface.

FIXTURES AND APPLIANCES

You can paint old scarred porcelain bathtubs and sinks with epoxy paint and renew stoves and refrigerators too. Look for a two-unit epoxy that you mix and apply immediately. These two-unit paints are expensive but are perhaps the hardest and most durable finishes available. For small noncritical jobs there are epoxy-based paints in spray cans.

COLOR SCHEMES

One note on using color in a renovation—painting different walls and woodwork with different colors can be tricky and expensive. Unless you have a natural or trained color and design sense you can get in trouble.

Most people want a unified look in their homes. The best way to ensure this is to choose one or two basic colors and stick with them throughout the entire house. Remember that color variety can be achieved through floor coverings, hangings, and furniture as well as with paint.

One easy way out of the problem is to use the "Architect's Solution." Use as much white paint as you can. White walls and ceilings brighten the dark spaces of old houses and throw focus to any natural woodwork that you may have. White paint reflects natural and artificial light and bounces it around in a way that is very flattering to people and furniture.

Certainly the various shades of white paint are inexpensive. You might use the money and time you save by painting white to buy and display some art on your walls. White paint is also consistent from batch to batch. Any paint retailer will tell you that colored paint differs from lot to lot, and matching colors exactly is especially difficult with custom-mixed intense colors. White paint offers you a good match even if you buy the paint over long periods of time. White paint is also available in economical 5-gallon plastic pails. These pails can save you 20 percent over single-gallon prices.

9

9

Carpentry Projects

⌐ HOW TO FRAME A WALL

Tools and supplies needed:

Hammer
Circular saw
Tape measure
Level
2 x 4 lumber
3½-inch common nails

Procedure:

Sometimes it is necessary to install a new wall or partition in an old home to replace a demolished one, create a new room, or subdivide an oversize room. The basic method for erecting new walls is to frame them with 2 x 4 lumber. The frame can then be covered with drywall, lath and plaster (or stucco), plywood, chipboard, or any other suitable sheathing material.

Install the top plate of the frame first. Cut a piece of 2 x 4 to the length of the partition. If the top plate is to be installed crossways to the joists, you can nail it to the joists with nails long enough to reach through the existing plaster and into the joists.

If the top plate is to be installed parallel to the joists, it must be nailed in place directly below a joist. If the placement of a parallel top plate falls between two joists, the plaster and lath must be removed and 2 x 6 or larger blocking pieces must be nailed between the joists at 2-foot intervals along the length of the partition for the top plate to nail into.

After the top plate is nailed into position, install the sole plate by nailing it into the floor. The sole plate should be the length of the top plate. To ensure that the wall will be straight and level, use the top plate to dictate where the

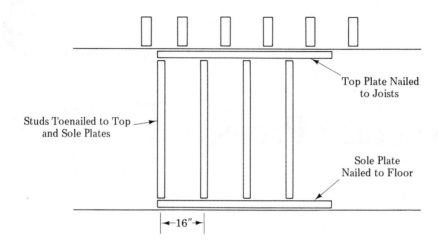

Top Plate Nailed
to Joists

Studs Toenailed to Top
and Sole Plates

Sole Plate
Nailed to Floor

←16"→

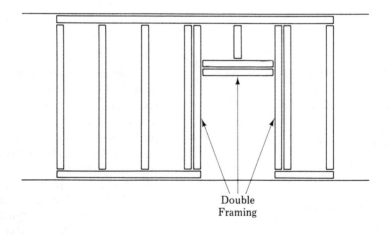

Double
Framing

Basic Framing.

sole plate is positioned. Hang a plumb bob from several points along the top plate and mark them on the floor, or use a straight piece of 2 x 4 and a level to mark points on the floor to position the sole plate.

After the sole plate is in position, measure and cut enough lengths of 2 x 4 to have one stud every 16 inches along the plate length. The studs should fit snugly between the top and sole plates. You should measure each stud because the distance between the top and sole plate may vary along the partition's length.

Toenail the studs to the top and sole plate by driving nails at a 45-degree angle into the sides of the studs and through to the top or sole plates. Any doorways in the partition are framed out with double 2 x 4 construction. Nail two 2 x 4s together and install on the edges and over the top of the doorway. The double 2 x 4 that spans the top of the doorway is called a *header*. Install a single vertical stud between the header and the top plate and toenail it in place to add stability to the doorway.

This basic frame is adaptable to just about any non-load-bearing interior wall. It can be adapted to build closets and alcoves as well as straight-line partitions.

The important thing is to nail the top plate securely to the ceiling joists and to install the sole plate in plumb with the top plate.

In Brief:

1. Cut a piece of 2 x 4 the length of the partition. Nail this top plate across the joists with nails long enough to reach through the wood and plaster and into the joist. If the plate runs parallel to the joists, it must be nailed exactly under a joist; otherwise blocking must be installed between joists for securing the top plate.

2. Use the top plate to position the sole plate. Hang a plumb bob from the top plate to mark the position of the sole plate on the floor, or use a straight piece of 2 x 4 and a level. Install the sole plate with nails into the floorboards.

3. Measure and cut enough vertical studs to place one every 16 inches along the partition's length. Measure each stud so that it fits snugly between the top and sole plate. Toenail the studs into the top and sole plates.

4. Frame any doorways with double 2 x 4 construction. Nail two 2 x 4s together and install them on the edges and over the top of the doorway. Install a single vertical stud between the header and the top plate and toenail it in place.

HOW TO INSTALL FURRING STRIPS

Tools and supplies needed:

Circular saw
Hammer
Tape measure
Level
Caulking gun
2-inch common nails
2-inch masonry nails
1 x 2-inch or 1 x 3-inch furring strips
Small wood wedges or shims
Tubes of mastic or panel adhesive

Procedure:

If you intend to cover a bare masonry wall with drywall or some other sheet material, you must first install furring strips so that you have a level nailing surface. Furring strips can also be used to provide an even, clean nailing surface over old, rough, and wavy plaster walls.

Furring strips are installed horizontally across the wall by driving nails into the vertical studs (in the case of old plaster walls) or driving masonry nails into the mortar joints between bricks (in the case of bare masonry walls).

Nail one furring strip across the bottom of the wall and one strip across the top of the wall, and then install one strip every 16 inches between these two starter strips. When installing, use the level to check various points across the strips to make sure that you are creating an even nailing surface. If necessary, use small wood wedges or shims behind the strips to bring them even with each other.

For greater support of the sheet material, you can nail vertical furring strips every 48 inches across the surface of the wall. Cut a supply of strips into the correct length to fit snugly between the horizontal furring strips. Install the strips on 48-inch centers, meaning that the center of the strip will be placed exactly 48 inches from the center of neighboring strips. If you are installing furring over bare brick, you can fasten the vertical strips directly to the wall with masonry nails. Use the level and shims to get each strip even with the rest of the furring.

If you install vertical furring over an existing wall you can't be sure to catch the studs at 48-inch spacing, so use industrial mastic or wallboard adhesive to attach the strips to the wall. Squeeze a wavy bead of mastic onto the back of the strip and press it to the wall. Use small finishing nails to hold the strip in place if necessary.

In Brief:

1. Nail one furring strip across the bottom of the wall and one strip across the top of the wall. Space other strips every 16 inches between these two starter strips. Use a level and wood shims to make sure that you are creating an even nailing surface.

2. Place vertical furring strips every 48 inches across the surface of the wall. Cut a supply of strips to fit between the horizontal strips and nail them in place. If you can't find a nailing surface for the vertical strips, they can be installed with a bead of mastic or wall adhesive and small finishing nails.

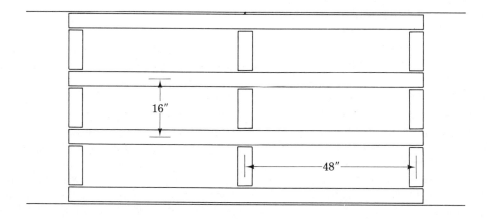

Furring Strip Pattern.

⤸ MAKING A PLANK DOOR FOR ALLEYS AND BACKYARDS

Tools and supplies needed:

Circular saw
Tape measure
Hammer
Board lumber, 1 or 2 inches thick
Galvanized roofing nails

Procedure:

If you need an exterior door for privacy and security to a backyard, courtyard, or alley you can make one up from board lumber. A plank door is ideal for exterior uses because it doesn't have any fancy carving or paneling to loosen and deteriorate in the weather. You can make your door as rough or as finished as you want by selecting different board lumber. Some suitable lumber would be 1 x 12-inch white pine, 1 x 6-inch tongue-and-groove roofing boards, 2 x 12-inch white pine, or random width 2-inch-thick rough-sawn scaffold or form lumber.

Measure the area to be secured and decide how high the door is to be. Cut the board lumber to the proper height and lay the boards down on the ground, butted next to each other. Keep cutting boards and laying them down until you come up with the proper width for the door. You may have to cut one board down its length to come up with the exact width you need.

Cut two lengths of board to the exact width of the door. Lay these planks down across the boards lying on the ground. Position these crosspieces one foot in from the top and bottom edges of the door. Make sure that the edges of the door boards align exactly and that the door is square. Nail the two crosspieces

to the door planks with galvanized roofing nails. Use two or three nails into each door plank. For extra strength you can use screws or bolts.

Lay a board across the door in a diagonal direction from the lower right-hand corner of the upper crosspiece to the upper left-hand corner of the lower crosspiece. Lay a ruler across the diagonal board and bring the ruler even with the bottom edge of the upper crosspiece. Mark a cut line on the diagonal board with a pencil. Move the ruler down the diagonal board and bring it even with the top edge of the bottom crosspiece. Mark a cut line with a pencil.

Cut the diagonal board with the circular saw along the cut lines. Lay the cut board down between the upper and lower crosspieces so that the three boards form the letter Z on the back of the door. Nail the diagonal board to the door planks with galvanized roofing nails.

Finish the door by brushing on a clear wood preservative, a penetrating wood stain, creosote oil, or exterior latex or oil paint. Attach the door to the doorway with strap hinges or T hinges. Use a double-cylinder deadbolt lock for maximum security.

In Brief:

1. Measure the area to be secured and decide how high the door is to be. Cut board lumber to the proper height and lay the boards down on the ground butted next to each other. Cut enough boards to come up with the proper width of the door. You may have to cut one board down its length to get the exact width of the door.

2. Cut two lengths of board the exact width of the door. Position these

pieces one foot in from the top and bottom of the door. Nail these pieces to the door planks with roofing nails or screw them in place for extra strength.

3. Lay a board across the door in a diagonal direction from the lower right-hand corner of the upper crosspiece to the upper left-hand corner of the lower crosspiece. Use a ruler and a pencil to mark cut lines on the board.

4. Cut the diagonal board with a saw, and lay it down on the door so that it fits between the upper and lower crosspieces to form the letter Z on the door. Nail or screw the diagonal piece to the door.

5. Finish the door by brushing on a wood preservative, penetrating stain, creosote oil, or exterior paint. Attach the door to the doorway with strap hinges or T hinges. Use a double-cylinder deadbolt lock on the door for maximum security.

Tips:

This same simple design can be used to make window shutters. Simply build two doors for each window and hang them with T-hinges. The shutters can be secured from inside with a crossbar or 2 draw bolts.

⤸ HOW TO REPAIR STICKY DOORS

Tools and supplies needed:

Screwdriver
Hammer
Cardboard or wood shims
Toothpicks or wooden matches
White glue

Procedure:

If you are having problems with sticky doors and your doorframes are square and the doors aren't warped, you should suspect that the hinges may have come loose and are allowing the door to sag against the frame. Doors in old houses often pull their hinges out of the door-frame from constant use. The solution is to tighten the screws that hold the hinges to the doorframe.

If the screws won't hold tight, remove them and pack the holes with toothpicks or matches until the hole is full of wood. Dip the filler pieces in white glue and place them in the screw holes. Break off the filler pieces even with the surface of the hole. Insert the old screws, and the hinge should hold securely.

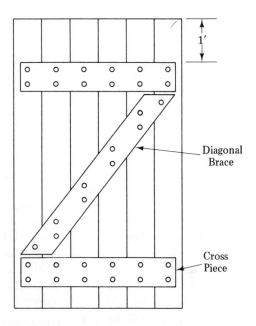

1′

Diagonal Brace

Cross Piece

Plank Door.

If the screws are tight and the door still sticks, it may be that the door is not sitting squarely in the frame. Inspect the door in the closed position and determine if putting a cardboard or wood shim under one hinge would correct the out-of-square condition. When the door is rubbing at the top edge of the doorframe, shim out the top hinge. When it rubs at the bottom edge of the doorframe, shim out the lower hinge.

Remove the screws from the affected hinges and insert one or two thicknesses of cardboard or thin wood (cut to size) under the hinge. Reattach the hinge with screws and check the operation of the door.

In Brief:

1. Tighten all hinge screws.
2. If the screws won't hold, pack the holes with filler dipped in white glue. Break the filler pieces off level with the surface and reattach the hinge with screws.
3. If the door still sticks try shimming one hinge. If the door rubs at the top edge, shim out the top hinge. If it rubs at the bottom edge, shim out the lower hinge.
4. Cut cardboard or thin wood to size and place one or two thicknesses under the affected hinge.

Tips:

Avoid sanding or planing doors. Most situations can be corrected by tightening hinges or shimming. When planing or sanding is necessary (if the door has swelled to oversize, for example), take the wood off the hinge side of the door so that you don't have to remove and reset the lock or latch.

When removing or replacing screws from hinges, use a magazine or wooden wedge under the bottom edge of the door to prevent the door from being suddenly unsupported and tearing out of the doorway.

Most doors can be removed for repair and refinishing by tapping out the pins in the hinges. Use a common nail and a hammer. Place the nail under the rim of the hinge pin and tap lightly upward until the pin is free. Always remove the topmost hinge pin last so that you are standing when the door comes free.

⤙ HOW TO DEAL WITH STICKY AND BALKY WINDOWS

Tools and supplies needed:

Putty knife

Screwdriver

Hammer

Candle or powdered graphite

Sash cord or metal sash chain

1-inch finishing nails

1-inch wood screws

Procedure:

When a window is stuck shut it is usually because of a buildup of paint around the window frame and the stop molding. Use a putty knife to separate the window from the stop molding. Go all along the edge, and cut and scrape any excess paint or dirt away.

Once the window is free, lubricate it with wax from a candle, or use powdered graphite lubricant. Rub the candle along the inside edge of the stop molding, or squirt powdered graphite between the window and the molding.

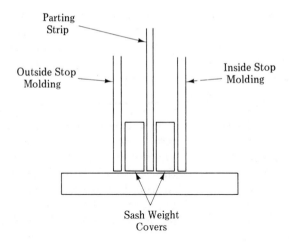

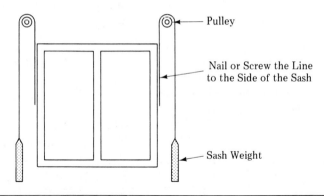

Replacing Sash Weight Cords.

If the window is balky because of broken sash weight cords you must remove the stop molding, bottom window sash, parting strips, and top window sash, in that order. Once everything is out, look at the inside of the window channel at the bottom, and locate the sash weight covers. There will be four of these covers, two on each side of the window channel. You may have to scrape with your putty knife to make out their outlines under the old paint.

Pry these covers open and find the sash weights. Remove the broken ropes or chains from the weights and from the window sashes. Cut new lengths of sash cord or chain by measuring the length of the two broken original pieces. The top sash will need a different length of cord or chain than the bottom sash.

Attach the new sash cord or chain to the sides of the window sashes with finishing nails or screws. Take the top sash, replace it in the window frame, and thread the new cord or chain over the two pulleys at the top of the outside channel. Let the cord or chain drop down into the sash weight chambers. Attach the weights to the end of the cord by knotting or wiring. Replace the two parting strips that hold the top sash in place and secure them with finishing nails.

Take the bottom sash, replace it in the window frame, and thread the new cord or chain over the pulleys at the top of the inside channel. Let the cord or chain drop down into the sash weight chambers. Attach the weights to the end of the cord or chain by knotting or wiring. Replace the sash weight covers on all four sash weight chambers and secure them with screws or finishing nails. Replace the stop molding that holds the bottom sash in place.

In Brief:

1. Scrape and cut any excess paint from between the sash and stop molding to free the window.

2. Lubricate the sash and molding with wax or powdered graphite.

3. To replace broken sash weight cord, remove the stop molding, bottom sash, parting strips, and top sash in that order.

4. Locate the four sash weight covers and pry them off.

5. Remove the broken cord from the weights and window sashes.

6. Cut new lengths of cord or chain by measuring the broken pieces of old cord.

7. Attach the new cord or chain to the sides of the sashes with finishing nails or screws.

8. Replace the top sash in the window frame, and thread the new cord or chain over the two pulleys at the top of the outside channel. Let the cord or chain drop to the weights.

9. Attach the weights to the cord or chain by knotting or wiring.

10. Replace the two parting strips that hold the top sash in place. Secure with finishing nails.

11. Replace the bottom sash in the window frame and thread the new cord or chain over the two pulleys at the top of the inside channel. Let the cord or chain drop to the weights.

12. Attach the weights to the new cord or chain by knotting or wiring.

13. Replace the sash weight covers on all four sash chambers, and secure them with screws or finishing nails.

14. Replace the stop molding that holds the bottom sash in place.

Tips:

Metal sash chain is a better choice than sash cord for most situations. Chain is more durable than cord, and because of its flat links, it rides over the pulleys very smoothly and evenly. It is available in steel and copper. The only time cord is better than chain is in salt-air locations. The salt will quickly rust and corrode metal chain.

↴ HOW TO FIX SQUEAKY STAIRS

Tools and supplies needed:

Hammer
Screwdriver
Drill and bits
Small-head ring nails
Wood screws
Glazier's points
Powdered graphite

Procedure:

Squeaky stairs are caused by one or more loose boards that rub when you step on them. The solution is to secure the boards so that they can't rub.

Drive nails or screws into the edges of the stair tread so that they will go into the wood below. You want to catch the riser, which is the board that supports the front of the stair tread, and the two stringers which are the supports for the sides of the tread. Drill pilot holes every 3 inches along the edges and drive nails or screws into the holes.

For squeaks that don't respond to securing the treads, you can try powdered graphite lubricant and glazier's points. Squirt the lubricant into the joints around the affected tread, and work several glazier's points into each joint with a screwdriver. This treatment will keep the boards from rubbing where you can't drive nails or screws.

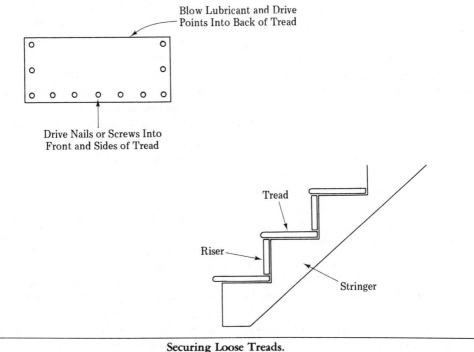

Securing Loose Treads.

If the stair is squeaking because a tread is cracked or so weakened that it bends, you should replace the tread.

In Brief:

1. Drill pilot holes every 3 inches along the front and side edges of the tread.
2. Drive ring nails or wood screws into the holes to secure the tread.
3. For squeaks in places that you can't nail or screw, blow powdered graphite lubricant into the joints.
4. Follow the lubricant by driving several glazier's points into each joint with a screwdriver.

Tips:

Most stairs in old houses are some variety of hardwood, and so you must use pilot holes when driving nails or screws or risk splitting the wood.

To find the proper place to place nails or screws along the front edge of the riser, measure the amount of overhang that the nosing of the tread has over the riser and add ⅜ inch to that.

↰ HOW TO REPLACE A TREAD ON A STAIRWAY

Tools and supplies needed:

Drill and bits
Keyhole saw or utility saw
Hammer
Wood chisel
Tape measure
Standard stair-tread stock
2-inch finishing nails
Industrial mastic

Procedure:

If a stair tread is broken or badly warped, the only real solution is to take it out and replace it. The process is tricky and time consuming, but it is worth it to have a safe and quiet stair.

Cut the damaged tread into thirds. Drill holes in the tread so that you can work a keyhole or utility saw into the tread and cut it into thirds. Stop your cuts just short of the riser pieces in front and back of the tread.

Split out the tread by using a wood chisel with a 1-inch-wide blade. Start on the middle third of the tread, and cut off the nosing over the riser first. After the nosing is gone, work your way back and chisel off 1-inch-wide sections of the tread. Carefully remove the last 1-inch section of tread from the back riser by prying it off the nails that hold it.

After the middle third of the tread is removed, work the chisel into the remaining tread sections from the sides and split them off the stair supports and nails. Carefully split the wood from around the vertical balusters (if they anchor into the tread). Remove and save any molding from around balusters. After all the tread is gone, cut off protruding nails and clean out the joint surfaces.

Saw a new tread to the required length. Make sure the tread is long enough to fit the slots at the sides of the stair. Cut a notch from one of the front corners of the new tread. This notch will help give the new tread enough free play to get it into position in the staircase. Cut the notch as wide as the depth of the slot on the side of the stair and as deep as that of the overhang of the tread nosing. Save the piece of scrap that comes out of the notch.

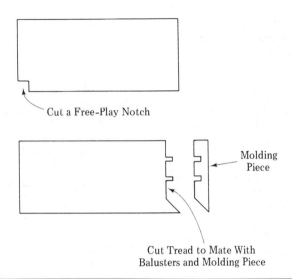

Cut a Free-Play Notch

Molding Piece

Cut Tread to Mate With Balusters and Molding Piece

Cutting New Treads.

Apply industrial mastic to the supports and joint surfaces for the tread. Insert the notched end of the tread into the slot at the side of the stair. Manipulate the tread into position on the stair using the free play that the notch gives you. Center the tread on the stairway and replace the scrap of wood into the notch (trimming the scrap if necessary), using adhesive and a finishing nail to secure. Nail the tread to the stair supports with finishing nails.

In Brief:

1. Cut the damaged tread into thirds. Drill holes in the tread, and work a keyhole saw into the tread. Stop the cuts just short of the riser pieces in front and back.

2. Split out the tread pieces with a wood chisel. Split the middle section out first and then split the side sections.

3. Carefully split the tread from around vertical balusters if they go into the tread, and remove and save any molding from the edges of the tread. Cut off any protruding nails and clean out all the joint surfaces.

4. Cut a new tread to fit. Cut a notch from one of the front corners of the tread. Cut the notch as wide as the depth of the slot on the side of the stair and as deep as the overhang of the tread nosing.

5. Apply industrial mastic to the supports and joint surfaces. Insert the notched end of the tread into the slot on the side of the stair. Manipulate the tread into position using the notch's free play.

6. Center the tread on the stairway and replace the scrap of wood into the notch with adhesive and a finishing nail. Nail the tread to the stair supports with finishing nails.

Tips:

If one side of the stair tread is open and vertical balusters are anchored into it you will have to do some fancy cutting and fitting on the new tread. You will have to cut one end of the new tread to match the molding pieces that help anchor the baluster.

Use a stiff-back saw to cut accurate lines on the end of the tread. Place the tread in position on the stair and mark the position of the baluster. Drill a hole or cut a slot for the end of the baluster. When you install the tread it is not necessary to cut a free-play slot in one corner of the tread since one side of the tread is open. Insert the plain end of the tread into the slot at the side of the staircase, and anchor the other end to the baluster and the old molding pieces that hold the baluster and dress the end of the tread.

↰ HOW TO REPAIR SIMPLE WOOD STAIRS

Tools and supplies needed:

Circular saw
Hand saw
Measuring tape
Steel square
Hammer
2 x 12-inch lumber
Stair-tread stock 9½ or 11½ inches wide
2½-inch finishing nails
Common nails
Metal connectors

Procedure:

Often when renovating an old house, you need to repair a run of simple open-style stairs. Porch steps, basement and attic stairs are all simple designs that can be repaired with standard materials.

The first step is to determine if the stair simply needs new treads. Inspect the stringers (the two large pieces of wood that are notched to hold the stair treads). If the stringers are in good shape (not cracked, sagging, or rotted), the stair can be repaired by replacing the worn treads.

Cut new treads to the length of the old ones from standard tread stock. Knock the old treads out of the stringers and replace them with the new tread. Do this procedure one at a time—knock an old tread out and nail a new tread in its place before going on to the next tread. Nail the new treads to the stringer with 2½-inch finishing nails; use about 10 nails per tread. Replace treads from the bottom of the stair and work up.

If the stringers are damaged, you will have to cut new ones from 2 x 12-inch lumber. Remove the treads from the old stringers and carefully remove the stringers from their supports on the top and bottom of the run. You want to preserve the old stringers as patterns for the new ones.

When the old stringers are down, clean up any nails that protrude from them and then lay them down on 2 x 12 lumber. Position the old stringers so that the outside points of the notches are right at the edge of the new lumber. Trace the outline of the stringer notches onto the new wood. If any notches are broken, use a steel square to continue the outline on the new wood.

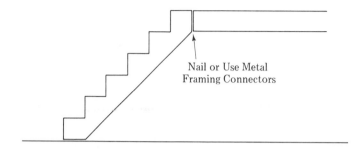

Nail or Use Metal
Framing Connectors

Lay the Old Stringer on New Lumber
and Trace Outlines

Use 8–10 Nails Per Tread

Simple Stair Building.

When the outline of the old stringer is traced onto the new lumber, remove the old stringers and cut new ones with a circular saw along the lines. Stop ½ inch short of the inside points of the notches with your circular saw, and finish cutting the notches free with a hand saw. You want to avoid nicking the wood with the circular saw.

Place the new stringers in position, and secure them with common nails. Toenail, or use metal framing connectors to secure. Cut new treads and nail them into position on the stringers with finishing nails.

In Brief:

1. Inspect the stringers to make sure that they are not cracked, sagging, or rotted.

2. Cut new treads and nail them to the stringers with finishing nails.

3. Knock out one old tread at a time and replace it with a new tread. Start at the bottom of the run and work up.

4. If the stringers are damaged, remove the old treads and carefully remove the stringers from their supports on the top and bottom.

5. Clean off any nails that protrude from the stringers and lay them down on 2 x 12 lumber. Position the old stringers so that the outside points of the notches are right at the edge of the new lumber.

6. Trace the outline of the stringer notches onto the new wood. If any notches are broken, use a steel square to continue the outline.

7. When the new lumber is marked, remove the old stringers and cut the new lumber with a circular saw. Stop ½ inch short of the inside points with the circular saw and cut the notches free with a hand saw.

8. Place the new stringers in position and secure them with common nails. Use metal framing anchors for extra strength.

9. Cut new treads and nail them into position with finishing nails.

Tips:

If the old stringer is unusable for a pattern, you can mark a new pattern on the 2 x 12 lumber with a steel square. Place the steel square along the best notch in the old stringer and mark the places where the outside points fall on the steel square. Use the marked steel square to mark the same number of notches on the new lumber as are on the old stringer.

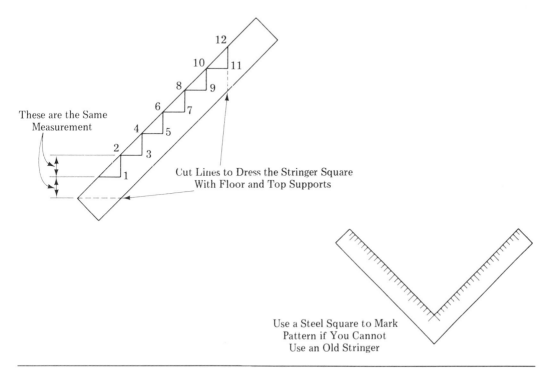

These are the Same Measurement

Cut Lines to Dress the Stringer Square With Floor and Top Supports

Use a Steel Square to Mark Pattern if You Cannot Use an Old Stringer

Cut Lines for a Stair Stringer.

To cut the bottom of the stringer so that it sits squarely, draw a line parallel to the first notch line and place it exactly as far away from that first line as the first line is from the third line. To cut the top of the stringer so that it sits squarely, simply continue the last notch line until it hits the other edge of the lumber.

⤸ HOW TO MAKE CABINET AND CLOSET DOORS WITH CHIPBOARD

Tools and supplies needed:

Circular saw
Drill and bits
Screwdriver
Tape measure
¾-inch chipboard
1½-inch or 2-inch loose pin butt hinges
Magnetic catches
Wood or porcelain knobs

Procedure:

Chipboard is a good, inexpensive material for cabinet and closet doors. The material has good dimensional stability, meaning that once it's cut and installed, it stays the same size and shape—obviously a good quality for a door to have. Three-quarter-inch chipboard can cover doorways up to 4 x 8 feet without undue flexing. Its greatest use will be for smaller size doors on closets and cabinets.

Measure the opening to be covered and cut a piece of chipboard to fit; then cut that piece in half, down the chip-board's length. Install two hinges on each door half for doors up to 2 feet long, three hinges for doors up to 3 feet long, and four hinges for doors over 3 feet long. Install the hinges flat on the chipboard, not on the edge. The reason for this flush mounting is for strength; the ¾-inch edge of the chipboard will not hold the hinge screws securely. Screw the other side of the hinges to the doorframe, also using flush mounting.

If you are bothered by the look of flush-mounted hinges on your doors, you can use a special cabinet hinge called a *pivot hinge* which will mount to the strong back sides of the door and frame and not show from the front. You can only use two pivot hinges for each door half, because they can be mounted only at the top and bottom of the door where there is space for the pivot mechanism. Another alternative to flush-mounted common butt hinges is to use flush-mounted ornamental hinges. These install and perform just like butt hinges but they come in many attractive designs and finishes. Select a finish and a design that reinforces the look of your general decoration scheme.

To hold the doors in place, install one magnetic catch to each side of the top doorframe. The best place for each catch is about 1 inch in from the point where the two doors meet. Set the catches back from the edge of the frame at a space equal to the thickness of the chipboard. Drill and fasten the catches to the wood, but leave the screws fairly loose. Drill and screw the catch plates to the back of the chipboard doors so that they will mate with the magnets mounted on the frame. Close the door and make sure that it's even with the surrounding surface. Tighten the magnetic catches so that they will hold the door closed in the proper position. Repeat this adjustment and tightening with the other door.

Finally, drill a hole in each chipboard door exactly in the middle of the door's length and set in from the edge by 1½ inches. Insert a porcelain or wood knob on a bolt into the holes and fasten with a washer and nut. Cut off any excess bolt on the back side of the doors with a hacksaw.

There are many different choices for knobs and handles for these doors. The simplest and safest choice is to use round porcelain or wood knobs. They are made of classic materials and will be in good taste and harmony with any decorating scheme.

Finish the chipboard by priming and painting. Epoxy- and oil-based paints will give a long-lasting, smooth finish that is easy to clean. Another possibility is to use plastic laminates, although this requires a great deal of skill to install.

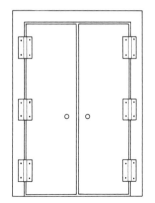

Hinges Are Installed Flat

In Brief:

1. Measure opening to be covered, and cut chipboard to fit.
2. Cut chipboard in half down its length.
3. Install hinges (butt, pivot, or ornamental) on doors and doorframe.
4. Install two magnetic catches loosely on the doorframe.
5. Install two catch plates to the back of the doors.
6. Adjust the doors so that they are flush with each other and the surrounding surface, and tighten the screws on the magnetic catches.
7. Drill two holes in the doors and install wood or porcelain knobs.
8. Prime and finish the chipboard with epoxy- or oil-based paint.

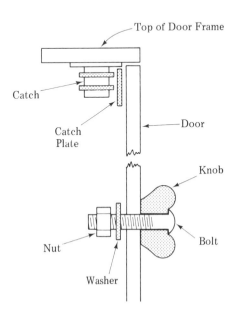

Simple Cabinet and Closet Doors.

ꙩ HOW TO FRAME AND COVER SIMPLE CABINETS

Tools and supplies needed:

Circular saw
Drill and bits
Screwdriver
Hammer
Tape measure
Level
⅝- or ¾-inch chipboard
2 x 4-inch lumber
3½-inch common nails
1½-inch finishing nails
Corner braces and screws
Wooden V-molding

Procedure:

Even if you install freestanding tubs, basins, and sinks and use open-hanging storage and bookshelf-style wall cabinetry, you will probably have to install at least one or two cabinets in your kitchen or bathroom. Cabinets provide counter space and they are a good way to hide dishwashers, garbage cans, and other utility items.

Custom-built or prefabricated cabinets are expensive and may not be exactly suited to the space available. The best route is to build your own cabinets right in place with simple framing and inexpensive chipboard covering. The money you save by building these simple cabinets can be used to provide top quality fixtures to put in them and to put a handsome and durable countertop (quarry tile or ceramic tile for example) on them.

Decide where the cabinet should go. Your cabinet will be strongest if it is built up against one or two walls. When you have decided on the dimensions, start cutting wood. Cut four pieces of 2 x 4 the length of the intended cabinet. Cut four pieces of 2 x 4 the width of the cabinet minus the thickness of two 2 x 4s (two 2 x 4s generally total a 3-inch thickness, but check yours). Cut four pieces of 2 x 4 the height of the cabinet (36 inches is recommended for kitchen cabinets, 18–36 inches for the bathroom cabinets).

Assemble the frame. Lay two length 2 x 4s on the floor on their edges. Place two width 2 x 4s down between them. Use one corner brace at each corner to tie the 2 x 4s together. Be sure to align the 2 x 4s so that their edges are even and square. Repeat the process with the other length and width pieces until you have two boxes the length and width of the cabinet.

Attach the height 2 x 4s to the boxes with nails or screws. Place the 2 x 4s in from the corners a few inches to avoid attaching them over the corner braces. The height 2 x 4s hold the boxes from inside the frame, leaving the boxes smooth to receive the cabinet skin.

You will now have a cabinet skeleton which is fairly flimsy. Carefully put the skeleton in place on the floor and next to the walls (if you are using any). Use the level to check that all surfaces are level and straight. Use shims on the floor and wall if necessary. Attach the bottom of the skeleton to the floor with four corner braces. Nail the skeleton to the studs in the wall below the plaster (if you are against any walls). These steps will stiffen the skeleton somewhat.

HOW TO FRAME AND COVER SIMPLE CABINETS

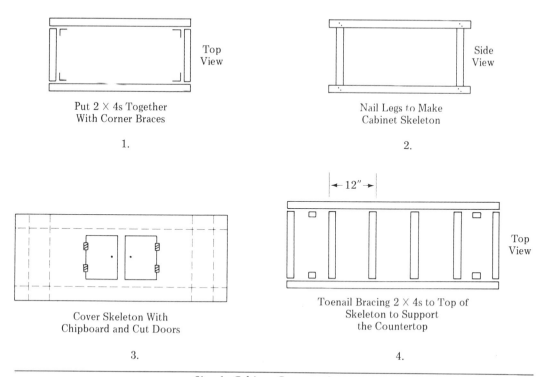

Top View

Put 2 × 4s Together
With Corner Braces

1.

Side View

Nail Legs to Make
Cabinet Skeleton

2.

Cover Skeleton With
Chipboard and Cut Doors

3.

Top View

Toenail Bracing 2 × 4s to Top of
Skeleton to Support
the Countertop

4.

Simple Cabinet Construction.

Cover the frame with chipboard. Use 1½-inch finishing nails and set them below the surface and putty over them. Simply butt the chipboard together at the cabinet edges. Cover the vertical edges with V-shaped wooden molding about 1 inch wide on each side. V-molding is available where wood paneling is sold, as it is used to cover outside edges on paneling jobs. Cut doors in one or more sides of the cabinet and install them as described under the how-to on chipboard doors.

Measure and cut a piece of ¾-inch chipboard for the countertop. Before installing, cut any openings needed for fixtures, sinks, etc. For countertops of 4 square feet or less, you can install the chipboard with no underbracing. For larger countertops, use 2 x 4 bracing pieces toenailed (or cornerbraced) into the skeleton top to support the countertop. The braces should occur every foot along the cabinet's length. Nail the countertop to the cabinet frame with finishing nails, and set the nails below the surface and putty them.

The cabinet sides can be finished by priming and painting with an epoxy- or oil-based paint; or the chipboard skin can be covered with colored plastic laminates, sheet aluminum, or thin veneer wood paneling. These sheet materials are installed with contact cement or mastic according to the manufacturer's recommendations. The cabinet countertop can be surfaced with prefabricated butcherblock planks (excellent for food preparation), quarry or ceramic tile (good for hard wear and easy cleaning), or various plastic or resin sheet materials.

In Brief:

1. Measure the space and decide on cabinet dimensions.

2. Cut 2 x 4s into 4 length pieces, 4 width pieces, and 4 height pieces.

3. Assemble two boxes with length and width pieces. Use corner braces and screws.

4. Attach the height 2 x 4s to the corners of the boxes with nails or screws. Place the height pieces within the frame and set in from the corners.

5. Place the cabinet skeleton in position and attach to the floor and walls. Check with the level and use shims if necessary.

6. Cover the skeleton with chipboard. Cover vertical edges with V-molding. Cut doors and install hinges, catches, and knobs.

7. Install 2 x 4 bracing to the skeleton top if needed to support a countertop.

8. Cut and install chipboard countertop.

9. Finish the sides of the cabinet.

10. Install a suitable countertop finish material.

↰ HOW TO REPLACE GLASS

Tools and supplies needed:

Putty knife
Tape measure
Utility knife or penknife
Glass panes
Glazier's points
Glazier's compound

Procedure:

Remove the broken glass from the frame and place the pieces in a cardboard box or sturdy brown bag. Clean the old glazing compound from the frame with a utility knife or penknife until the bare wood shows. Measure the frame for new glass. Allow ⅛-inch clearance between the new glass and the window frame. Take the measurements to a glass store and have glass cut or cut your own from stock-size sheets.

Put a thin coating (⅛ inch) of compound along the window frame. This provides a cushion and a seal for the glass pane. Place the new glass in the frame and press it gently against the bead of compound. Drive 8 metal points (2 at each corner of the frame) into the wood frame with a driver or the putty knife. The points provide strength and will keep the glass from moving while you apply compound.

Scoop the compound from the can and form it into a ball with your hands. Knead the ball to make it more pliable. Roll the ball between your hands into a thin strip about ⅜ inch in diameter. Place the strip along the frame and glass.

Use the putty knife to press the compound into the joint. Draw the putty knife smoothly along the compound to make a bead that is even with the height of the wood on the other side of the glass pane. Repeat this process until all of the glass and wood has been covered.

In Brief:

1. Remove broken glass from the frame and discard. Clean the old glazing compound from the frame with a utility knife or penknife.
2. Measure the frame for new glass. Allow ⅛-inch clearance between the glass and the wood frame.
3. Have glass cut or cut your own from stock-size sheets.
4. Put a ⅛-inch coating of compound around the window frame.
5. Place new glass in the compound bedding and press in place.
6. Drive 8 glazier's points into the wood frame.
7. Form compound into ⅜-inch strips and place strips along the joint between frame and glass.
8. Draw the putty knife along the compound to press it into place and work it into a bead the height of the wood on the other side of the glass.

Tips:

If the putty knife sticks and pulls compound out of the joint as you move it, try keeping it lubricated in kerosene or linseed oil. Keep the blade clean and dip it into lubricant from time to time to tool a smooth bead.

The joint compound should be soft and pliable in order to create a uniform, watertight bead around the frame. Kneading compound in your hands and rolling it into strips helps. You should be able to form the compound easily into a V-shape with the putty knife. The point of the V is in the seam between the glass and the wood and the top of the V comes even with the wood frame on the inside and outside of the glass pane.

When dealing with an irregularly shaped piece of glass, clean the frame thoroughly and then draw an outline of the glass on cardboard. Lay the frame on a piece of cardboard (outside down) and trace the outline of the shape with a pencil. Cut the cardboard smaller than the frame so that the glass will have a clearance of ⅛ inch all along the frame. You can use the cardboard template to cut the unusual shape or have the glass store do it for you.

⤶ HOW TO CUT GLASS

Tools and supplies needed:

Glass cutter
Wooden yardstick or straightedge
Gloves and goggles
Tape measure
Kerosene or sewing machine oil

Procedure:

If you are replacing window glass and you can't buy precut glass in the size you need, or if your glass supplier charges you for cutting, you can cut your own glass at home. Glass cutting is a skill, and you will have to practice with some scrap glass to do it well. Whenever you cut glass you *must* wear gloves and goggles. Even when you become experienced with glass you will find that it can break and splinter in unexpected ways, so you should always wear hand and eye protection.

Lay the glass on a flat table so that the whole piece is supported. Measure the size needed on the glass and mark the cut with a felt-tipped pen by placing two marks on the edge of the glass. Place the wooden yardstick over the two marks and hold it firmly with one hand.

Lubricate the cutter by dipping the wheel in kerosene or sewing machine oil. Do this for every three cuts. Place the cutter against the yardstick, holding it absolutely vertical, and lightly draw it down the edge, scoring a line in the glass. Don't press hard on the cutter because you will make a rough score line that will tend to break unevenly. The cutter will make a small sound like tearing thin paper when you draw it down the glass with the proper pressure.

Remove the yardstick and move the glass across the table so that the score line is just over the edge of the table. Hold the pane flat on the table with one hand and gently press downward on the waste piece to break it off. The thumb of your hand should be across the score line and the knuckles of your index finger should be below the score line on the underside of the glass. The proper position of the breaking hand is about three inches in from the bottom of the glass.

In Brief:

1. Lay the glass on a flat table. Measure and mark the cut by placing two marks with a felt tipped pen on the edges of the glass. Place the straight-edge over the marks and hold firmly against the glass.

2. Lubricate the glass cutter by dipping the wheel in kerosene or sewing machine oil. Place the cutter against the yardstick, hold it vertical, and draw it lightly down the edge, scoring a line in the glass. The cutter will make a sound like tearing paper when the proper pressure is applied.

3. Remove the yardstick and move the glass so that the score line is just over the edge of the table. Hold the pane flat on the table and press downward on the cut piece to break it off.

Tips:

If you are having a hard time getting the glass to break off evenly, try tapping the underside of the score line with the ball on the end of the glass cutter. Start about ¼ inch in from the edge of the cut and tap on the underside of the score line to start a crack. Tap the ball directly on the underside of the score line. When the crack has started, press down on the cut piece to break the rest of it off.

When you are cutting long pieces of glass (over 24 inches), you may have to modify your breaking technique to get a clean edge. As you feel the glass start to break under the pressure of your thumb and knuckles, pull the scrap piece of glass away from the score line. The sensation is very much like tearing a folded sheet of newspaper. If this technique is done properly, even very long cuts separate cleanly.

Any small pieces of glass that hang onto the score line after the main break is accomplished can be broken off with the grooves in the head of the glass cutter. Fit the glass into one of the grooves and push outward on the cutter to break the bits of glass off. The edge of the groove should be even with the score line.

If you try to recycle old glass that you find around your house by cutting it to fit, you may be disappointed. Old glass is much more brittle and full of surface tensions than new glass, and it simply may not cut and break cleanly.

↖ HOW TO SAND WOOD FLOORS

Tools and supplies needed:

Commercial drum sander (8-inch drum)
Commercial disk edger (5-inch disk)
Respirator and goggles
Old leather or canvas belt
Earplugs or sound muffs
Coarse, medium, and fine grades of sandpaper to fit drum and disk machines

Procedure:

Sanding an old wood floor, either wide-wale floorboards or strip hardwood, is a basic project in old houses. Sanding brings up the natural beauty of the original wood and can completely transform the look of a room.

Before renting equipment, systematically go over the floor on your hands and knees and tap all nails below the surface of the wood. Use the hammer and nail set and put the nails ⅛–¼ inch

below the surface of the wood. You won't get all the nails but at least try to get the obvious ones because exposed nails will quickly ruin a piece of sandpaper. Before going to rent equipment, measure the square footage of the room to be sanded.

Rent an 8-inch drum sander and 5-inch disk edger from a paint store or tool rental shop. The retailer should also be able to sell you the three grades of sandpaper you will need. Tell him the kind of wood floor you have, the finish that is now on the floor, and the square footage of the area. In general, the retailer should set you up with a 20–50-grit coarse paper, an 80-grit medium paper, and a 100-grit fine paper. He will give you more paper than you need for a margin of safety, but you can return unused sheets for a refund.

Load the drum machine and the disk edger with *coarse* paper. Loop an old belt around the handle of the drum sander and fasten it around your waist. This belt arrangement will help you to control and hold the machine with your body as well as your arms and will prevent fatigue. Put your respirator and safety goggles on, and insert earplugs or use sound muffs before starting the drum machine.

Check to make sure that the drum lever is in the up position (holding the drum off the floor) before starting the machine. Start the machine, drop the drum lever down and begin sanding. The first sanding is done at a 45-degree angle to the floorboards. This tends to knock off any high spots and curls in the wood. The drum machine will pull you forward; your job is to control it and keep it at the proper angle to the wood.

When you want to stop or turn, pull the drum lever to the up position and the machine will stop pulling forward. After the main floor area is coarsely sanded, use the disk edger to sand all the tight areas that the big machine missed.

For the second sanding, load the drum machine and the edger with *medium* paper. Proceed as before but this time guide the sander parallel to the boards. Follow the drum machine with the edger and sand all the tight areas.

For the third sanding, load the drum machine and the edger with *fine* paper. Proceed as before and guide the sander parallel to the boards. Follow the drum machine with the edger.

In Brief:

1. Use a hammer and nail set to tap all nailheads ⅛–¼ inch below the surface of the wood floor.

2. Measure the square footage of the area to be sanded.

3. Rent equipment and buy three grades of sandpaper.

4. Load the drum machine and the disk edger with coarse paper. Sand the floor at a 45-degree angle to the floorboards. Use the edger to sand tight areas. Repeat procedure using medium and then fine paper, sanding parallel to the boards.

Tips:

For a professional look, take up all the quarter-round shoe molding from the baseboards before sanding. This will allow you to get right to the baseboard with the edger. After refinishing, replace the old molding or buy new quarter-round molding.

If you are hitting a lot of nails, stop after the coarse sanding and tap them down again with the nail set and hammer. The nails should be more visible after the first sanding.

If you have a large area to sand or are doing multiple rooms, you will want to have the sander for as long as possible. You may be able to get more use of the equipment for the same 24-hour rate by picking up the machines Saturday afternoon and returning them Monday morning. Check with the retailer on this.

On some older machines there may not be a drum position lever to move it onto or off the floor. In this case you should always start the machine with the drum tilted off the floor (push down on the handle) so that you don't dig a hole in the floor. The drum should always be tilted off the floor when turning or stopping the machine as well as when starting it.

Even with the edger, there may be very tight places that are impossible to power sand. Use a 4-inch razor-blade scraper to remove the old finish from these areas, and then sand with medium and fine sandpaper wrapped around a thin stick. The stick will let you sand areas around pipes, behind radiators, etc.

HOW TO EVEN FLOORS

Tools and supplies needed:

Circular saw
Hammer
Tape measure
Putty knife

Chipboard, ¼ or ⅜ inch or tempered hardboard, ⅛, 3/16, or ¼ inch
Roofing nails or ring nails, ¾ or 1 inch
Latex crack filler or latex wood putty

Procedure:

It is often necessary to even a floor to provide a smooth surface for tile or other floor covering. Evening a floor is usually required when dealing with wide-wale floorboards in old houses, and it is recommended whenever the original floor is rough or has a lot of seams in it.

Use sheets of chipboard or tempered hardboard to cover the floor. Remove the shoe molding from all baseboards. Simply cut the 4 x 8-foot sheets to fit the space. Secure the sheets with roofing nails or ring nails (which provide a very strong hold).

To fill seams and gaps around pipes and other obstructions, use a latex crack filler or wood putty. Press the material in place with a putty knife and smooth it even with the surface of the underlayment. Check the material when it is dry, and apply a second coat if it has shrunk.

In Brief:

1. Remove all the shoe molding from around the baseboards.
2. Cut 4 x 8-foot chipboard or hardboard to fit the area.
3. Nail the pieces to the floor with roofing or ring nails.
4. Fill gaps and cracks around obstructions with latex putty.
5. Check for putty shrinkage and apply more if necessary.

Tips:

Chipboard in the ⅜-inch thickness will bridge gaps in the floor more successfully than the thinner hardboard. Chipboard is indicated for floors that have boards that are cupped or curled by age.

Space your nails approximately every 8 inches across the surface of the underlayment. Start nailing from the center of each sheet of underlayment to avoid making the underlayment bow up in the center where it has no place to expand as you nail it to the original floor.

HOW TO MAKE CHIPBOARD FLOOR COVERING

Tools and supplies needed:

Circular saw with carbide blade
Floor-adhesive trowel with ⅛-inch notches
Tape measure
Hammer
Finishing nails, 1 or 1½ inches
Heavy-duty tile adhesive or industrial mastic
Chipboard, ½ inch or ⅝ inch thick

Procedure:

Chipboard makes a durable and low cost floor covering. Use it to cover large floor areas that have poor quality floors not worth sanding and refinishing.

Prepare the base floor. Repair any holes and tap any nails down so that you have a smooth surface to work with. Re-

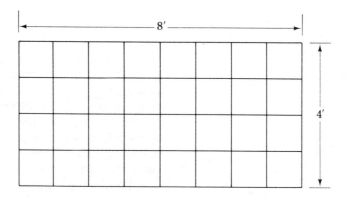

Cutting Chipboard Into 1 Foot Square Tiles

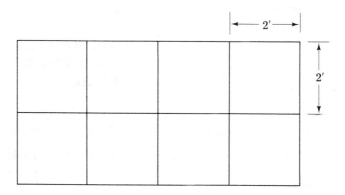

2 Foot Square Tiles

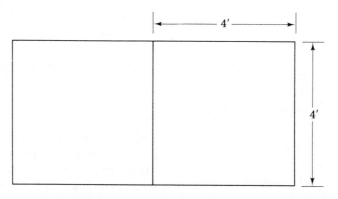

4 Foot Square Tiles

Chipboard Floor Covering.

move shoe molding and baseboards from the base of the walls. Measure the area to be covered to come up with a square footage figure.

Cut the chipboard into tiles. You can go with one-foot-square tiles, two-foot-square tiles, or four-foot-square tiles. Cut all the tiles you will need at one time. Each 4 x 8-foot sheet of chipboard will yield 32 square feet of floor covering.

Work on about one-fourth of the floor at a time. Lay the chipboard tiles on the floor with heavy-duty tile adhesive or industrial mastic. Trowel the adhesive on to a thickness of about ⅛ inch. If your floor is very rough you will need to trowel the adhesive on even more thickly to provide a good bond. You may need to secure the larger tiles by driving a few finishing nails.

Butt the tiles together until you have laid the whole floor down. Trim the border tiles, and use a contour gauge to measure and cut tiles for fitting around obstructions. Finish the job by installing the old baseboards and shoe molding. If the old shoe molding is cracked or encrusted with old paint, buy and install new quarter-round molding. Install a beveled wooden threshold (flooring shops sell these) wherever the chipboard meets a lower floor.

The chipboard should be finished by applying three coats of urethane. The urethane will darken the chipboard and protect it, giving the whole job the look of cork flooring. The chipboard can be stained with a dark oil-based penetrating stain before any urethane is applied. The stain and urethane will make the chipboard very dark and hard looking, imitating the look of earthenware or stone flooring.

In Brief:

1. Prepare the base floor. Repair any holes, and tap nails down.

2. Remove the baseboards and shoe molding from the base of the walls.

3. Measure area to be covered and get a square footage figure.

4. Cut the chipboard into tiles. Use one-, two-, or four-foot-square tiles.

5. Trowel the adhesive on the floor. Work about one-fourth of the floor at a time.

6. Press the tiles into the adhesive and butt each tile tightly with its neighbor. Secure any balky tiles with a few finishing nails.

7. Trim border tiles and use a contour gauge to measure and cut tiles for fitting around obstructions.

8. Install the old baseboards and shoe molding. Install a beveled wood threshold to mate the chipboard with lower floors.

9. Finish the chipboard by applying three coats of urethane. For a darker look apply one coat of a dark penetrating stain before the urethane.

↰ HOW TO USE 1″ x 6″ BOARDS FOR FLOORING

Tools and supplies needed:

Circular saw

Hammer

Tape measure

1 x 6-inch tongue-and-groove roofing boards

2-inch finishing nails or cut nails

Procedure:

Another option for covering an undistinguished floor is to use inexpensive 1 x 6 tongue-and-groove roofing boards. Roofers of this size are knotty and burly, but they lie straight and mate tightly and can be finished with urethane to make a handsome floor.

The 1 x 6 size is available up to 20 feet in length, so it is ideal for flooring because in most cases you can cover the whole width of a room with one board and avoid butting and piecing shorter boards together.

Clean and prepare the original floor for the new boards. Take up the old shoe molding from the baseboards so that the new floor will butt the baseboards and be covered with new molding. For a stronger and more professional edge, you can carefully remove the baseboards and lay the new floor right to the wall. After the floor is down, replace the baseboards and apply new molding to the space between the baseboards and the floor.

Make sure that the 1 x 6 boards are dry. You want to minimize any chance of the boards shrinking once they are in place. If you have any suspicions that the wood is wet, store the boards, laid out flat in an unused room, for two weeks. Turn the boards over every three or four days to let them adjust to the normal humidity of the house.

Nail the boards crosswise to the existing floor. This will tend to minimize any unevenness in the old floor and make for a stronger floor overall. Nail each board in place with finishing nails. Put the nails about ½ inch in from each edge and space them every two feet along the board's length. You can leave the nail-heads flush or set them down ⅛ inch with a nail set and cover with wood putty.

Start nailing boards with the groove side facing the baseboard. This will let the board sit securely against the wall or baseboard. Lay each new board down and mate the tongue-and-groove edges together. Use a hammer and a piece of scrap wood to tap the boards tightly together and to seat the tongue and groove.

If you are covering only part of a room or come to a doorway, use a beveled wood molding or threshold piece (sometimes called a *clamshell reducer strip*) to bind the last board and make an edge for the floor where it meets a lower floor.

After the floor is down, replace the baseboards and install new wood shoe molding. Clean up any rough spots on the floor with a sander, and finish with three coats of urethane floor varnish.

In Brief:

1. Buy 1 x 6-inch boards; lay out to dry and adjust for two weeks.

2. Prepare old floor, take up old molding, and remove baseboards.

3. Lay 1 x 6 boards crosswise to the old flooring and nail in place. Nail flush, or set nails and cover with putty.

4. Install edge molding or threshold where new floor meets old floor.

5. Replace baseboards, and install new shoe molding.

6. Sand rough spots and nail holes, and finish with three coats of urethane.

You can install these boards with cut nails. Cut nails have squarish shanks and oblong heads. They have good holding power and you can use fewer of them to install the floor than if you used finishing nails. Cut nails also are classic nails (most original wide-wale floorboards in old houses have cut nails), and they can be left flush with the flooring as part of the design. Install them in the same position as finishing nails but space them every three feet along the board's length. The nails should be 2 or 2½ inches long. Install them with the thin portion of the nailhead parallel to the board seams.

⤻ HOW TO LAY FLOOR TILE

Tools and supplies needed:

Paint brush
Toothed adhesive trowel
Heavy-duty shears
Tape measure
Mini-hacksaw
Hammer
Contour gauge
Tile
Adhesive (paintable or trowel-spread type)
Metal molding
1-inch finishing nails

Procedure:

Floor tiles come in many different materials. The more common materials are asphalt, rubber, vinyl, and vinyl-asbestos. These tiles are resilient and will provide a certain amount of softness and sound-deadening quality to the floor. For the greatest selection and proper advice on materials and installation, shop at a store that sells only floor tiles.

Prepare the floor by cleaning, tapping exposed nails down, laying smooth underlayment (if needed), and taking up the shoe molding from the bottom of all baseboards. Measure the area to get a square footage figure. Most tiles are one foot square and are sold in boxes of 45 tiles.

At the store buy enough tiles to cover your floor plus an extra 10 percent for wastage. Most stores let you return unused tiles for a refund. It is important to buy all the tiles you will need at one time, because different tile lots can vary in color and texture. Also buy enough metal molding to bind the places where tile will butt bare floor.

Follow the store's recommendation and the manufacturer's suggestion for the proper adhesive for your particular tile. In general, you have two choices. There is a paintable tile adhesive that goes on with a paint brush and is very easy to clean up; and there is a troweled-on adhesive that is a bit more tricky to apply and clean up but which may provide a better bond for the tile you buy. Some tiles come with an adhesive already bonded to their backs. These self-adhesive tiles are easy to apply, but the floor must be absolutely clean and smooth for them to bond strongly.

When you are ready to lay tile, divide the area into quarters. Draw a line from the center of two opposite walls and then divide that line by drawing another line from the center of the other two walls. (The easiest way to draw the lines is to snap two chalk lines, but if the space is small a yardstick or straight piece of lumber will do.)

Lay some uncemented tiles from the center of the two lines to a sidewall to see if the space between the last whole tile and the sidewall is less than 6 inches. If it is you should draw a new center line 6 inches closer or farther from that wall. The idea is to lay the tile in such a way that you avoid having to lay narrow strips of tile near the wall. Check this in the other direction along the bisecting line and draw a new line 6 inches closer or farther if necessary.

When you have established a good layout you can spread the adhesive. Cover a quarter of the floor at a time, using the lines that you drew as a guide. Use a paint brush or trowel to spread adhesive according to the package directions. Let the adhesive set for the recommended time. Start to lay tile from the center point of the room, where the two lines come together. Lay, don't slide, the tiles into place. Butt the tiles tightly together. Lay all the whole tiles in place before cutting any border tiles.

When you have laid all the whole tiles down in that quarter, spread adhesive over a second quarter and lay the whole tiles there. Repeat this process with the remaining two quarters until the floor is covered with whole tiles.

Now work on the border tiles. To cut border tiles, lay a tile exactly on top of the last full tile in the row. On top of this tile put another tile and slide it toward the wall until it is butted against it. Use the edge of this tile to make a pencil line on the tile below it. Cut the marked tile with a pair of shears. The cut tile will fit the border area perfectly. Repeat this

fitting, marking, and cutting operation with the rest of the border tiles.

To cut tile around irregular shapes, use an inexpensive tool called a *contour gauge*. This tool consists of slim metal slats held together by a frame and clamp. To use it, simply loosen the slats up by slackening the clamp and pushing it against the irregular shape that the tile must butt. The slats will take the contour of the shape. Tighten the clamp to hold the shape and remove the tool from the area. Use the contour gauge to trace the shape on to the tile. Cut the shape with shears or use a mini-hacksaw or power sabre saw.

Finish the job by installing quarter-round shoe molding where the tile butts baseboards and flat metal molding where the tile meets the bare floor.

In Brief:

1. Prepare the base floor by cleaning, tapping nailheads, and laying smooth underlayment (if needed). Remove the shoe molding from the baseboards.

2. Measure the area for square footage and buy what you need to cover plus an extra 10 percent for wastage. Purchase adhesive and enough metal molding to bind the exposed edges of the tile.

3. Divide the area into quarters. Lay some tiles out dry to check that the last tile in each row will be 6 inches or more wide. Draw new lines 6 inches from the old ones if necessary.

4. Spread the tile adhesive over one quarter of the floor area. Let adhesive set. Begin to lay tile from the center point of the floor.

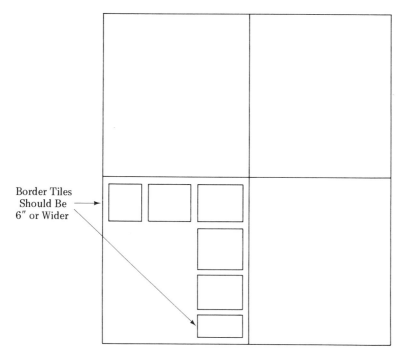

Border Tiles
Should Be
6″ or Wider

Lay Tiles Out Before Applying Adhesive

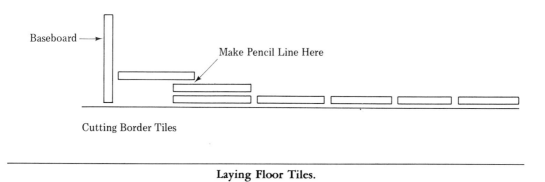

Baseboard

Make Pencil Line Here

Cutting Border Tiles

Laying Floor Tiles.

5. Lay, don't slide, tiles into place. Butt the tiles tightly together. Lay all the whole tiles you can in that quarter.

6. Repeat the process with the other three quarters, doing one quarter at a time.

7. Cut border tiles by placing a tile exactly over the last full tile in a row. Place another tile over this tile and slide it to the wall until it butts the wall. Use the edge of this tile to make a pencil line on the tile below it. Cut the marked tile with shears and place it in the border area.

8. Use a contour gauge to make a model of any irregular shapes that must be fitted. Trace the shape on to the border tile and cut with shears, mini-hacksaw, or sabre saw.

9. Complete the job by installing new quarter-round shoe molding where the tile butts the baseboards. Bind the tile with flat metal molding where it meets bare floor.

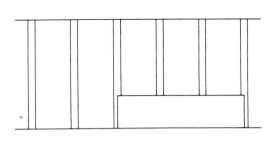

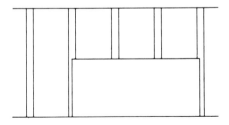

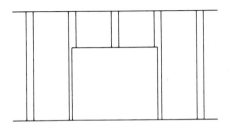

10

Plaster, Paint, and Wallpaper Projects

↶ HOW TO INSTALL DRYWALL

Tools and supplies needed:

Hammer

Taping knife

Scissors

Bucket

Paint brush

Utility knife

Tape measure

Step ladder and T stick

Rubber sponge

Drywall sheets

Drywall joint tape

Self-adhesive wall-repair tape

Galvanized roofing nails or drywall nails

Metal corner bead

Prepared joint compound

Procedure:

Drywall is one of the most useful materials for new construction and renovation work. It eliminates the costly, tricky, and time-consuming work of applying plaster over lath. It can be applied to new or old wood studs, old damaged plaster walls, wood joists, or furring strips. It can be applied in single sheets or as a double layer for extra sound deadening. In any case, the nailing and finishing procedures are the same.

Simply place the drywall sheets over a nailing surface and secure them with roofing nails or drywall nails. Drive the nailhead slightly below the surface of the drywall, creating a dimple with the hammer head. For wall surfaces, nail every 8 inches along each nailing surface. For ceiling surfaces, nail every 5 inches along each nailing surface.

Drywall is cut with a razor-blade utility knife. Measure and mark the cut

139

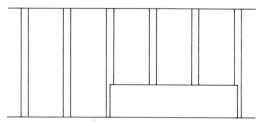

Plan Drywall Installation So That There Is Always
a Nailing Surface For Each End

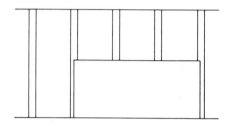

Horizontal Application

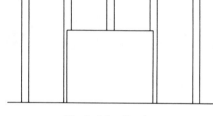

Vertical Application

Drywall Techniques.

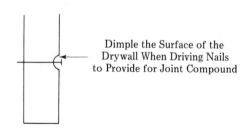

Dimple the Surface of the
Drywall When Driving Nails
to Provide for Joint Compound

Side View of a Drywall Joint Showing
a Layer of Compound, a Layer of Tape,
and Then Two More Layers of Compound

Drywall Details.

lines on the drywall finish side. Run the utility knife down the cut line. Press hard enough to break the finish paper. Score the finish paper at the top and bottom edge of the drywall. Bend the drywall back from the cut line. It will break easily. Keeping the drywall bent back, run the utility knife down the backside of the cut line, breaking the backing paper and freeing the cut piece.

After all of the drywall is in place the joints and nailheads are finished to provide a smooth and seamless surface. Treat the nailheads first. Scoop joint compound out of the container, and press it into the dimple around each nailhead. Draw the taping knife across the filled dimple to bring the joint compound even with the surface of the drywall.

After all the nailheads are covered, treat the joints between the drywall sheets. Work on an area about as long as your outstretched arms. Spread joint compound over the drywall seams with the taping knife. The joint compound should be about ⅛ inch thick. Cut a length of drywall joint tape and stretch it over the joint compound. Press the tape firmly into the compound with the taping knife. Draw the knife smoothly over the tape to bed it into the compound. After the tape is in place, let it dry for a moment. Then apply another thin layer of joint compound over the tape, and smooth it with the taping knife. Go over the joint immediately with a wet sponge to make the compound smoother, and feather the edge even with the surface of the drywall.

Repeat this procedure until all but the corner joints have been covered with compound and tape. The corner joints require special treatment. After the

compound has dried on the joints and nailheads, you must go over the drywall again with joint compound. Cover the nailheads again, and draw the compound even with the surface of the wall. Apply another coat to all joints, and smooth with the taping knife and wet sponge. This second application of compound is usually enough, but if the nailheads are deep they may require a third application of compound to compensate for shrinkage.

Inside and outside corners are treated differently than flat joints. The easy way to finish inside corners is to apply self-adhesive wall-repair tape. The tape is soaked briefly in water and then stretched across the inside joint. Press it in place with your fingers and smooth it out with a wet paint brush. Wall-repair tape requires no further finishing and is a good choice for inside corners, because it is resilient and flexible and will resist cracking.

Outside corners need the protection of a metal corner bead to protect the drywall edges from chipping. The bead is in the shape of a V with legs about ½ inch long. The legs have holes in them to allow you to nail the bead along the corner. Cut the bead to length and install it with roofing or drywall nails into the drywall and studs. Use one nail every 4 inches along the bead's length.

Finish the corner by applying a coat of joint compound to each side of the bead. The coat should be about 6 inches wide. Smooth it with the taping knife and a wet sponge. After the compound is dry apply a second coat to each side about 9 inches wide. Finish this coat with the taping knife and a wet sponge.

After all the applications of joint compound have dried, go over the compound with a vibrating power sander loaded with fine-grit paper. Use the sander to bring the compound over joints and nailheads to an absolutely smooth surface and to make the edges of the compound even with the drywall sheets.

In Brief:

1. Attach drywall sheets over a nailing surface with roofing or drywall nails. Nail every 8 inches for walls and every 5 inches for ceilings. Drive the nailheads slightly below the surface of the drywall.
2. Cut drywall with a utility knife. Break the finish paper with the knife, bend the drywall back from the cut, and break the backing paper to free the cut piece.
3. Cover all nailheads with joint compound. Draw the compound smooth with a taping knife.
4. Treat joints by spreading joint compound, pressing tape into the compound, waiting a few moments, and then spreading more compound over the tape. Smooth the compound with a taping knife and a wet sponge.
5. After the compound is dry, go over all nailheads and joints with a second application of compound.
6. Inside corners are finished with self-adhesive wall-repair tape. Soak the tape in water and press it in place along the corner. Smooth the tape with a wet paint brush.
7. Cut and install metal corner bead for all outside corners. Use one nail every 4 inches.

8. Finish the corner bead by applying a 6-inch-wide coat of compound to both sides of the bead. Smooth with the taping knife and a wet sponge. After the first coat is dry apply a second 9-inch-wide coat and smooth it with the taping knife and wet sponge.
9. After all applications of joint compound have dried, go over the compound with a power sander loaded with fine paper. Smooth the compound and bring it even with the surface of the drywall.

Tips:

Use only roofing or drywall nails to install drywall. Most other nails will rust out or pull out. Drywall nails have a smaller and thinner head than roofing nails, but roofing nails are more readily available (especially in the longer lengths needed for double-layer construction or for securing to old plaster and studs).

Drywall can be installed vertically or horizontally. Choose the method that makes for the least cutting and fitting in your situation. In double-layer construction it is recommended that you apply the first layer vertically and the second layer horizontally. This method staggers the joints in the two layers for a strong, soundproof wall.

Inside corner joints can be finished with the conventional tape and compound procedure if you wish. You must buy a special V-shaped corner taping knife to do it. This knife lets you press the tape smoothly and accurately into the inside corner and bed it into the compound. Finish the corner with more compound and smooth it with the taping knife and a wet sponge.

For single-layer wall construction, ⅜-, ½-, or ⅝-inch drywall is recommended. For double-layer construction, ¼- or ⅜-inch drywall is used for each layer. For drywall over existing plaster and studs, ¼- or ⅜-inch is adequate. Ceilings use ½-inch drywall in a single layer or two ¼-inch layers for better soundproofing and easier handling of the individual sheets.

⤿ HOW TO INSTALL A DRYWALL PATCH

Tools and supplies needed:

Hammer
Tape measure
Utility knife
Mini-hacksaw
Taping knife
Vibrating power sander
Drywall sheets or scraps
Roofing nails
Prepared joint compound
Wood shim material
Fine sandpaper

Procedure:

If a section of plaster is damaged and you can't repair it with a simple application of joint compound, you can install a patch of drywall. Putting a patch in is easier than mixing plaster and other materials necessary to cover lath. Using drywall patches may be necessary when removing heating registers or other built-in fixtures from a wall.

Remove a square or oblong section of the plaster from around the damage.

Use a mini-hacksaw, keyhole saw, or a power sabre saw to cut the plaster and lath from around the damage. Remove enough plaster to expose a portion (at least ½ inch) of the nailing surfaces on each side of the damage.

Measure and cut a piece of drywall to fit. Measure the drywall thickness and depth of the plaster and lath, and determine if you will have to put shims under the drywall to bring it up even with the rest of the wall. Thin pieces of plywood, paneling, or wood shingles make good shims. Nail shims to the studs until you have the right depth for the drywall. You want the drywall to sit even with the rest of the wall when it is nailed in place.

Nail the drywall patch to the shimmed studs with roofing nails. Set the nails below the surface of the drywall, creating a dimple in the drywall.

Finish the job by filling in the gaps between the patch and the wall with joint compound. Cover the nailheads with compound too. Let the compound dry and apply another coating. Keep applying compound until the gaps and nailheads are level with the rest of the wall.

After everything is dry, smooth the compound with the power sander loaded with fine-grit paper. Smooth the compound and bring it even with the plaster and drywall surface.

In Brief:

1. Remove a square or oblong section of plaster and lath from around the damage. Expose ½ inch of nailing surface for the patch.

2. Measure and cut the drywall to fit the hole. Nail shims to the studs to

achieve the right depth for the drywall thickness.

3. Nail the patch to the shimmed studs with roofing nails. Set the nails below the surface of the drywall.

4. Apply joint compound to all nailheads and the joint around the plaster and the drywall. Let compound dry and apply a second coat. Check for shrinkage and apply more compound if necessary.

5. Finish the patch by sanding the compound smooth and even with the surrounding wall.

Cut a Regular Shape Around
a Large Hole

1.

Expose Two Nailing Surfaces and Shim Them
so the Drywall Will be Even With the Wall

2.

When the Patch is in Place,
Apply Joint Compound and Sand Smooth

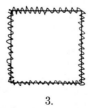

3.

Installing a Drywall Patch.

↘ HOW TO PATCH HOLES AND CRACKS IN PLASTER

Tools and supplies needed:

Taping knife
Vibrating power sander
Punch-style can opener
Prepared joint compound
Fine sandpaper

Procedure:

Old plaster walls generally have lots of small nail holes and a system of small cracks. These imperfections are easy to fix and require only patience and a few tools to do the job right.

For holes up to the size of a half dollar, simply push a blob of joint compound into the hole with a taping knife. Draw the knife across the filled hole to wipe off the excess compound.

Undercut cracks with the point of a punch-style can opener to provide a good key for joint compound. Run the opener point under the edges of the crack and dig out an undercut about ⅛ inch deep. Use the taping knife to push joint compound into the crack. Wipe the compound across the crack in a series of moves down the crack's length. Clean the taping knife and then draw it down the length of the crack to smooth the compound.

After the initial application of joint compound, let the repairs dry and then check for shrinkage. Apply more compound to bring the crack or hole level with the rest of the wall. For some deep holes or cracks you will have to apply three or more coats of compound. Let each coat dry before applying more.

After all the compound has dried, go over the repairs with a power sander loaded with fine-grit paper. Sand the compound smooth and bring the repair level with the rest of the wall.

In Brief:

1. Push a blob of joint compound into the hole and draw the taping knife across the hole to wipe off excess compound.

2. Undercut cracks to provide a key for the compound. Use a can opener point to dig out a ⅛-inch key under each edge.

3. Fill the crack with joint compound. Push the compound into the crack by wiping the taping knife across the crack. Smooth the compound by drawing a clean knife along the length of the crack.

4. Let the compound dry and check for shrinkage. Reapply compound if necessary.

5. After all compound has dried, go over the repairs with a power sander loaded with fine paper. Sand the compound smooth, and level the compound even with the rest of the wall.

Tips:

Use prepared joint compound in 1- or 5-gallon pails. Joint compound is stronger and more easily worked than spackle or patching plaster. Make sure that the brand you buy contains no asbestos and that you use a respirator when sanding.

For "bottomless-pit" holes where there is no backing or lath to hold the joint cement, stuff the hole with wads of newspaper until there is something for the joint cement to grab on to.

For larger holes (2 to 6 inches) with no backing, cut a piece of stiff wire mesh about 2 inches larger than the dimensions of the hole. Tie a piece of string to the middle of the mesh. Insert the mesh into the hole and hold it in place by keeping the string taut. You can tie the other end of the string to a piece of furniture or a nail in a wall to keep the mesh in place while you fill the hole. Fill the hole slowly, working from the sides. Apply at least 4 or 5 coats of joint compound to close the hole, letting each coat dry before applying more. When the hole is filled, cut off the string flush with the surface.

Some very small nail holes and chips will not be visible until after the first coat of wall paint. The first coat of paint often makes small imperfections stand out. You should be ready for this and have your taping knife and joint compound ready for making small repairs after the first coat of paint. The holes are often so small that one swipe of compound will fill them and no sanding will be required.

⤸ HOW TO DEAL WITH CORNER CRACKS IN PLASTER WALLS

Tools and supplies needed:

Bucket
Paint brush
Step ladder
Scissors
Putty knife
Self-adhesive wall-repair tape

Procedure:

A favorite place for cracks to appear is in the inside corners of a room. After you take old wallpaper off, you may find large gaps and cracks in just about every corner. You can try to fill them with joint compound or spackle, but it is difficult to do well and the corners may open up later with changes in temperature and moisture.

An easy way to deal with the problem is to use self-adhesive wall-repair tape. Buy a brand that is rubberized so that the tape will take tension without cracking. Wall-repair tape doesn't require any finishing before painting, and so it is a very quick and superior treatment for corners.

Clean up any roughness on the plaster edges with a putty knife. Cut a length of tape about as long as your outstretched arms. Soak the tape briefly in water to moisten it and activate the adhesive. Lay the moistened tape along the crack. Press it into place with your fingers and smooth it out with a wet paint brush. Use the brush to drive any air bubbles out from under the tape. Repeat the process until all the cracks and gaps are covered, simply butting the tape edges together as you work along.

As soon as the tape is dry (approximately 2 hours) it can be painted. Wall-repair tape is not visible under two coats of latex wall paint.

In Brief:

1. Use a putty knife to clean up rough edges along the cracks and gaps.
2. Cut a length of tape and soak it briefly in water to moisten it.

3. Lay the tape along the crack and press it into place with your fingers.

4. Smooth the tape with a wet paint brush. Drive out any air bubbles.

5. Repeat the process until all the cracks and gaps are covered, butting the tape edges together as you go along.

↜ HOW TO DEAL WITH CRACKED OR BROKEN CORNICES

Tools and supplies needed:

2-inch-wide paint brush
Saucepan
Circular saw
Tape measure
Hammer
Powdered spackle mix
Household vinegar
1 x 12-inch white pine
3-inch finishing nails
Fine-grit sandpaper

Procedure:

Often an ornamental plaster cornice in a ceiling will have a system of unsightly cracks. It is impossible to fill the cracks in an ordinary way because of the tight curves of the cornice. If the cornice is worth saving, you can fill the cracks with a spackle slurry.

Make a mix of powdered spackle and water about the consistency of heavy whipping cream. Add three tablespoons of vinegar to each cup of slurry to retard the setting time of the spackle so that you can paint the slurry into the cracks.

Apply the slurry to the cornice cracks with a paint brush. For deep cracks you will have to apply several coats. Always let the spackle dry before applying more.

After the spackle dries in the cracks, go over the cracks with fine sandpaper. Sand the cracks by hand and use a balled-up cloth under the sandpaper, if necessary, to form the sandpaper to the curve of the cornice.

If the cornice is beyond repair, with chunks missing or whole sections crumbling, you can cover it with strips cut from 1 x 12-inch white pine. The strips bridge the broken cornice and make a simple covering which can be painted or finished to match the wall. Covering the damaged cornice is much simpler than demolishing it and replastering the wall and ceiling.

Measure the width of the strip needed to cover the cornice and cut the white pine to fit. Cut 45-degree bevels in the top and bottom edges of the white pine so that it fits neatly against the wall and ceiling. At the corners of the room where the white pine strips meet, cut matching 45-degree bevels in the ends of the strips so that they make a neat joint.

Attach the strips with finishing nails driven into the wall and ceiling. Space the nails every 12 inches along each strip's length. The nails should hold the lightweight white pine strips securely without having to catch the hidden studs below the plaster and lath.

In Brief:

1. Mix water and powdered spackle to the consistency of heavy whipping cream. Add three tablespoons of vin-

egar to every cup of slurry to retard its setting time.

2. Apply the slurry to the cornice cracks with a paint brush.

3. Allow the slurry to dry and then reapply. For deep cracks, keep applying slurry until the crack is filled.

4. After the slurry is dry, go over the repairs with fine hand sanding. Use a cloth ball to form the sandpaper to the contour of the cornice.

5. If the cornice is beyond simple repair, cover it with white pine strips. Cut

white pine to the width needed to bridge the cornice.

6. Cut 45-degree bevels in the top and bottom edges of the strips to mate them smoothly with the ceiling and wall.

7. Cut matching 45-degree bevels in the edges of the strips where they meet in the corners of the room.

8. Attach the strips over the cornice with finishing nails driven into the ceiling and wall. Space the nails every 12 inches along the strip's length.

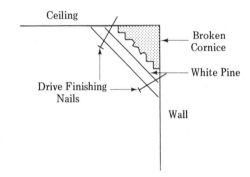

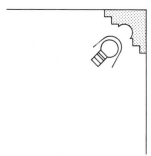

Use a Cloth Ball to Form the Sandpaper
to the Curve of the Cornice

Dealing with Plaster Cornices.

↪HOW TO DEAL WITH BROWN SPOTS IN PLASTER WALLS

Tools and supplies needed:

Paint brush
Alkali-resistant oil- or epoxy-based paint

Procedure:

When painting old plaster walls with light-colored latex paints, you may encounter brown spots on the walls that will bleed right through the new paint. These spots are often found on walls and ceilings where there has been water seepage in the past. The spots are water soluble alkalis and stains that have been carried by water from the lath and base coats of plaster to the finish coat.

Applying more latex paint is not the solution. You must use an oil-based or an epoxy-based paint that will seal and resist these deposits. Buy a paint that is labeled alkali-resistant, and get a color that is near to the color of the latex paint you are using.

Make sure that the spot is dry, and use a brush to apply the sealing paint. Wait for the paint to dry and apply a second coat. When the second coat is dry, you can apply the original latex paint and it will not be affected by the browning.

In Brief:

1. Buy an oil- or epoxy-based paint that is alkali-resistant.
2. Apply the paint to the spot with a brush and let dry.

3. Apply a second coat to the spot and let dry.
4. Resume painting with latex paint.

Tips:

You should try to identify and treat these problem spots before using latex paint. It is a real time-waster to come across these spots while you are rolling paint. Most, but not all, brown spots will be visible on the naked plaster before you start painting. They look like water marks, tan to deep brown in color. They will be found most frequently on the ceiling and walls of the top-floor rooms. Treat suspected spots immediately after the wall has been stripped of wallpaper and repaired with joint compound and sanding. You won't get them all, but you will keep them to a minimum.

↪HOW TO DEMOLISH PLASTER WALLS

Tools and supplies needed:

2-foot wrecking bar
Claw hammer
Shovel
Wheelbarrow
Gloves, goggles, dust mask
Hard hat or motorcycle helmet
2-inch-wide masking tape
Step ladder
Push broom
Wide-blade brick chisel
Cardboard liquor boxes
100 feet of thick twine

Procedure:

Plaster walls and ceilings in old houses are very easy to demolish. The plaster is applied over wood lath which is nailed to framework, joists, or furring strips. In some cases the plaster is applied directly over brick or stone and can be more difficult to remove.

You should have a plan for what you intend to do with the debris. If you have hired a truck or container, you should have a clear route from the room to the dumping place so that you can guide the wheelbarrow or hand-carry the boxes easily. If you intend to put out the debris in boxes and bundles for the trash men, you should have an area clear to store the boxes and bundles until trash day. If the room is on an upper floor, use boxes to carry the loose debris down steps, or build a plywood chute out of a window to guide the debris into a container.

The first step is to clear everything out of the room. The only things you want in the room are your tools and yourself. Place all tools in a cardboard box and keep returning them there so they don't get lost in the rubble.

When you are ready to start, seal off the room from the rest of the house. Close all interior doors and seal them with strips of 2-inch masking tape. Open all exterior doors and windows to the room. Wear heavy boots, thick clothes, hand, head, eye, and mouth protection. Remove all woodwork from around windows, doors, and floor. If you don't want to save and reuse it, you can rip it out quickly with the wrecking bar. If you do want to recycle it, use a claw hammer and be slow and careful as you pry it away from the studs and framing.

Start demolishing at a corner of the ceiling farthest from your exit door.

Climb onto the ladder with the wrecking bar, and use the plain end of the bar to poke a small hole (about 3 inches) in the plaster. When you have the hole, insert the crooked end of the wrecking bar into it and hook it under the plaster and lath. Pull down on the bar. If the plaster won't come away, you can try jerking the bar up and down, but be careful not to lose your balance.

When you expose a large hole (about 2 feet wide), you should be able to see the direction of the joists and the lath. Notice that the lath is nailed crosswise to the joists. You want to get your wrecking-bar crook crosswise to the lath to pull it away from the joists. The movement is a pulling one; you want to pull the lath away from one or two joists and then let it swing free on one or two others so that you don't get hit by it or the plaster clinging to it. Apply your crook close to the joists and always work to the sides of the ladder, never directly overhead. Once the lath is swinging, you can knock it free by hitting it with the crook of the bar. Hit the lath close to the joist where the nails are holding it.

Move the ladder frequently to get a good position on each section of lath and plaster. The work goes quickly and it can tempt you to take chances, but most lath is about four feet long and you will have to keep repositioning to get a good grip on each section.

As you pull and knock lath and plaster away from the joists, it will fall to the floor and create lots of dust and rubble. You should stop frequently and let the dust settle so that you can see what you're doing and also to move debris out of the way of the ladder. When the whole ceiling is down, your floor will have a uniform coating of dust, rubble, and lath to a depth of about one foot. It's a good time to stop, take a break, and come back to clean up and cart the debris before starting on the walls.

Gather up the wood lath from the floor and bundle it with twine into 2- or 3-foot-diameter bundles. If you have pulled rather than cracked the lath, it should be in pieces about 4 feet in length. Carry out the lath bundles and store or dump them. You can use lath for fire kindling and a small amount might be saved for shims, but that's about it for recycling possibilities.

When all the lath has been taken out, use a heavy push broom to sweep the plaster rubble into large piles. Use a flat-bladed shovel to load the plaster into liquor boxes or a wheelbarrow. Carry the plaster out and store it or dump it.

Now you are ready to start on the walls. Once again start on a corner away from your exit door. Climb on the ladder and start pulling lath and plaster away from the framing or furring at the top of the wall. Place your crook near the nailing surface and pull. You will have to pull at each nailing surface, because you don't have gravity helping you to swing the lath free of the frame as you did with the ceiling.

Work all the way across the wall at one height until you have cleared all you can from your position on the ladder. Start at the corner again, this time standing on the ladder where you can reach the next run of plaster and lath. Use the ladder to keep pulling strips of lath and plaster from the wall until you have cleared to about four feet off the floor. At this point you can stand on the floor and pull from there.

Most of the debris will fall to the base of the wall and pile up there, and so you will have to keep cleaning up as you

work that wall. Bundle lath and sweep plaster rubble into piles so that you have a secure floor to stand on. After one wall is down, take the time to bundle and load the rubble and remove it before starting the next wall.

Continue with the rest of the walls until the whole room is down. Leave framing, furring, and joists intact. Remove lath and plaster from around doors and windows carefully. Use the claw hammer for pulling lath from these tight spaces. Be especially careful near pipes, ducts, and electrical boxes.

After all the plaster and lath is down and out of the room, go around and inspect the framing, joists, and furring. If these items are to be left in place and covered with something else, you should pull any remaining lath nails out with the claw hammer. If you are going to expose brick or stone walls, you should remove furring strips from the masonry with the wrecking bar.

If you have demolished the plaster on both sides of a frame wall and you wish to remove the frame, now is the time to knock it apart. Use the wrecking bar and claw hammer to knock the studs free from the floor and ceiling plates. Pry off the floor and ceiling plates after the upright studs have been removed. Save all the framing wood that you remove. Pull all the nails, cut off the bad ends, and store the wood for future projects.

In Brief:

1. Make a plan for the debris. Hire a container or collect boxes to hold the plaster.

2. Clear the room of everything. Seal the doors with strips of masking tape. Open all windows and exterior doors. Remove all the woodwork

from around windows, doors, and floor.

3. Start with the ceiling at a corner away from your exit door. Poke a small hole in the ceiling with the wrecking bar. Insert the crooked end of the bar into the hole and hook it around lath and plaster. Pull down on the bar.

4. When you establish the direction of the lath, always get the crook crosswise to the lath to pull large hunks of ceiling down. Pull the lath away from one or two joists and let it swing free away from you. When it's swinging, hit it off the joists with the wrecking bar.

5. Stop frequently and let the dust settle. Move your ladder often to get a secure grip on each section of ceiling. When the whole ceiling is down, clean up the debris before starting on the walls.

6. Gather the lath into bundles and secure them with twine. Use the twine to carry the bundles out, and dump them or store them. Use a heavy push broom to sweep the plaster rubble into large piles. Load the rubble into liquor boxes or a wheelbarrow.

7. Start on the walls from the top and work across each wall at one height before moving down to pull away another level of plaster and lath. Use the same technique as with the ceiling, but pull at each nailing surface because the wall lath won't swing away as easily as ceiling lath.

8. Keep cleaning rubble and bundling lath because it will pile up very quickly at the base of the wall. Clean up completely after each wall is demolished before moving on to the next wall.

9. Use a claw hammer to remove lath and plaster carefully from around doors, windows, ducts, pipes, and electrical boxes.

10. Pull any nails remaining in the furring or framing if they are to be covered with something else. If you want to remove the framing, pry and knock it out with the wrecking bar. Pull nails and cut off bad ends, and store the lumber for future projects.

Tips:

In some situations, you may encounter one or more walls with plaster applied directly over brick. If you decide to demolish the plaster to expose the brick, you have got a real job on your hands. You must chip and chisel the plaster off the wall with a wide-blade brick chisel and hammer. In some spots the plaster will fall off in large hunks with just a few hits. In most places, however, you must work on each section with the chisel. Try to get the chisel under the plaster and nearly parallel to the wall. It is slow, frustrating work. The only quick way to do the job is to rent an air-driven hand chisel.

Even if you manage to get the plaster off the brick, you will find that the brick is still dirty with bits of plaster and fiber binder. You can sandblast this off with a rental machine if you want to expose clean natural brick. One easy treatment is simply to paint the wall with oil- or epoxy-based paint to even the color and texture of the masonry.

◟ HOW TO REMOVE PAINT

Tools and supplies needed:

Saucepan

Paint brush

4-inch razor-blade scraper

Wire brush

Rubber gloves

Goggles

Putty knife

Steel wool

Waste container

Semipaste paint remover (water-wash type)

Procedure:

Paint stripping is a very common old-house project. Most woodwork in old houses is coated with thick encrustations of paint and varnish. The wood must be stripped to bring out the original details and to provide a good surface for new paint or finishes.

For most work, a semipaste chemical paint remover is best. It will cling to vertical surfaces and won't dry out too fast. If you buy a water-wash type of stripper, you can polish the wood and remove deep stains with stripper, water, and steel wool. (See "Tips" at end of section.)

Pour out the remover into a saucepan and apply it to the wood with a paint brush. Keep applying remover until it will sit for 20 minutes without drying up. Busy yourself with something else so that you are not tempted to rush the process. After 20–30 minutes, check the remover. If the remover is still wet you can scrape it off. If it has dried out, apply more remover and wait another 20 minutes.

Scrape the softened paint off with the razor-blade scraper and deposit it in a waste container. Use a putty knife and wire brush to clean out grooves and carving.

If any paint remains after scraping and brushing, you must apply more stripper and wait while it works. Semipaste stripper will remove about 3 coats of paint with each application. The key is giving the stripper time to work and keeping enough stripper on the wood so that the stripper and paint remain liquid. After scraping down to bare wood, polish the wood with a piece of dry steel wool while the wood is still wet with stripper.

In Brief:

1. Apply paint remover to the wood with a paint brush. Apply enough so that it will sit for 20 minutes without drying up.

2. After 20–30 minutes, scrape the softened paint with a razor-blade scraper. Use a wire brush and putty knife to clean tight places.

3. If any paint remains, repeat the above process.

4. Polish the bare wood with steel wool while it is still wet with stripper.

Tips:

It is advisable to wear rubber gloves and eye protection when using chemical stripper. The stripper will burn and irritate your skin if it is not washed off immediately. Goggles are especially important when you are using a wire brush or steel wool to clean off softened paint;

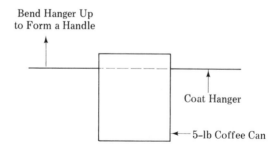

Bend Hanger Up
to Form a Handle

Coat Hanger

5-lb Coffee Can

Making a Waste Can for Paint Scraping.

bits of stripper can fly off in unexpected directions when you are brushing an ornate piece of carving.

Make a waste container by taking a five-pound coffee can and punching two holes in opposite sides near the rim. Take a straightened coat hanger and insert it through the two holes. Twist the two ends of the hanger together to form a handle like a paint can's. The wire between the two holes can be used to clean softened paint off the razor-blade scraper and putty knife.

To polish the wood after the paint is off and to remove any stains, brush a thin coating of stripper on the bare wood. Take a wet piece of steel wool and rub the stripper into the wood. The water and stripper will clean out any stain in the wood and will smooth the grain of the wood. Clean the wet wood with dry rags.

If a still lighter shade of wood is desired, bleach the wet wood with full-strength household bleach. Apply the liquid bleach with a rag or sponge. This bleach treatment has a way of evening out the color of the wood.

Doors are best stripped when taken off their hinges and laid flat on the floor or across sawhorses. Wood shutters must

be taken down to be stripped. Baseboards, stair woodwork, and door and window woodwork can be stripped in place.

Paint can also be removed with a propane torch. Buy a flame-spreader fitting for your hand torch. Move the tip of the flame over a small portion of the wood at a time and scrape the paint off as it blisters and softens. Flame removing is best suited to rough outside work such as porch woodwork or exterior doors. If you use flame indoors, make sure that the area is well-ventilated and that you have a fire extinguisher handy.

Another variation on flame paint removing is to use an electric heat gun. This device softens and blisters paint with an electric coil. You move the gun over the paint and scrape with a putty knife or razor-blade scraper. After you get most of the paint off the wood you should follow with a light application of chemical stripper and then polish with steel wool to get all the finish off. If you get proficient with a heat gun, you can remove thick paint quite quickly and economically and then bring out the subtleties of the wood with chemical stripper and steel wool.

If you have a large quantity of strip-

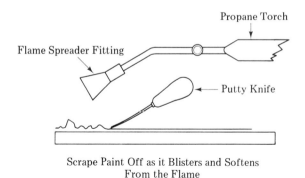

Propane Torch

Flame Spreader Fitting

Putty Knife

Scrape Paint Off as it Blisters and Softens
From the Flame

Paint Stripping Techniques.

ping to do (all the doors in a large house for example), it may be easier and more economical to send out your wood to be stripped in commercial lye baths. These commercial strippers will often give you a good price if you have a large quantity of items to be stripped. You must remove the wood and take it down to the stripping shop, and so it makes sense only for items like doors, window shutters, removable mantels and shelves, and other items that can be easily taken out and reinstalled.

⤳ HOW TO REMOVE WALLPAPER

Tools and supplies needed:

Step ladder
Plastic tarp
5-gallon bucket
Stiff-bristled scrub brush
4-inch razor-blade scraper
Extra blades for the scraper
Plastic trash bags
Masking tape

Procedure:

Most old houses have several layers of old wallpaper covering most of the walls and ceilings. The paper is often torn and peeling, and it must be removed to bring out the detail in the plaster work. Even old wallpaper that is in good condition has a disturbing tendency to peel off or bleed through when painted over. One of the first tasks you should undertake in an old house is to strip off all wallpaper.

Lay a plastic tarp on the floor to protect the wood and prevent loose wallpaper from sticking to it. Secure the tarp to the baseboards with strips of masking tape. Fill the bucket with hot water. Use the scrub brush to wet the wallpaper thoroughly with the water. Work on an area of about 15 square feet at one time.

Keep wetting the area until all layers of the wallpaper are soaked. Test the wallpaper with the razor-blade scraper and keep wetting until the paper comes off the wall with a moderate stroke of the scraper.

Put the waste paper into large plastic trash bags, and keep cleaning up after yourself so that you don't slip on old wallpaper. Any bits of wallpaper that still cling to the wall can be spotted with water and scraped off after the bulk of the paper is down.

In Brief:

1. Lay a plastic tarp on the floor, and secure it to the baseboards with masking tape.

2. Fill a bucket with hot water, and use the scrub brush to apply the water to the paper.

3. Keep wetting the paper until all layers are soaked. Test with the scraper and keep wetting until the paper comes off in large sheets.

4. Put the waste paper into trash bags and keep cleaning up as you work to avoid slipping on wet paper.

5. Spot small sections of tough paper with water and scrape them after the bulk of the paper is down.

Tips:

Hold the scraper as near to parallel with the wall as possible to avoid gouging the plaster and to get under all of the paper. The paper will tend to strip off in large sheets with this method.

Keep putting fresh blades in the scraper. You can save the dull blades for less demanding work, such as scraping off softened paint.

If there are many layers of paper on the wall, you may have to strip the first few off and rewet the underlayers to get to bare plaster. However, the wallpaper should strip off in one sheet if you have thoroughly wet it down from the beginning.

If there is oil-based paint on one of the layers of paper, it will prevent water from soaking through and releasing the paste from the wall. In this case you should score crosshatch lines in the paper with a utility knife to let water get through to the paste.

Really tough wallpaper demands a steamer rented from a paint store or rental shop. The steam from this machine is applied to the wallpaper with a hand-held pan, and it quickly releases the paste from the wall. If you own an electric heat gun you can use it to release tough wallpaper. Move the gun slowly over the wallpaper and follow it closely with the scraper. Don't use too much heat or you will fuse the paste to the wall.

You can do the walls and ceilings in any order you wish. If you start on the ceiling first, you do have the advantage of a clean and dry floor on which to place the ladder. When you do the walls you should start at the top to take advantage of gravity pulling the water onto and into the wallpaper below.

If you have one, a tank-type garden sprayer is an ideal tool for wetting the wallpaper. You can also try using a thick-nap paint roller to coat the wallpaper with water.

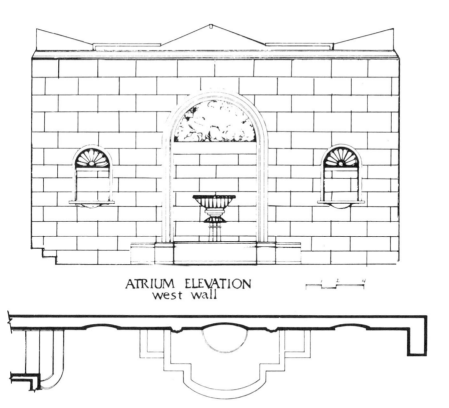

ATRIUM ELEVATION
west wall

11

Masonry Projects

⌥ HOW TO MIX MORTAR

Tools and supplies needed:

Mortar tray or wheelbarrow
Square-blade shovel
Garden hoe
Premixed mortar
or
Mortar cement and sand
or
Portland cement, hydrated lime, and sand

Procedure:

Mortar is the basic material for laying bricks, concrete blocks, and stone. It is also used for pointing the old mortar joints in an existing masonry structure.

For small jobs a premixed mortar in a bag is the easiest to work with. You simply add water to the mix, and blend until you get the right consistency.

For economy when working large jobs, you can use mortar cement to which you add sand and water. The mortar cement is composed of portland cement and hydrated lime and can be obtained in various shades ranging from a dark gray to a pure white.

For maximum economy and to allow freedom to experiment with proportions, you can make your own mortar by using portland cement, hydrated lime, and sand. You must measure the ingredients separately and blend them together before adding water.

Measure all the dry ingredients with a shovel. Mix the dry ingredients together in a wheelbarrow or mortar pan with a garden hoe. Scoop out a hollow in the middle of the material and add water slowly to the hollow. Mix and chop the mortar with the hoe until you come up with a smooth, plastic mix. Mixing is what brings the mortar to its proper consistency, not excessive water.

In Brief:

1. Measure all ingredients with a shovel and place them in a mortar pan or wheelbarrow.

2. Mix the dry ingredients with a garden hoe. Scoop a hollow in the middle of the material.

3. Add water slowly to the hollow, and begin to mix the mortar. Add water as you mix, and chop the mortar with the hoe.

4. Continue working the mortar with the hoe until you have a smooth, plastic mix. Mixing, not excessive water, is what produces a smooth mortar.

Tips:

The general formula for mixing mortar cement and sand is one part mortar cement to four parts clean sand.

The general formula for mixing mortar from scratch is one part portland cement, one-half part hydrated lime, and four parts clean sand.

There are other mortar formulas for special situations. For masonry that is in contact with the earth, a cement-rich mortar is called for. Use one part portland cement, one-fourth part hydrated lime, and three and one-half parts clean sand.

A medium-strength mortar with easy workability for above-ground work is one part portland cement, one part hydrated lime, and five parts clean sand. The extra lime in this formula makes the mortar easy to work with a trowel.

For maximum strength, mortar should be mixed with clean, pure water. Mix only what you can use in about an hour. You can retemper mortar one or two times by adding water and remixing as the mortar dries out. Mortar sets by a chemical reaction, not by drying out, so don't use two-hour-old mortar that you soften with water.

➥ HOW TO POINT BRICK JOINTS

Tools and supplies needed:

Tuckpointing trowel ¼ x 6-inch blade
Mixing bucket
Mortar hawk
Chisel and hammer
Wire brush
3-inch masonry nails
1 x 2 x 12-inch wood stick
Mortar

Procedure:

Cleaning out old crumbling mortar from between bricks and replacing it with new mortar is called *pointing*. Pointing protects the brick wall from the elements and reconditions its appearance. You will probably have to point only a few small sections of the walls where water or wind has worked on the joints. Check the walls near gutters and downspouts for water damage to the joints.

Clean out the joints to be pointed with a wire brush or chisel. You can make a joint raker by drilling a pilot hole in the end of a 1 x 2 x 12-inch stick and driving a round masonry nail halfway into the stick. Use the pointed and blunt end of the masonry nail to clean out the joints down to solid mortar.

Wet the joints and surrounding

bricks with plenty of water. Play a mist of water over the area for at least ten minutes.

Mix your mortar in small batches in a five-gallon bucket. Place a heap of mortar on the mortar hawk and carry it to the wall. Start pointing from the highest joint and work your way down the wall. Place the edge of the hawk even with the joint to be filled. Use the tuckpointing trowel to cut a small quantity of mortar from the heap. Push the mortar into the joint from the edge of the hawk.

Draw the trowel across the joint to spread the mortar into the joint. Keep moving the hawk along the joint's edge to keep up with the trowel. Cut any excess mortar off the joint with the edge of the trowel and let it fall to the ground.

For the short vertical joints, place the hawk even with the bottom of the vertical joint. Push mortar into the joint with the trowel, and move the hawk higher along the joint until it is filled.

After an area has been pointed so that all the joints are filled flush with the surface of the brick, you should tool the joints smooth. For a flush joint (the most common in old houses), simply draw the tuckpointing trowel smoothly along the mortar to smooth it. For a concave joint, draw a concave jointer tool (available at a masonry supply store) across the mortar to remove a bit of the mortar and produce a concave surface.

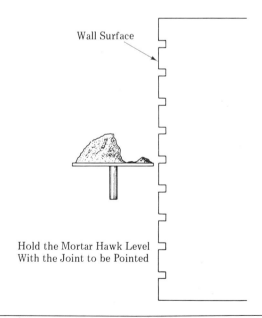

Wall Surface

Hold the Mortar Hawk Level
With the Joint to be Pointed

Pointing Brick Joints.

In Brief:

1. Clean out all loose and crumbling mortar from the joints with a joint raker, wire brush, and chisel.

2. Play a mist of water over the joints and bricks for at least ten minutes.

3. Mix a small quantity of mortar in a bucket. Place a heap of mortar on the mortar hawk.

4. Start pointing from the top and work down. Place the hawk even with the joint to be filled. Cut a small quantity of mortar from the hawk and push it into the joint with the pointing tool.

5. Keep moving the hawk along the joint as you spread the mortar into the joint. Cut any excess mortar off of the joint with the edge of the trowel and let it fall to the ground.

6. For vertical joints, place the hawk even with the bottom of the joint. Push mortar into the joint and keep moving the hawk up the joint as it is filled.

7. After the area is pointed, tool the joints smooth with the trowel or a concave jointing tool. Simply draw the tool across the mortar to smooth and shape it.

Tips:

Small areas of pointing on a wall can be done using a ladder. If you have to point all of a large wall, it is worth it to rent a scaffold so that you can work efficiently and safely over the entire surface.

The homemade joint raker is useful for small jobs, but if you have a lot of pointing to do you should buy a skate-wheel joint raker. This inexpensive device lets you run a nail quickly down a joint to clean it out and will save you time (and a few barked knuckles).

Stone foundations and walls sometimes need pointing too. The procedure is the same, but you must use a small triangular trowel to push the mortar into place. The best size for this trowel is 5 inches long by 2½ inches wide. This small trowel will let you get mortar into the odd-shaped cracks and crevices of a stone wall.

↳ HOW TO REPAIR CONCRETE CRACKS AND HOLES

Tools and supplies needed:

Medium-size trowel
5-gallon bucket
Paint or whitewash brush
Hammer
Chisel
Portland cement
Sand
Pea gravel
Plastic sheeting

Procedure:

Small cracks and holes in concrete are common around an old house. You will want to patch sidewalks, concrete steps, and basement floors. For holes up to 12 inches in diameter and 3 inches deep, the standard patching mix is one part portland cement, two parts sand, and two parts pea gravel, with just enough water to make a stiff mix. For narrow cracks use a patching mortar of one part portland cement to three parts sand, with just enough water to make a stiff mix.

For either holes or cracks, the procedure is the same. Use a chisel to break up and remove any loose or flaking material from the area to be patched. Thin cracks must be chiseled out to at least ¼ inch wide to receive the patching material. The patching material will hold much better if the crack or hole is undercut slightly with the chisel to provide a mechanical key. Sweep the area clean of any debris with a brush.

Wet the area to be patched. Use plenty of water, but don't apply so much that there is standing water in the area. Mix a small quantity of pure portland cement and water into a very thin bonding grout. Brush this grout into the crack or along the sides of the hole.

Trowel the patching mix into the crack or hole. Force it into the area with the trowel and tamp with a piece of scrap wood if necessary. Overfill the area slightly with patching mix to allow for some slight shrinkage when the patch dries. Tool the surface with the trowel and feather the edge of the patch even with the surrounding concrete. Cover the patch with plastic sheeting, and secure with boards or stones. Leave the sheeting in place for at least five days to let the patch damp-cure.

In Brief:

1. Use a chisel and hammer to break up and remove any loose and flaking material from the area. Chisel thin cracks to at least ¼ inch wide. Undercut the cracks and holes slightly to provide a mechanical key.

2. Wet the area with water. Mix a thin bonding grout of pure portland cement and water. Brush the grout into the crack or hole.

3. Trowel the patching mix into the crack or hole. Press or tamp the material firmly. Overfill the area slightly to provide for shrinkage as the patch dries. Tool the surface with the trowel, and feather the edge even with the surrounding concrete.

4. Cover the patch with plastic sheeting, and leave the sheeting in place for five days to let the patch damp-cure.

Tips:

For vertical holes or chips in a wall or set of steps, build a wood form to keep the patching material in place until it hardens. Use plywood or 1-inch-thick boards for the form. Chisel the top of the hole (or chip) out so that you can add patching material from above. Prepare and apply bonding grout to the hole. Set the form against the hole, and prop it in place with a wooden strut or heavy cement block. Use the trowel to put the patching material into the area from the gap between the top of the form and the edge of the hole. Use a wooden dowel or thin piece of wood to tamp the material firmly into place. Leave the form in place for 24 hours and then dampen the patch and cover with plastic.

↰ HOW TO STUCCO

Tools and supplies needed:

Wheelbarrow or mortar tray
Flat-blade shovel
Garden hoe
5-gallon bucket
Mortar hawk (1 foot square or larger)

Rectangular mason's trowel (12 x 6 inches)

Hammer

6-inch paint brush or whitewash brush

Rough wire whisk or scratcher

Portland cement

White portland cement

Clean sand

Masonry nails

Expanded-wire stucco lath (¼–½ inch)

18-gauge tie wire

Procedure:

Stucco is a mortar composed of portland cement and sand. It is a very durable material for covering exterior and interior walls. For exterior masonry walls that are too deteriorated to be brought back with cleaning and pointing, stucco is ideal for appearance and protection from the elements. You might, for example, run a band of stucco around the base of your house 3 feet high to cover and protect masonry that has sustained physical and water damage.

Inside the house, stucco can be used to finish and waterproof rough basement walls. Stucco can also be applied to interior brick walls and troweled smooth to make a very durable surface that stands up to high moisture and rough use. The restorer will find little use for interior stucco except in the basement, but the person who guts and redesigns his home will be able to make use of stucco in living areas, bathrooms, and kitchens.

Stucco can be applied directly to rough-surfaced, clean, unpainted masonry surfaces. Exposed brick, stone, and concrete block can all be covered with stucco without any other preparation beyond cleaning.

Dirty, smooth, or painted surfaces must first have expanded-wire lath applied to them to give the first coat of stucco a good bond. The use of wire lath is also recommended for any large job (the whole side of a building, for example) or when maximum strength and resistance to cracking is desired (as in finished interior stucco walls).

If you use wire lath under stucco, you must nail it securely to the surface to be covered. Use masonry nails every 16 inches over the surface of the lath. Each separate piece of lath must be overlapped with neighboring lath pieces by 1 inch on each side. The overlaps should be tied together using 18-gauge tie wire.

The lath must be made to stand out from the backing surface by ¼ inch. Some styles of lath do this automatically by the use of built-in furring channels or dimples punched in the lath. If you are not using a self-furring lath, install the lath with furring nails that have built-in lath stand-offs. Regardless of the nails you use, they should penetrate the wall to a depth of at least three-quarters of an inch.

When the surface is lathed or otherwise prepared for the application of stucco, you are ready to mix. Don't mix more stucco than you can use in half an hour. You will be mixing a stiff mortar, and you don't want to mix so much that you have to keep rewetting it in order to use it.

The proper proportions for stucco base coats are one part portland cement to three parts clean, well-graded sand. (Well-graded means that there is an equal mix of large and small particles.)

Don't be tempted to use more portland cement in an effort to produce a stronger stucco—cement-rich stucco tends to crack easily.

Mix the dry ingredients well with a garden hoe. Scoop out a hollow in the middle of the material and add water slowly to create a stiff mix. The stucco should be stiff enough to hang on vertical surfaces without sagging. Thorough mixing will bring what seems like a dry mass to a smooth, plastic mortar.

If the mortar seems too stiff after you start working with it, you can add some more water—but this is no substitute for proper mixing. The constant addition of more water to increase workability will reduce the bonding strength of the mortar.

Start applying stucco from the top of the wall, and work your way down. This first coat (called the *scratch coat*) will be about ¼ inch thick. Heap the stucco mixture onto the mortar hawk and carry it to the wall. Place the edge of the hawk right on the wall. Cut a quantity of stucco off a corner of the hawk onto the rectangular trowel, and apply it to the wall. Spread the stucco over the wall until it is ¼ inch thick. Avoid excessive troweling with this coat—try to spread each trowelful of stucco in one or two movements. If you are using lath, the mortar should be just thick enough to show some of the pattern of the lath on its surface. If you don't feel comfortable using the hawk to carry stucco, try using a 5-gallon bucket. Scoop stucco out of the bucket with the trowel, and apply it to the wall. If the stucco is the right consistency, you shouldn't have any trouble keeping it on the trowel as you take it out of the bucket.

About 15 to 20 minutes after you apply the stucco, you should scratch it with a wire whisk or straight-line scratcher (available at the masonry supply house). The scratches should be about ½ inch apart. Scratch the stucco in all directions and go over the entire surface. These scratches will provide a good mechanical key for the next coat of stucco.

Let the scratch coat cure for a minimum of two days. Dampen the stucco with a spray of water once or twice during this period. When you are ready to apply the next coat (called the *brown coat*), dampen the scratch coat with a fine mist of water from a hose. This will improve the bond and allow for smoother working of the brown coat with the trowel.

For the brown coat, mix stucco exactly as you did for the scratch coat: one part portland cement to three parts sand, with just enough water to make a plastic mix. Apply the brown coat with a trowel and hawk (or bucket). Again, stucco from the top of the wall and work down. Apply enough stucco to make this coat about ½ inch thick, and you can trowel it enough to make the surface fairly smooth. If you are working a large area, you can use a wooden float (shaped like a rectangular trowel but larger and made of wood) to smooth out the surface. Use the float after the water gloss has disappeared from the surface of the stucco. Press the float against the stucco to compact it and straighten the surface, and then move it in broad, circular strokes across the surface to smooth it. Use a wide brush soaked in water to smooth the stucco further while using the float. Lightly scratch (about ⅛ inch deep) the brown coat after troweling and floating to provide a key for the finish coat.

Let the brown coat cure for two days, keeping it moist with an occasional misting of water. Let the brown coat dry for seven days after this first cure before the finish coat is applied.

The finish coat of stucco is composed of white portland cement and sand. White portland cement is specially formulated to harden into a white color. Most people prefer it to regular portland cement, which hardens into a gray color. The proportions are the same as for the base coats: one part white portland cement to three parts sand, with just enough water to make a stiff, plastic mortar. Powdered coloring materials can be mixed dry with the stucco materials to provide different pastel colors. These coloring materials should not equal more than 6 pounds of color to each 90-pound bag of cement.

Dampen the brown coat with a fine mist of water prior to applying the finish coat. The finish coat should be troweled on to a depth of ⅛ to ¼ inch to bring the total thickness of the stucco to about 1 inch. As with the other coats, start applying stucco at the top of the wall and work your way down to the bottom.

In Brief:

1. If you use wire lath, nail it with masonry nails every 16 inches over the surface of the lath. Overlap each piece of lath by 1 inch. Tie the overlaps with 18-gauge wire. The lath should stand out from the backing surface by ¼ inch. Use a self-furring lath or use furring nails with lath stand-offs.

2. Mix the stucco mortar. Use only enough water to create a stiff mix. Use more mixing to make the mortar plastic, not more water.

3. Start applying stucco from the top of the wall and work down. Carry stucco to the wall with a mortar hawk. Cut the stucco off the hawk with a trowel and spread it over the wall until it is ¼ inch thick. Avoid excessive troweling. The pattern of the lath (if used) should show through this first coat.

4. Fifteen to twenty minutes after application, scratch the stucco with a wire whisk or scratcher to provide a mechanical key. Let this coat cure for at least two days. Dampen it with a mist of water several times during the cure and just before the application of the brown coat.

5. Mix stucco exactly as you did for the first coat. Apply a ½-inch-thick coat to the wall. Trowel this coat sufficiently to make a fairly smooth surface. Use a wooden float to press the stucco and straighten the surface, and then move it in broad strokes across the surface to smooth it.

6. Lightly scratch the brown coat after floating it to provide a mechanical key. Let this coat cure for two days, wetting it with water several times during the cure. Let the brown coat cure for an additional seven days after this damp cure before applying the finish coat.

7. Wet the brown coat with a mist of water before applying the finish coat of stucco. The finish coat is composed of white portland cement and sand, with dry coloring materials added if desired. The stucco should be thoroughly mixed to make it a stiff plastic consistency as with the other coats.

8. Apply the finish coat in a thickness of ⅛–¼ inch to bring the total thickness of the stucco to about 1 inch.

Tips:

There are many textures that can be troweled or tooled into the finish coat of stucco. One of the most common is called the *French trowel texture.* In spite of its fancy name it is quite easy to do. The finish coat of white portland cement stucco is applied quickly and worked with the steel trowel until it is ⅛–¼ inch deep. The trowel marks are simply left in the wet stucco to make their own texture.

Another simple technique is to float the finish coat with a wooden or rubber-faced float just as you did with the brown coat. This leaves a fairly even, smooth-looking coat that highlights the texture of the sand in the stucco. One more simple finish can be created by floating the surface and then tooling it with a whisk broom. Just apply the broom lightly to the surface, and let the bristles make a pattern in the stucco.

If you are applying stucco to a masonry surface without lath, be sure to wet the masonry thoroughly before applying stucco. This will provide a better bond and prevent the first coat from drying out too fast. Be sure to keep the stucco coats damp as they cure. If you are working outside, you should plan to work in the shade as much as possible to prevent premature drying. The stucco must be kept damp until it reaches its initial strength (seven days with conventional cements, three days if you are using cement marked "high early strength").

⤳ HOW TO LAY BRICK

Tools and supplies needed:

Medium trowel (about 8 x 5 inches)
Brick chisel
Hammer
Level and line
Mortar tray or wheelbarrow
Bricks
Mortar

Procedure:

Most of your bricklaying projects around an old house will be small ones. You will be repairing tumbled chimney tops, edges of window frames, and other small problems. In addition you may want to use brick to close up a basement window or unused doorway for security and privacy. Bricklaying is a skilled procedure, and you should first get the feel of small repairs before you go on to bigger projects.

Wet the bricks before laying them in mortar. Soak the bricks in water or play a mist of water over them for at least half an hour. Lay out the bricks in a dry run and check for any problems. Use a ⅜-inch gap between bricks to simulate mortar joints. You may find that you will need to cut a full brick to fill the space neatly.

Cut a brick by scoring all around the top, bottom, and edges of the brick with a brick chisel. Score a cut about ⅛ inch deep. Lay the brick on soft ground, and put the chisel into the cut on the broad side of the brick. Strike the chisel sharply with a hammer and the brick will break cleanly on the line.

When you have checked your layout and cut all the half bricks you need, mix mortar to the consistency of soft mud. Mix only what you can use in an hour.

Use the running bond pattern when laying brick. This is where the brick is placed halfway over the tops of the bricks below it. This means that there will be a half brick at the ends of every other row in the wall. Those half bricks could be the ends of full bricks if you are turning a corner with your project.

Begin building at the corner of your project. Lay the brick three rows (also called *courses*) high with ⅜-inch joints. Use a level to check for trueness as you lay each course of brick. Then build up another corner, keeping it level with the first corner by using a straightedge and a level.

When you have two corners built up, push two nails into the mortar between the bricks, and stretch a line between the two corners. Use this line to lay the

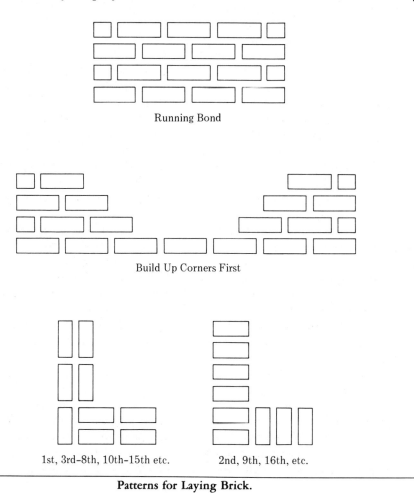

Running Bond

Build Up Corners First

1st, 3rd–8th, 10th–15th etc.   2nd, 9th, 16th, etc.

Patterns for Laying Brick.

other bricks. Keep moving the line up with each new course of bricks.

Laying the brick consists of putting enough mortar down to lay three bricks. Furrow the mortar a few times with the trowel. Take a brick, and butter one end with a swipe of mortar. Lay the brick down, squeezing the mortar out of the joint until it is ⅜ inch thick.

Cut the excess mortar from the joint with the edge of the trowel. Butter the end of another brick, and place the buttered end next to the unbuttered end of the first brick. Continue buttering and placing bricks until you come to the middle of the row and the last brick. Butter this brick on both ends, and place extra mortar in the socket. Carefully lower this brick into place, and tap it into position with the handle of your trowel.

Always use the corners of the project to guide the rest of the work. When you build the middle up level with the corners, start up with the corners again and then fill in the middle using the nails and line as a guide for each course of bricks.

In Brief:

1. Soak the bricks in water or play a mist of water over them for at least half an hour.

2. Lay out a row of bricks in a dry run to check for fit. Score and cut bricks with a chisel and hammer.

3. Mix mortar to the consistency of soft mud.

4. Begin building at the corner of your project. Lay the bricks three courses high with a ⅜-inch joint. Build up a second corner level with the first.

5. Use nails and a line to guide the individual courses of brick between the two corners.

6. Put down enough mortar to lay three bricks. Furrow the mortar with your trowel.

7. Take a brick, and butter one end with a swipe of mortar.

8. Place the brick on the mortar and squeeze it into place, letting excess mortar come out of the joints. Cut the excess mortar from the joint with the edge of the trowel.

9. Repeat the buttering-and-placing process until you come to the last brick in the row. Butter both sides of this brick, and place extra mortar in the socket. Carefully lower the brick into place, and tap the brick into position with the handle of your trowel.

10. When the wall is even with the corners, start up with the corners again and use them to guide the rest of the brick.

Tips:

Most brick construction is of double thickness. To construct a double-thickness wall you must tie the brick together by laying an occasional course of brick across the two running bond walls. The crosswise course occurs directly on top of the first course and then every sixth course after that. The only difference in laying this crosswise course is that the broad sides of the brick are buttered, not the ends.

⤳ HOW TO LAY CONCRETE BLOCK

Tools and supplies needed:

Medium-size trowel
Level and line
Brick chisel
Hammer
Mortar tray or wheelbarrow
Mortar
Concrete block

Procedure:

Hollow concrete block is useful for filling or repairing masonry openings that you plan to stucco later to provide a uniform surface. Block lays faster than brick and doesn't require a double layer for strength.

Block is laid dry so the only preparation is to lay out a trial course and cut block to fit. Concrete block can be rough cut with a chisel and hammer in the same manner as brick. Score a line ⅛ inch deep all around the sides and faces of the block. Hit the chisel smartly along the line, and the block will break apart. Chisel off any rough spots on the edges. For a perfect cut you can put a masonry saw blade in your circular saw and cut along the line.

Mix mortar to a stiff mud consistency. You want the mortar to be stiff enough to support the weight of the blocks without squeezing out of the joint.

Use the running bond pattern as with brick. Begin building at the corners and use a ⅜-inch joint. When you have two corners built up and level with each other, fill in the middle using a line an-chored in the corner mortar joints as a guide for the rest of the blocks.

Put down enough mortar on the footing to lay three blocks. Lay the blocks with the small-size core holes facing up. Butter the ends of the block with mortar, and place them in the mortar bed. Tap the blocks in place with the handle of your trowel until you have a ⅜-inch joint. Cut excess mortar off the joint with the edge of your trowel.

When you come to the last block in the course, butter both ends and place extra mortar in the socket. Carefully lower the block into place, and tap it into position with the handle of your trowel.

The upper courses are laid in the same way. A mortar bed is put on the top of the lower blocks, and a block is buttered with mortar on the ends and placed in position.

In Brief:

1. Lay out a trial course of block and cut any half-blocks needed. Cut block with a hammer and chisel or use a masonry saw blade in your circular saw.

2. Mix mortar to a stiff mud consistency.

3. Build up the corners of your project first. Put down enough mortar on the footing to lay three blocks. Butter the ends of the blocks and lay them, small holes up, in the mortar bed. Tap the block with the handle of your trowel to get a ⅜-inch joint. Cut excess mortar off the joint with the edges of your trowel.

4. When you have built two level corners, stretch a line between two nails driven into the corner mortar joints. Lay the middle blocks to the line. Lay

a mortar bed, butter the ends of the blocks, and tap the blocks into position with the handle of your trowel.

5. When you come to the last block in the course, butter both ends and place extra mortar in the socket. Lower the block into place and tap it into position with the handle of your trowel.

⤙ HOW TO LAY BRICK IN SAND

Tools and supplies needed:

Shovel

Rake

Brick chisel

Hammer

Circular saw

Broom

Paint brush

2 x 4-inch or 4 x 4-inch lumber

Clean sand

Creosote oil

Face brick, paving brick, or used brick

Procedure:

Laying brick in a bed of sand is an easy and inexpensive way to make a walkway or terrace. The combination of brick and sand is surprisingly strong, and any repairs are easily done. There are brick and sand sidewalks that have held together beautifully for over ninety years.

You can use new face or paving brick, or you can buy or salvage used brick. If you use old brick, make sure it's face brick and not soft interior (some-times called *wad*) brick. Face brick is harder and darker than wad brick and holds up better because of superior clay and firing.

Lay out the walkway or terrace, and dig the area out to a depth that equals the thickness of the brick plus two inches for sand. Build a frame for the project with 2 x 4s or 4 x 4s. Paint the wood with two coats of creosote oil, and hold the frame in place with small creosoted wood stakes. Install the framing pieces along the edge of the hole, with the top edge of the wood level with the surrounding ground.

If you want to prevent grass and weeds from growing up between the bricks, put down 4-mil or thicker black plastic sheets or roll roofing. Overlap the edges of the sheet material by 6 to 8 inches.

Dump sand into the area and rake it to within a brick thickness of the top edge of the frame. Use a long piece of 2 x 4 to level and smooth the sand further. Use the frame as a guide for your leveling operations.

Choose a pattern and begin to lay brick in the sand. Simply start at any corner and begin to lay the brick. Butt the edges of the bricks tightly together. If one brick sits higher than the others, scoop a little sand out from under it and re-lay it. Reverse the process for any brick that sits too low.

Cut any bricks that are needed for small places with a wide-blade chisel and a hammer. Score all around the brick with the chisel. Place the brick on the soft ground and hit the score line on the top surface smartly with the chisel and hammer. The brick will come apart cleanly.

When all the bricks are laid, shovel

sand over them and work it into the joints with a broom. Go over the bricks repeatedly with sand and the broom. Wet the job down with water from a hose to pack the sand further into the joints. Follow with more sand and sweeping. The bricks will soon firm up, and the sand will lock in place.

In Brief:

1. Lay out the project, and dig the area to a depth that equals the thickness of the brick plus two inches of sand.

2. Build a frame with 2 x 4 or 4 x 4 lumber. Paint the wood with creosote oil, and hold the frame in place with small creosoted stakes.

3. Put black plastic sheeting or roll roofing down in the hole if you want to prevent grass and weeds from growing up between the bricks. Overlap the sheeting by 6 to 8 inches.

4. Choose a pattern and begin to lay brick. Butt the edges of the bricks tightly together. Level each brick as you lay it by removing or adding sand under it.

5. Cut any bricks for small places. Score the brick all the way around with a chisel and hammer. Lay the brick on soft ground, and strike the score line smartly with the chisel and hammer.

6. When all the bricks are laid, shovel sand over the bricks and work it into the joints with a broom. Wet the job down with water to pack the sand. Follow this with more sand and sweeping.

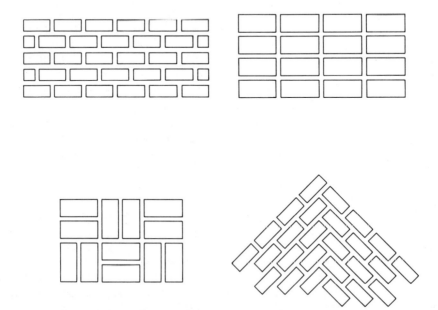

Patterns You Can Use for Paving Brick

Tips:

If you buy new standard face brick for your project, you can calculate the number of bricks to order by expecting to use five bricks for each square foot of the project. Five-hundred bricks will cover 100 square feet with a 10 percent allowance for wastage.

Paving brick is slightly larger than standard brick, so you can calculate about four paving bricks to the square foot. The advantage of paving brick is that it is exactly half as wide as it is long, and so you can easily accomplish some of the tricky patterns that use the brick in two or more directions. Pavers will cost more than standard brick and may not be available in a large selection of colors.

If you use old salvaged brick you will find that the sizes can vary. In general four bricks will cover a square foot. Broken bricks can be used if you cut off rough edges and use the common bond to lay them. Good sources for used brick include demolition sites, old brick walkways that are being taken up, salvage yards, and classified-ad publications.

It is cheaper to buy sand by the ton and have it delivered to your house than to buy it by the bag and take it home yourself. Bags are adequate for small projects, but for anything over 15 square feet you should buy sand by the ton. Reserve a large parking space in front of your house with your car or some lumber and concrete blocks. When the truck comes, have the sand dumped in the parking space. You can then transfer the sand by wheelbarrow to your project. Any extra sand can be shoveled into heavy plastic bags (the bags fertilizer comes in are great) for storage.

⤙ HOW TO LAY QUARRY TILE

Tools and supplies needed:

Taping knife

Mixing bucket

Tape measure

Rubber window squeegee

Clean rags

Quarry tile

Tile adhesive

Dry grout mix

Procedure:

Quarry tile is a hard, red earthenware tile that is resistant to heat, liquids, and scratching. It is an excellent choice for countertops and floors that take hard wear. The standard size is 6 x 6 inches. It is sold by the square foot, which means that the price you are quoted will be for four tiles.

Measure the area to be covered. Order enough tiles to cover your square footage plus 10 percent for wastage. Buy your tiles at a store that will lend or rent you a tile cutter heavy enough to cut quarry tile. Some places will not give you a cutter but will let you come back with the tiles that you need cut and do it for you with a diamond-tipped saw. Also buy quarry-tile adhesive and a dry grout mix. Grout is available in many different colors. A dark or black grout is easier to keep clean looking than lighter shades.

At home, lay the tiles out in a dry run with a ¼-inch space between them. This space will be filled with grout after the tiles are cemented in place. A piece of thin wood or a straight piece of metal is useful for spacing the tiles uniformly. Mark the tiles that will have to be cut.

Cut the tiles with the borrowed (or rented) cutter, or bring them back to the store and have them cut for you. Lay the cut tiles in place and check for proper fit. Take all the tiles up.

Spread adhesive over the surface to be tiled. Use the taping knife and follow the package directions for the proper thickness of the adhesive. When the surface is completely covered, lay the tiles down using the spacing stick. When all the tiles are down and correctly spaced, press them firmly into the tile adhesive. Use the spacing stick to correct any gaps that have gotten out of line.

Let the tile adhesive cure according to the package directions. When everything is firm, prepare the grout in the mixing bucket. Use only enough water to bring the grout to a stiff plastic consistency.

Use the taping knife and the rubber-bladed squeegee to press the grout into the gaps between the tiles. Go over each joint two or three times to make sure that it is completely filled. When all the joints are grouted, scrape off any excess with the clean rubber squeegee. Keep cleaning the squeegee with a rag as you use it to remove excess grout from the surface of the tiles.

Do a final cleaning of the tiles with clean, wet rags. Wipe each tile with a rag to clean it of grout. This is tedious labor, but it must be done before the grout cures. Keep using fresh rags to avoid fouling clean tiles.

Let the grout cure according to package directions before using the surface.

In Brief:

1. Measure the area to be covered and come up with a square footage figure. Order enough tiles to cover plus 10 percent for wastage. Buy enough tile adhesive and grout to take care of the area you are covering.

2. Lay the tiles out in a dry run with a ¼-inch gap between tiles. Use a spacing stick to make uniform gaps.

3. Mark tiles that will have to be cut. Cut the tiles yourself, or take them back to the tile store and have them cut for you on a saw.

4. Lay the cut tiles down and check for proper fit.

5. Take all the tiles off the surface and spread the adhesive over the area with a taping knife. Lay the tiles on the adhesive and use the spacing stick to gap them evenly. After everything is down, press the tiles into the adhesive. Use the spacing stick to correct any gaps that have gotten out of line.

6. Let the tile adhesive cure according to package directions. When everything is firm, prepare the dry grout mix. Use only enough water to bring the grout to a stiff plastic consistency.

7. Use the taping knife and rubber squeegee to press the grout into the gaps between tiles. Go over each joint two or three times to make sure it is completely filled.

8. When all the joints are flush with the surface, use a clean squeegee to scrape off any excess grout. Do a final cleaning of the tiles with wet rags. Wipe each tile completely clean, and

keep changing rags to avoid fouling clean tiles.

9. Let the grout cure according to package directions.

Tips:

If you are tiling a large floor area, follow the procedure for laying floor tile. Divide the floor into quarters, and work on a quarter of the floor at a time.

You can follow the quarry-tile procedure to lay and grout other materials. Slate, milk glass, and glazed ceramic tile can all be laid and grouted this way.

If you use quarry tile to line the floor and sides of a fireplace, bed the quarry tile in mortar instead of tile adhesive. Clean the masonry surface with a wire brush, wet the masonry down, and trowel a ¼-inch bed of mortar. Lay the tile in the wet mortar and press into place. When the tiles are firm, they can be grouted with mortar.

↰ HOW TO STACK AND INSTALL TERRA-COTTA FLUE LINING

Tools and supplies needed:

Rope
Gloves
Medium trowel
Terra-cotta flue lining
Mortar

Procedure:

Terra-cotta flue lining is an excellent product for reconditioning and sealing an old flue. The terra cotta provides a smooth surface for the inside of the flue, and each piece rests tightly on its neighbor to provide a smoke-tight joint.

Select a flue liner that will fit in the old flue with about ½ inch clearance. All flue liners are two feet in length. The common dimensions of flue liners are as follows:

4 x 8″	4 x 12″	4 x 16″
8 x 8″	8 x 12″	8 x 16″
12 x 12″	12 x 16″	
16 x 16″	16 x 20″	
20 x 20″	20 x 24″	
24 x 24″		

Drop a line down the old flue and measure its length. Buy enough liners to run the entire length of the chimney and to extend 4 inches above the top edge of the chimney.

Make sure that the first piece of flue lining will rest on a secure surface. You may have to install angle iron or brick with mortar to provide a secure footing for the first liner.

Get on the roof with the liners and enough rope to reach the bottom of the flue and back again. Remove the chimney cap, if there is one. Slip one end of the rope through a liner. Pull the rope through until both ends are even. Pick up the liner by grasping the twin ropes near its top.

Insert the liner into the chimney. Lower the liner by letting the twin ropes drop hand-over-hand. When the liner touches bottom, remove the rope by pulling one side of the rope until the whole length comes free. Recover the rope, and repeat the process until all the liners are in place.

Mix a small batch of mortar, and apply a sloped coping of mortar to the topmost liner and the chimney top. The coping should run from the outer edge of the chimney to within 2 inches of the liner top. This coping will prevent water

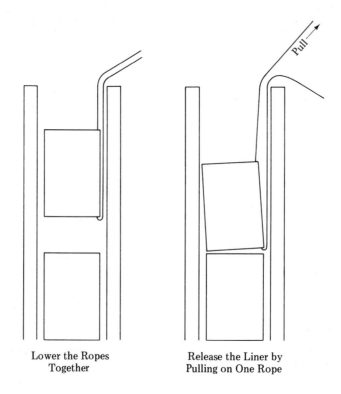

Lower the Ropes Together

Release the Liner by Pulling on One Rope

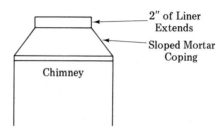

2″ of Liner Extends

Sloped Mortar Coping

Chimney

Lining an Old Flue.

from entering the old flue and will improve the draft characteristics of the new terra-cotta flue.

In Brief:

1. Measure the length of the flue by dropping a line down it. Buy enough flue lining to run the length of the old flue and extend 4 inches above the top edge of the chimney.

2. Prepare the footing for the first piece of liner. Install angle iron or brick and mortar if needed.

3. Go to the roof with the liners and enough rope to reach the length of the flue and back again. Remove the chimney cap, if any.

4. Slip one end of the rope through a liner. Pull the rope through until both ends are even. Pick up the liner by grasping the twin ropes near the top of the liner.

5. Insert the liner into the chimney. Lower the liner by letting the twin ropes drop, hand-over-hand. When the liner touches bottom, pull one end of the rope until the whole length comes free.

6. Recover the rope and repeat the process until all the liners are in place.

7. Mix a small batch of mortar, and apply a sloped coping to the topmost liner and the chimney top. The coping should run from the outer edge of the chimney to within 2 inches of the liner top.

Tips:

If you have to cut a liner, the safest way is to use a masonry blade in your circular saw. Simply mark the cut lines with a pencil, and cut them with the circular saw. Be sure to use goggles when cutting a liner.

If you want to use a chimney cap on the flue after you have installed liners, you can strap a prefabricated metal cap directly to the top liner. These metal caps are available for the standard sizes of flue liners, and they install quickly with a screwdriver and adjustable wrench.

Flue liners are suitable for any kind of flue. They can be used for coal-, oil-, or gas-fired furnaces, gas hot-water heaters, woodburning stoves, and conventional fireplaces.

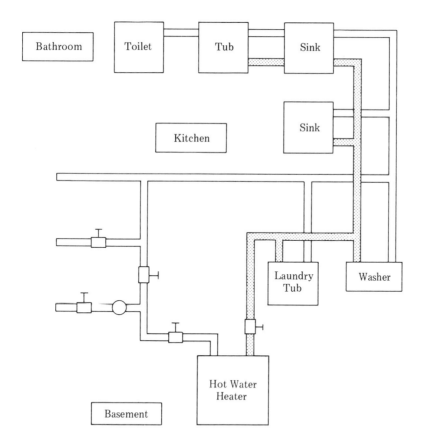

Bathroom	Toilet	Tub	Sink

Kitchen

Sink

Laundry Tub

Washer

Hot Water Heater

Basement

12

Plumbing Projects

⤻ HOW TO SWEAT COPPER PIPE AND FITTINGS

Tools and supplies needed:

Propane torch with medium-flame fitting (½ inch in diameter)
Tubing cutter and reamer
Wire solder
Flux
Steel wool

Procedure:

Sweating copper pipe and fittings together is the basic operation in putting together water-supply lines and attaching them to fixtures. Sweated joints are very strong and reliable and should be preferred to clamp joints or flared joints whenever there is a choice. If you practice with a few pieces of copper pipe and some simple fittings, you can become proficient at making these joints with about an hour of practice.

Cut copper pipe with a tubing cutter. Place the cutter on the pipe, and tighten the cutter around it. Turn the cutter around the pipe, and tighten it every second turn until the pipe is cut. Ream the inside of the pipe to clean out any burrs with the triangular reamer that is part of the cutter.

Clean the ends of the pipe with steel wool until the copper is bright. With your finger, apply a coating of flux to the end of the pipe. Insert the fluxed end into the fitting, and lay the assembly across two bricks or blocks.

Apply flame from the torch to the fitting, not the tube. Keep the flame on the fitting for about 30 seconds. Touch the solder wire to the joint between the fitting and the pipe, keeping the torch flame on the fitting. When the joint is heated to the right temperature, it will

181

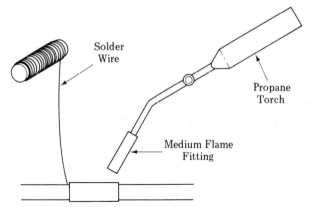

Point the Flame at the Fitting, Not the Joint

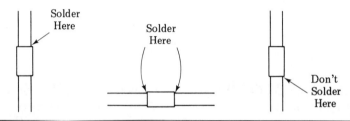

Soldering Techniques.

draw molten solder into itself—all you have to do is apply a gentle pressure on the solder.

Feed the solder to the joint by pushing the solder wire around the fitting. Remove the solder when an excess forms on the underside of the fitting. Remove the flame from the fitting, and leave the assembly undisturbed for two or three minutes while the solder hardens.

In Brief:

1. Cut copper pipe with a tubing cutter. Turn the cutter around the pipe and tighten it every second turn until the pipe is cut. Ream the cut end of the pipe.

2. Clean the ends of the pipe with steel wool until the copper is bright. Use your finger to apply a coating of flux to the end of the pipe. Insert the fluxed end of the pipe into the fitting. Lay the assembly across two bricks or blocks.

3. Apply flame from the torch to the fitting, not the tube. Keep the flame on the fitting for about 30 seconds. Touch the solder wire to the joint between the fitting and the pipe. Keep the flame on the fitting; when the joint is the right temperature, it will draw molten solder into itself.

4. Remove the solder when a drip of excess forms on the underside of the fitting. Remove the flame from the fit-

ting, and leave the assembly undisturbed for two or three minutes.

Tips:

The most important thing to remember when sweating joints is that the flame should always be on the fitting, never on the pipe or solder. Let the heated fitting suck the solder into itself by capillary action.

Don't be afraid to use plenty of flux. Flux cleans the joint and prepares the metal for a good bond with the solder. Any extra flux will simply melt and drip off the pipe when you apply heat.

When working with a complicated assembly, try to arrange your work so that you will never have to sweat a fitting in the upside-down position. You don't want gravity working against the capillary action of the heated joint. Sweat fittings from above or on the side. This means that you may have to sweat two or three subassemblies on the ground and then put them together with sleeves.

Keep a wet rag handy for wiping a joint cool after letting it sit undisturbed for a full minute. Be careful, however, because a hot joint can still produce a handful of steam after the solder hardens.

When sweating valves, take the valve stems out of the body with an adjustable wrench. Sweat the body to the pipe, and then reinstall the valve stems after the body has cooled down. You want to protect the plastic and fiber washers in the stems from melting.

When you are sweating copper pipe larger than 1 inch (for drain lines and heating pipes, for example), use a hacksaw to cut the pipe, and smooth the edge of the pipe with a file. You must also buy a large-flame fitting (1-inch diameter) for your propane torch so that the fittings get enough heat.

↘ HOW TO FIT THREADED PIPE

Tools and supplies needed:

Two pipe wrenches (14-inch length)
One 3-foot length of steel pipe that fits over the end of the pipe wrench
Can of pipe joint compound or pipe joint tape

Procedure:

Fitting threaded steel pipe is the basic skill for repairing and modifying gas-supply lines and heating lines. It is straightforward work, but there is a specific procedure that should be followed to make tight and reliable joints.

Coat the male threads of the pipe with joint compound, or wrap the threads with pipe joint tape. Screw the threads into the fitting hand-tight. Apply one pipe wrench to the body of the pipe in a counterclockwise fashion. Apply another pipe wrench to the fitting in a clockwise fashion. Stand on the first wrench, or have an assistant hold it to keep the pipe from turning. Tighten the fitting with the second wrench until it becomes hard to turn. Then tighten the fitting one quarter turn past that point. You should have two or three unused male threads showing.

In Brief:

1. Coat the male threads with joint compound, or wrap them with pipe joint tape.

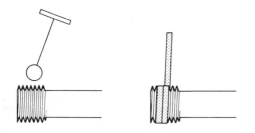

Coat the Male Threads of a Pipe with Joint Compound or Wrap Them with Joint Tape.

Leaks are obvious when running water through pipes but less obvious when piping gas. Check for gas leaks by mixing liquid dish detergent and warm water and brushing the solution on all joints. Gas leaks will make bubbles in the detergent solution.

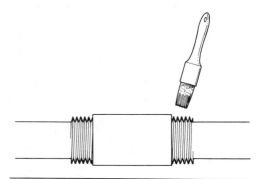

Brush Gas Pipe with Detergent in Water to Check for Leaks.

2. Screw the threads into the fitting hand-tight.

3. Apply one wrench to the body of the pipe in a counterclockwise fashion.

4. Apply a second wrench to the fitting in a clockwise fashion.

5. Secure the first wrench by standing on it, or have an assistant hold it.

6. Tighten the fitting with the second wrench until it becomes hard to turn.

7. Tighten the fitting one quarter turn beyond that point.

Tips:

Use plenty of joint compound. Any excess can be wiped off later. The pipe joint tape is neater than compound, but either method is acceptable.

Use the three-foot-long extender pipe over the end of a wrench to provide extra leverage when assembling or dismantling tight joints. If you are going to be doing a lot of work with pipe that is more than 1½ inches in diameter, you should buy a 24-inch wrench, which will give you a good grip and plenty of leverage for those big pipes.

⤳ HOW TO INSTALL A TOILET

Tools and supplies needed:

Adjustable wrench
Screwdriver
Soldering supplies
Wax gasket for toilet
Set of closet bolts
Toilet water-supply kit with shut-off valve

Procedure:

Installing a new toilet is very easy and can be accomplished by the homeowner in about two hours. Buy a new reverse-trap toilet, a wax gasket, and a set of two closet bolts with washers and nuts. To make installation of the water supply easy, purchase a toilet water-supply kit with a shut-off valve. This kit provides everything necessary to connect the toilet tank with the ½-inch copper cold-water supply pipe.

Assemble the toilet according to the manufacturer's directions. In general, you will have to fit a rubber gasket to the back of the toilet bowl and then place the toilet tank on top of the gasket. The tank and bowl are secured with three or four brass bolts and rubber washers.

Unwrap the wax gasket and press it onto the horn on the underside of the toilet bowl. Put the two closet bolts into the slots on the sewer pipe flange. Gently lower the toilet onto the two closet bolts, getting the bolts through the mounting holes in the toilet's base. Twist the toilet slightly when it is seated to ensure a positive seal between the wax gasket and the toilet flange.

Assemble the washers, coverplates, and nuts onto the closet bolts. Tighten the nuts until the toilet is secure and steady on the floor. Cut the toilet bolts with a hacksaw so that they are flush with the nuts. Snap the cover bubbles onto the coverplates to dress up the ends of the closet bolts.

Solder the water-supply shut-off valve to ½-inch copper pipe. (These supply valves usually come mated to a chrome-plated sleeve which slips over the ½-inch pipe for soldering.) Attach the fitting end of the ⅜-inch flexible supply tube to the toilet water input. Turn the nut until it is hand-tight. Bend the supply tube gently until you have the shape required to mate it with the fitting on the shut-off valve. Mark where the tube will have to be cut to mate it with the shut-off valve.

Remove the tube from the toilet, and cut it with a hacksaw. Smooth the cut end with a file and steel wool. Ream the inside of the cut with the reamer on your tubing cutter. Unscrew the fitting from the shut-off valve. Note that it consists of a threaded brass nut and a tapered brass ring called a *ferrule*.

Reattach the cut supply tube to the toilet, hand-tight. Slip the nut over the end of the supply tube, and follow it with the ferrule. Insert the assembly into the shut-off fitting, and tighten the nut with an adjustable wrench. Tighten the nut on the toilet with an adjustable wrench as well. Turn on the water supply, and check for leaks.

In Brief:

1. Assemble the toilet according to manufacturer's directions.

2. Unwrap the wax gasket and place it on the outlet horn on the underside of the toilet bowl. Put the two closet bolts into the slots on the toilet flange.

3. Gently lower the toilet onto the two closet bolts, getting the bolts through the mounting holes in the toilet's base. Twist the toilet slightly when it is in place to ensure a positive seal.

4. Assemble the washers, coverplates, and nuts onto the closet bolts. Tighten the nuts until the toilet is secure. Cut the toilet bolts flush with the nuts. Snap the cover bubbles onto the coverplates to dress the closet bolts.

5. Solder the water-supply shut-off valve to ½-inch copper pipe. Hand-tighten the ⅜-inch flexible supply tube to the toilet water input. Bend

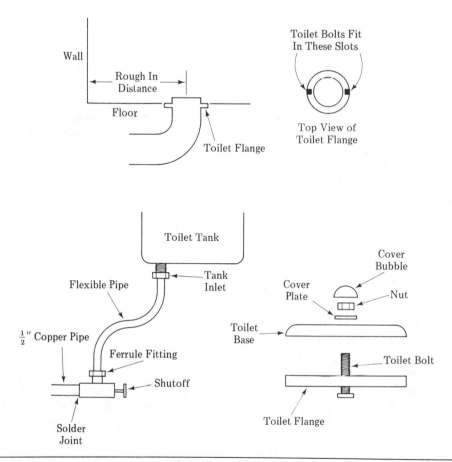

Installing a Toilet.

the supply tube gently until you have the shape needed to mate it to the shut-off valve. Mark where the tube will have to be cut.

6. Remove the tube from the toilet, and cut it with a hacksaw. Smooth and ream the cut end of the supply tube. Unscrew the fitting from the shut-off valve.

7. Reattach the cut supply tube to the toilet, hand-tight. Slip the nut and ferrule over the end of the supply tube. Insert the assembly into the shut-off fitting, and tighten the nut. Also tighten the nut on the toilet inlet. Turn on the water supply, and check for leaks.

Tips:

Tighten the ferrule fitting very gently. It is better to see a few drops of water come out and then snug it up than to over-tighten and strip the soft brass of the fitting.

Always use a new wax gasket when installing a toilet or resetting an old one. If you damage it, get a new one—they're cheap. For a good seal, the wax should be about 70 degrees. If it's cold and stiff, warm the seal on a radiator or in the sun.

Toilets come in different rough-in sizes—this means the distance from the wall to the center of the sewer-pipe flange. The common rough-in sizes of toilets are 10, 12, and 14 inches. Twelve inches is the most common size. To determine your rough-in size, simply measure the distance from the mounting slots in the toilet flange to the finished wall behind the toilet.

⤺ HOW TO INSTALL A SINGLE-LEVER FAUCET

Tools and supplies needed:

Soldering supplies
Adjustable wrench
Single-lever faucet
2 soldering adaptors, ½ inch to ⅜ inch

Procedure:

A single-lever faucet is a good choice for kitchen or bathroom sinks. The single-lever design makes for easy maintenance, because all the interior parts can be replaced when necessary with an inexpensive rebuild kit.

Attach the faucet to the sink with an adjustable wrench. Slip the rubber or fiber gasket over the mounting bolts on the underside of the faucet. Put the faucet and gasket in place on the sink. Align the mounting bolts with the holes in the sink, and feed the supply tubes down the center hole in the sink. Secure the faucet

by slipping the washers and nuts onto the mounting bolts, and tightening with an adjustable wrench (or a basin wrench if the space is tight).

When the faucet is secured to the sink, bring the flexible ⅜-inch tubes of the faucet parallel to the ½-inch copper supply pipes. Solder the adaptors to the ½-inch pipes. Bend and cut the ⅜-inch tubes to mate with the adaptors, and solder the tubes to the adaptors.

In Brief:

1. Slip the rubber gasket over the mounting bolts on the underside of the faucet. Place the faucet and gasket on the sink.

2. Secure the faucet by slipping the washers and nuts onto the mounting bolts and tightening with a wrench.

3. Bring the flexible ⅜-inch tubes parallel to the ½-inch supply pipes. Solder the adaptors to the ½-inch pipes.

4. Bend and cut the ⅜-inch tubes to mate with the adaptors on the ½-inch pipes. Solder the tubes to the adaptors.

Tips:

After all the joints are made and you are ready to turn on the water, unscrew the strainer on the faucet neck. This will allow the debris of soldering to pass out of the faucet with the first burst of water. If you don't unscrew the strainer, it will become quickly clogged with metal chips, slag, etc., from your soldering.

If you want to install shut-off valves so that the faucet can be isolated from the main water supply for servicing and replacement, simply buy two ½-inch valves for copper pipe. Remove the

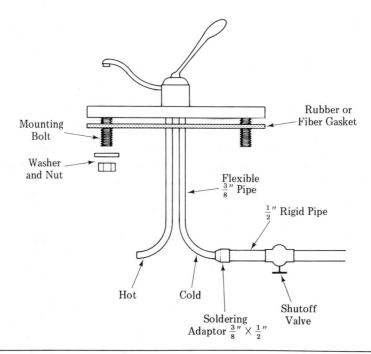

Mounting Bolt

Washer and Nut

Rubber or Fiber Gasket

Flexible $\frac{3}{8}''$ Pipe

$\frac{1}{2}''$ Rigid Pipe

Hot

Cold

Soldering Adaptor $\frac{3}{8}'' \times \frac{1}{2}''$

Shutoff Valve

Installing a Single-Lever Faucet.

stems from the bodies of the valves and sweat them to the ½-inch pipe about 3 inches from the adaptors. When the valves are cool, reinstall the stems in the bodies.

↜HOW TO INSTALL A DOUBLE-LEVER FAUCET

Tools and supplies needed:

Adjustable wrench
Soldering supplies
Double-lever faucet
Two basin supply sets to mate with ½-inch copper pipe

Procedure:

A double-lever faucet is often needed to recycle an old-fashioned porcelain sink. The double-lever design has been around for many years, and any leaks are repaired by installing new washers on the valve stems and smoothing worn valve seats with a seat-dressing tool.

Double-lever faucets are sold to fit sinks by what are called *centers*. A center is the distance between the middle of the two outside holes in your sink. There are many different center measurements available but the common ones are 6 inches for a bathroom sink and 8 inches for a kitchen sink.

Slip the rubber or fiber gasket over

the threaded inlet pipes on the underside of the faucet. Position the faucet and gasket on the sink. Secure the faucet by slipping washers and nuts over the threaded inlet pipes and tightening with a wrench.

When the faucet is secure, attach the two basin supply sets to the threaded inlet pipes. Hand-tighten the nuts on the supply sets. (A basin supply set consists of a flexible copper tube flared at one end to mate with the inlet pipe on the faucet using a captive nut. The other end of the tube is flared to fit over ½-inch copper pipe and is sweated in place.)

Cut and fit the ½-inch copper supply pipes to mate with the basin supply sets. The copper pipe should extend at least 1 inch into the flared bottom of the supply set. Unscrew the supply sets from the faucet and sweat them to the copper supply pipes. After the sweated joints are made, reinstall the sets to the faucet and tighten the captive nuts with a wrench. The nut will draw the flared end of the supply set tight with the inlet pipe

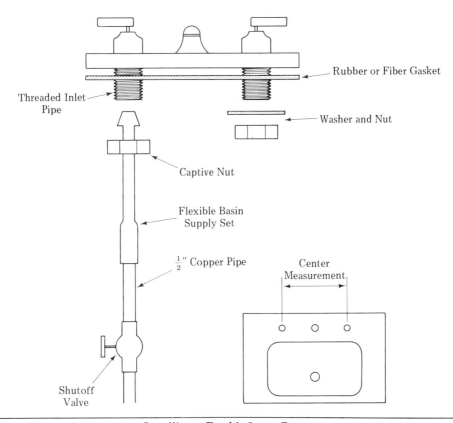

Installing a Double-Lever Faucet.

and make a watertight joint—no joint compound or tape is needed.

In Brief:

1. Measure your sink to get a center. Order the proper size of faucet.
2. Slip the rubber or fiber gasket over the threaded inlet pipes on the underside of the faucet. Place the faucet and gasket on the sink and secure by tightening washers and nuts over the threaded inlet pipes with a wrench.
3. Attach the two basin supply sets to the threaded inlet pipes. Tighten the nuts on the sets hand-tight. Cut and fit ½-inch copper supply pipes to mate with the supply sets. The copper supply pipes should extend at least 1 inch into the flared ends of the supply sets.
4. Unscrew the sets from the faucet and sweat them to the copper supply pipes. Reassemble the sets to the faucet, and tighten the captive nuts to the threaded inlets with a wrench.

Tips:

As you did with the single-lever faucet, unscrew the strainer on the faucet neck before turning on the water supply. Let the first stream of water blow out any soldering debris; then reattach the strainer to the faucet neck.

If you wish to install shut-off valves on the water-supply pipes to enable the faucet to be isolated for repair or replacement, the place to put them is on the ½-inch copper supply pipes about 3 inches from the bottom of the basin supply sets.

⤷ HOW TO REPLACE A FAUCET IN AN OLD-FASHIONED BATHTUB

Tools and supplies needed:

Soldering supplies
Adjustable wrench
Double-lever tub faucet
Pipe joint compound or tape
Two supply elbows with nuts
Two female threaded adaptors to ½-inch copper pipe

Procedure:

To recycle a freestanding cast-iron bathtub you need to install a new faucet and a waste-water kit. Both are easy to do. To install the faucet, measure the existing holes in the bathtub. Measure from the center of each hole to come up with the proper center. The most common center in an old tub is 4 inches. When you buy the faucet, also order two matching supply elbows to fit it and two female threaded adaptors that fit the elbows on one side and ½-inch copper pipe on the other.

Attach the faucet to the tub with an adjustable wrench. Fit the faucet through the holes and tighten washers and nuts to the inlet pipes with a wrench. When the faucet is secure, assemble the supply elbows to the faucet inlets, hand-tight. Also screw the threaded adaptors to the elbows, hand-tight. Measure your ½-inch copper supply pipes and cut them to mate with the adaptors.

Remove the adaptors from the supply elbows. Solder the ½-inch copper supply pipes to the adaptors and allow the joints to cool. Remove the supply elbows from the faucet and coat their male threads with pipe joint compound or joint tape. Assemble the elbows to the adaptors. Use a wrench to hold the adaptors rigid while you apply another wrench to the elbows and tighten them securely. Make sure that the elbows face the inlet pipes on the faucet on the last turn you make to tighten them to the adaptors.

When the elbows and adaptors are tight, replace the elbows into the faucet inlets and hand-tighten the nuts to the inlet threads. Make sure that the elbows and the inlets are aligned correctly before tightening the nuts with a wrench to make a watertight joint.

In Brief:

1. Measure the tub to obtain the proper center. Purchase a double-lever faucet, supply elbows, and female threaded adaptors.

2. Attach the faucet to the tub with washers and nuts tightened onto the threaded inlet pipes.

3. Assemble the supply elbows to the faucet inlets, hand-tight. Assemble the threaded adaptors to the elbows, hand-tight. Measure the ½-inch copper supply pipes to mate with the adaptors, and cut to fit.

4. Remove the adaptors from the elbows. Solder the ½-inch pipes to the adaptors and allow the joints to cool.

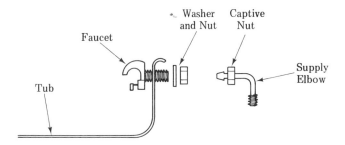

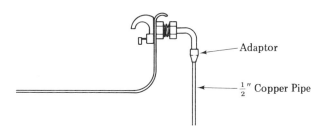

Installing a Faucet in a Tub.

5. Remove the supply elbows, and coat their male threads with joint compound or joint tape. Assemble the elbows and adaptors with a wrench holding the adaptor rigid and another wrench turning the elbow.

6. When the elbows and adaptors are tight and the elbows are properly turned toward the faucet inlets, replace the elbows into the inlets and hand-tighten the nuts to the inlet threads.

7. Tighten the elbows to the inlets with a wrench to make a watertight joint.

Tips:

If you want your tub to have a stand-up or telephone shower, simply buy a tub faucet that has a diverter valve and a shower outlet built into it. Connect a flexible telephone shower to the shower outlet, or solder ½-inch copper pipe to the outlet and mount a shower head to the other side of the pipe about 6 feet off the floor.

For a shower curtain you can buy a prefabricated metal frame that hangs from the ceiling above the tub (available at the plumbing supply store). The frame is roughly the same shape as the tub but a little smaller. The shower curtain hangs from the frame and falls inside the tub walls.

╲ HOW TO INSTALL A SINGLE BASIN DRAIN TRAP

Tools and supplies needed:

Pipe wrench
Hacksaw
File
Trap kit

Procedure:

Every plumbing fixture must have a trap. Traps hold a plug of water in the drain line and seal the system so that sewer gases and odors can't enter the living space. Toilets have built-in traps; tubs and showers use traps that are part of a drain line; and sinks and basins use traps that start right under the fixture and terminate at the branch drain line.

Buy an S-shaped trap if your branch line terminates in the floor. Buy a P-shaped trap if your drain line terminates in the wall. Measure the tailpiece on the fixture and determine its diameter. Order a 1½- or 1¼-inch trap kit to fit the tailpiece. It is not usually necessary to measure the distance from the fixture to the floor or wall, because the trap kits come with plenty of extra pipe.

Fit the trap assembly together to establish the proper length of the downtube. Slip a nut (threads facing down) and a washer over the end of the tailpiece. Put the U-shaped trap piece onto the tailpiece and hand-tighten the nut and washer to it. Now take the downtube and hold it so that it looks like an upside-down letter J. Slip a nut (threads facing up) over the bottom end of the downtube, and bring it around to rest on the metal flange. Slip a washer onto the top end of the tube, and push it up to rest against the flange. Now fit the downtube to the other end of the trap piece and hand-tighten the nut.

Now that the trap is assembled, you can turn it and adjust it and measure how much of the downtube will have to be cut to mate it with the adaptor on the branch drain line. Mark where the tube will have to be cut and disassemble the trap.

Cut the downtube with a hacksaw. Smooth the cut with a file, and ream the inside of the tube with the edge of the file. Insert the cut end into the adaptor on the branch line, and tighten the adaptor. Reassemble the rest of the trap hand-tight, and check for proper fit. Turn the pieces of the trap to make it stand square between floor and fixture. When everything lines up, tighten the nuts on the tailpiece, trap piece, and adaptor with a pipe wrench.

In Brief:

1. Measure the tailpiece on the fixture and buy a trap of the proper diameter. Buy an S trap for a floor branch line, or a P trap for a wall branch line.

2. Fit the trap assembly together to check for fit. Slip a nut (threads down) and a washer over the end of the tailpiece. Fit the U-shaped trap piece onto the tailpiece and tighten the nut and washer hand-tight.

3. Hold the downtube so that it looks like an upside-down letter J. Slip a nut (threads up) over the bottom end of the downtube and bring it up to rest on the metal flange near the other end of the tube.

4. Slip a washer onto the top end of the tube and push it up to rest against the flange. Fit the downtube to the other end of the trap piece, and tighten the nut hand-tight.

5. Turn and adjust the trap so that it will mate with the adaptor on the branch line. Mark where the downtube will have to be cut to fit the adaptor.

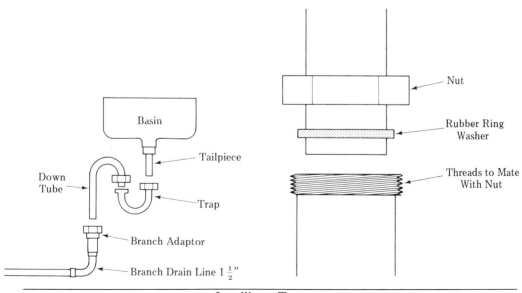

Installing a Trap.

6. Cut the tube with a hacksaw. Smooth the cut with a file, and ream the inside of the tube with the edge of the file.

7. Insert the cut end into the adaptor on the branch line, and tighten the adaptor hand-tight. Reassemble the rest of the trap hand-tight.

8. Turn and adjust the trap to make it stand square between floor and fixture. When everything lines up, tighten the nuts on the trap and adaptor with a pipe wrench.

Tips:

When installing a trap, it is helpful to think of the entire system from basin to branch line. At the bottom of the basin there is a strainer or simple outlet. Attached to that outlet is a tailpiece which fits inside the trap piece and is secured with a nut and a rubber washer. After the trap piece is a straight run of tube which fits into an adaptor on the branch line and is secured with a nut and a washer at the trap end and the adaptor end.

13

Electrical Projects

⤙ HOW TO INSTALL OUTDOOR SECURITY LIGHTING

Tools and supplies needed:

Electric hand drill
½-inch masonry drill bit
Penknife
Screwdriver
Hammer
½-inch masonry anchors
Double exterior floodlight fixture
14-gauge exterior electrical cable
Industrial time switch SPST
Cable clamps for masonry wall
Electrical cable staples
Two 150-watt PAR floodlights

Procedure:

Assuming that your home has adequate locks and security hardware, the next best step you can take to provide good security is to install good exterior lighting. Bright lights are an excellent deterrent to crime. Many homes have nothing more than a dim porch light in the way of exterior lighting.

Examine your home to determine the best placement for the light fixture. Pay special attention to the back and sides of the building. You want light to flood dark areas in corners, behind bushes, and near any vulnerable area of your house. If you plan well you can mount a single fixture with two lights high on a corner of the house, and it will flood two separate areas. The higher you mount the fixture, the better. Light will spread out more from a high fixture than a low one. The fixture must be at least high enough to be out of the reach of someone on the ground who might try to tamper with it.

Assemble the floodlight fixture. Screw the floodlight sockets to the fixture faceplate. Strip 4 inches of exterior insulation from the electrical cable to

197

expose the two insulated wires and the single bare wire. Insert the stripped end of the cable through a cable clamp, and tighten the clamp around the cable. Insert the cable and clamp into the body of the fixture, using a side or bottom hole, and tighten the clamp to the fixture.

Strip about ¾ inch of insulation from the wires inside the fixture and connect them with wire nuts. Connect all black wires together and all white wires together. Ground the bare wire to a cable clamp or to a screw on the body of the fixture.

When everything is hooked up, assemble the coverplate and the body of the fixture. Be sure to use all gaskets, plugs, and screws provided so that the fixture is watertight.

Drill two holes in the wall with the masonry bit. Use the mounting ears on the fixture to place the holes. Set anchors in the holes and drive them with the setting tool. Attach the fixture to the wall using the mounting ears on the body of the fixture. Turn the necks of the floodlight sockets in the general direction you want them to go. Screw the 150-watt exterior floodlights into the sockets.

Mount the electrical cable to the wall with anchors and cable clamps. Use one clamp every four feet along the length of the cable. Run the cable to a basement window. Drill a ½-inch hole for the cable in the wood frame of the basement window opening. Feed the end of the cable through the hole and into the basement.

In the basement, run the cable to an industrial-style time switch mounted on the wall or on a joist. Use electrical cable staples to attach the cable to basement joists. Connect the cable to the switch

as described in the section on time switches. Connect the time switch to an electrical line with a splice box.

Program the time switch to turn the floodlights on and off at the desired times. When the floodlights are on, go back up the ladder and adjust them so that light falls exactly where you want it.

In Brief:

1. Plan the best placement of the floodlight fixture.

2. Assemble the floodlight fixture by screwing the floodlight sockets into the coverplate.

3. Strip 4 inches of outside insulation from one end of the cable and insert it into the fixture with a clamp.

4. Strip ¾ inch of insulation from the wires inside the fixture and connect them with wire nuts—black to black, white to white, bare wire to fixture body.

5. Assemble the cover and body of the fixture. Plug unused holes in the fixture.

6. Drill holes in the wall, and mount the fixture with masonry anchors.

7. Adjust the necks of the floodlight sockets, and install the floodlights.

8. Mount the electrical cable to the wall with masonry anchors and clamps. Use one clamp every 4 feet.

9. Drill a ½-inch hole through the wood frame around a basement window. Insert cable through the hole and feed it into the basement.

10. Run the cable to a time switch. Attach the cable to basement joists with cable staples.

11. Connect time switch to cable. Con-

nect time switch to a branch electrical line with a splice box.

12. Program timer, and adjust the necks of the floodlight sockets for best coverage.

Tips:

One refinement of the above setup would be to buy a photocell switch that screws into one of the holes on the floodlight fixture. This switch will turn the lights on at dusk and off at dawn by responding to daylight. If you use a photocell switch, you can eliminate the time switch in the basement and simply splice the end of the cable to a branch electrical line. Follow the manufacturer's instructions for wiring and placement of the photocell switch on the body of the floodlight fixture.

⤶ HOW TO INSTALL A TIME SWITCH

Tools and supplies needed:

Screwdriver
Penknife
Needle-nose pliers
Industrial-style 24-hour time switch
Two cable clamps
12-gauge plastic cable

Procedure:

A time switch is useful for a variety of jobs. The most common situation is to use a time switch to turn hall and outside lights on at dusk and off at dawn. You could install several time switches to control your interior lighting circuits; by programming them to different sched-

ules, you can create the illusion that the house is occupied, even when no one is home.

There are many different kinds of switches available, but the most rugged and reliable switch is the commercial/industrial time switch, or tour clock. This switch is housed in a metal utility cabinet and has replaceable parts. Inside it has a large 24-hour dial on which you screw "on" and "off" trippers which will repeat their jobs day after day until you reset them.

Buy your switch at an electric supply house, and get an SPST type for light control. They are sold with one set of trippers included, but you can buy more if you need them.

Install the switch in the basement by screwing its casing to a joist or by anchoring it to masonry with ½-inch masonry anchors. Use 12-gauge plastic cable to hook the switch to the fixture circuit and the power source.

Strip 6 inches of cable covering from the ends of the plastic cables to expose the white, black, and bare wires. Knock out two holes in the sides or bottom of the utility box (there are plenty of precut holes in the box). Insert a cable clamp in each hole and tighten it to the box. Insert the stripped cable ends into the clamps, and tighten the clamps around the cable.

Strip ½ inch of insulation from the ends of the black and white wires. Take the white wire from the fixture circuit and the white wire from the power-supply circuit, and attach them to the silver-colored neutral screw on the switch. Form the wires into loops with the pliers and place them around the screw and tighten.

Take the black wire from the power-

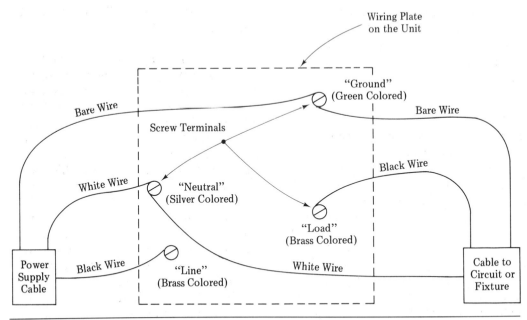

Industrial Time Switch.

supply circuit and attach it to the brass-colored line terminal on the switch. Take the black wire from the fixture circuit and attach it to the brass-colored load terminal on the switch. Take both bare wires and attach them to the green-colored ground terminal on the switch.

At the other end of the fixture cable, attach the cable directly to the fixture. At the other end of the power supply cable, attach the wires to a power line using a splice box and wire nuts. Turn off power to the line, cut the line, insert the three loose ends of cable into a splice box with clamps, and attach the wires. The time switch is now ready to supply or interrupt power to the fixture or circuit.

In Brief:

1. Install the switch in the basement by screwing the utility box to a joist or anchoring it to a masonry wall.

2. Strip 6 inches of cable covering from your hook-up cables. Knock out two blanks in the side or bottom of the utility box. Insert a cable clamp in each hole and tighten. Insert the cables into the clamps and tighten.

3. Strip ½ inch of insulation from the cable wires. Attach the two white wires to the silver-colored neutral terminal.

4. Take the black wire from the power supply cable and attach it to the brass-colored line terminal. Take the black wire from the fixture cable and attach it to the brass-colored load terminal.

5. Take both bare wires and attach them to the green-colored ground terminal.

6. Attach the other end of the fixture cable to the fixture. Attach the other end of the power cable to a power

line. Splice into the line and use wire nuts and a splice box.

Tips:

There are many other electrical control devices. Security lighting can be controlled by a photocell switch on a threaded stem. This switch would be screwed into the exterior lighting fixture and wired between the fixture and the power source. It will turn on power at dusk and off at dawn.

Another useful device is a spring-wound switch for lights and equipment in public places that are often left on unnecessarily. This switch replaces the normal on/off switch in a switch box; in order to turn power on, its handle must be turned against a spring. Once the switch is on, it starts to work its way back to off and will shut off automatically if not reset. These switches are available in ranges of 0–5 minutes, 0–15 minutes, and 0–60 minutes, and others.

An interesting variation of the industrial timer is known as a *seven-day programmer*. This switch looks like a standard tour clock, but it provides up to four different switching operations for each day of the week. It could be wired to control a very sophisticated security lighting program or to operate mechanical equipment (furnaces, air conditioners, water heaters, etc.) on a precise schedule for energy savings.

↰ HOW TO INSTALL A DOORBELL

Tools and supplies needed:

Screwdriver
Drill and bits
Penknife
Hook-up wire
Doorbell or buzzer
Doorbell transformer
Pushbutton switch

Procedure:

Most doorbells in old houses are unreliable because they are usually worn and damaged by age and moisture. A completely new doorbell system is easy to install, and the basic elements are inexpensive.

Buy your system at an electrical supply house or discount department store. All you need is a simple bell or buzzer, a pushbutton, and a low-voltage transformer. Also buy plastic-insulated hook-up wire and an AC power cord and plug or plastic cable and a splice box.

Mount the transformer in the basement and connect the primary side to a power source, either through a power cord and plug or plastic cable spliced into a power line.

Mount the doorbell switch at the front door, and place the doorbell or buzzer high on a wall in a central hallway.

Use the plastic-insulated hook-up wire to run one wire directly from a low-voltage terminal (secondary side) on the transformer to one terminal on the bell or buzzer. From the other low-voltage terminal on the transformer, run a wire to one terminal on the doorbell switch. From the other terminal on the doorbell switch, run a wire to the remaining terminal on the bell or buzzer.

In Brief:

1. Mount the transformer in the basement, and connect the primary side to a power source.

2. Mount the doorbell switch at the front door, and mount the doorbell or buzzer high on a wall in a central hallway.

3. Run one wire directly from a low-voltage terminal on the transformer (secondary side) to one terminal on the bell or buzzer. From the other low-voltage terminal, run a wire to one terminal on the doorbell switch. From the other terminal on the doorbell switch, run a wire to the remaining terminal on the bell or buzzer.

Tips:

This basic wiring scheme can be followed for some of the fancier doorbell arrangements. Chimes or other musical doorbells are powered and controlled by the same kind of switch and transformer. If you do buy a chime or fancy musical doorbell, you should be sure to get a matching transformer for that particular device. Large devices need up to 24 volts to function properly.

If you want to have a doorbell for a front and a back door, you should buy an extra doorbell switch and a bell or buzzer. It would be a good idea to buy a bell for one door and a buzzer for another so that you will know which door to answer. You can use a single transformer to power both systems. Simply wire the second bell or buzzer and switch to the secondary side of the transformer in the same manner above.

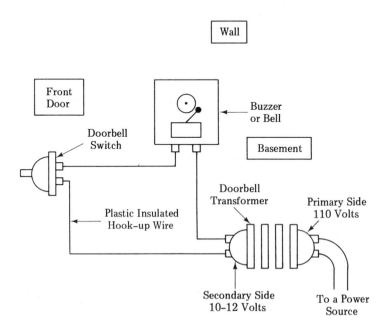

Diagram for a Doorbell.

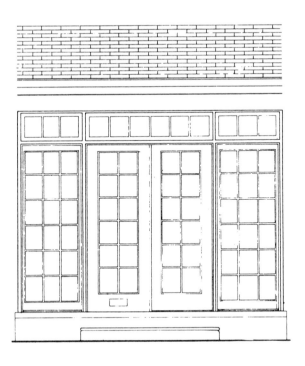
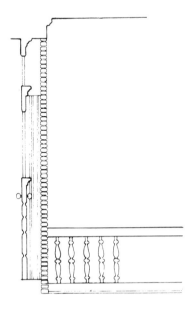

14

Heavy Duty Projects

⤷ HOW TO BUILD A FENCE

Tools and supplies needed:

Shovel
Hammer
Measuring tape
Level
Paint brush
4 x 4-inch posts about 12 feet long
1 x 6-inch roofing boards, tongue and groove
Creosote oil
Galvanized roofing nails, 2 inches long

Procedure:

Making a board fence for security and privacy is a basic project for back and side yards. There are many different styles and varieties of wood fencing, but one basic design uses 1 x 6-inch roofing boards and 4 x 4-inch posts. The posts are anchored in plain earth and tamped in place, which makes a surprisingly strong and quick support for the fence boards.

Dig holes for setting the 4 x 4 posts. Dig the holes 4 feet deep and about 1½ feet around. Space the holes every 5 feet across the area to be fenced. If the fence runs more than 10 feet (the standard length of the 1 x 6 boards), make sure that the post that runs behind the joint between two sections of board is centered to provide a nailing surface for both sets of boards.

Paint the ends and sides of the posts that will go into the holes with three coats of creosote oil to protect them from the elements. For extra protection against rot, you can trowel plastic roof cement on the parts that will be underground.

Place the posts in the holes, and tamp earth back into the hole around

205

the post (use a scrap piece of 2 x 4 for tamping). Use a level to check the post for straightness. Wetting the fill earth while tamping will speed setting.

When the posts are secure, erect the fencing boards from the ground up. Place the first board across the posts, tongue end up, and nail it in place while holding a level on it to ensure straightness. Place and nail the rest of the boards, mating the tongue-and-groove surfaces for strength. Use two galvanized roofing nails for each board and post.

The fencing boards will further stabilize the posts. After about a week, tamp the posts again and add more earth to the area around the posts.

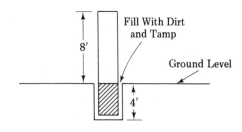

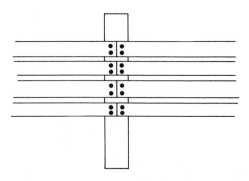

Center Post to Provide a Nailing
Surface For Joints

Making a Board Fence.

In Brief:

1. Dig holes for setting 4 x 4 posts. Dig the holes 4 feet deep and 1½ feet around. Space the posts every 5 feet across the area to be fenced.

2. Paint the ends and sides of the posts with three coats of creosote oil to protect them.

3. Place the posts in the holes, and tamp earth back into the holes. Check each post with a level while tamping to make sure the posts are straight.

4. Erect the fencing boards from the ground up. Nail the first board in place, tongue end up, using a level to ensure straightness. Place and nail the rest of the boards, mating the tongue-and-groove surfaces for strength.

5. After about a week tamp the posts again and add more fill earth to the holes.

Tips:

If your ground is soft or you want to provide a rock-solid footing for your posts, you can pour gravel-mix concrete into the holes around your posts to anchor them. Drive about 6 masonry nails into the sides of the posts to key them to the concrete. You must level each post in the wet concrete and then prop the posts from two sides with long pieces of 1 x 2-inch furring strips. Nail the furring strips into the posts with finishing nails driven partway into the wood. Anchor the other end of the strips with stakes driven into the ground. Leave the props in place for 48 hours while the concrete cures. After the props are taken away you can nail the boards to the posts as described above.

You can protect the wood with a clear preservative and a colored penetrating stain. For a low cost and durable finish you can paint the whole fence with the same creosote oil that you used for the posts. The creosote will stain the wood a dark brown. The deep color will mellow over the years, and creosote oil can be reapplied as desired.

⌐HOW TO CUT AND HANG SECURITY BARS

Tools and supplies needed:

Hacksaw
Adjustable wrench
Measuring tape
Brace and bit
Two one-foot lengths of steel pipe (⅝-inch inside diameter)
Salvaged iron or steel fence
1-foot-long concrete bolts ½-inch diameter, with washers and nuts

Procedure:

Security bars for first-floor windows are an excellent way to prevent break-ins. Many homeowners in urban and suburban locations are installing them, and some houses from the late 1800s have them as part of the original design. You can have custom bars made up by a welding shop to any design you choose, but you can make your own very cheaply from lengths of old salvaged fence. Good places to obtain fencing would be salvage yards, demolition sites, and local classified-ad publications.

Select lengths of fence at least 4 feet high. Cut the fence with a hacksaw to fit over the window and frame. You should be able to cover two windows with one length of fence.

Bore four holes into the corners of the window frame with a brace and ½-inch bit. Place the holes about ½ inch in from the outside edge of the window frame to avoid drilling through the sash-weight channels. Bore the holes all the way through to the inside of the window frame.

Buy a bag of 24 concrete-setting bolts from a steel-supply house or industrial hardware store. The bag will include washers and nuts for the bolts. Cut the bent end of the bolts off with a hacksaw so that you have a steel rod with threads on one end.

Slip a length of steel pipe over the threaded end of the bolt until you have about 3⅓ inches of plain rod showing. Slip the other steel pipe over the bare rod and bend it until you have an L with a 3½-inch leg. Move the second pipe up to the middle of the leg and bend again until you have a J shape on the plain rod. Remove both pipes from the bolt. Repeat this process until you have enough J bolts to secure your bars.

Hold the bars to the window frame, and insert the threaded end of the J bolts into the holes. Hook the J end around a bar, and push the bolt snug against the bar.

When the bars are held in place by the bolts, go inside and put a washer on each end of the bolts and tighten the nuts down on the washers with an adjustable wrench. Cut any excess threaded end off at the nut with a hacksaw.

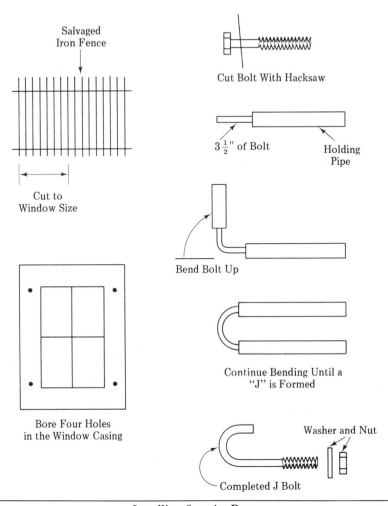

Salvaged Iron Fence

Cut to Window Size

Cut Bolt With Hacksaw

$3\frac{1}{2}''$ of Bolt

Holding Pipe

Bend Bolt Up

Continue Bending Until a "J" is Formed

Bore Four Holes in the Window Casing

Washer and Nut

Completed J Bolt

Installing Security Bars.

In Brief:

1. Cut fencing with a hacksaw to fit over the window and frame.

2. Bore four holes into the corners of the window frame with a brace and ½-inch bit. Place the holes about ½ inch in from the outside edges of the window frame.

3. Cut the formed end of the concrete

bolts off with a hacksaw to produce a steel rod with threads on one end.

4. Slip a length of pipe over the threaded end of the bolt until you have 3½ inches of plain rod showing. Slip the other pipe over the bare rod and bend it until you have an L with a 3½-inch leg. Move the second pipe up to the middle of the leg and bend again until you have a J shape on the

bolt. Repeat the process until you have enough J bolts to secure the bars.

5. Hold the bars to the window frame, and insert the threaded end of the J bolts into the holes. Hook the J around a bar, and push the bolt snug against the bar.

6. On the inside, put a washer and nut on each bolt and tighten with an adjustable wrench. Cut off any excess bolt even with the nut using a hacksaw.

Tips:

Instead of using a brace and bit to bore the ½-inch holes in the window frame, you can buy a 1-foot-long ½-inch auger bit with a ⅜-inch shank. The shank end will have a diamond-shaped head on it. Cut this head off with a hacksaw, and you can use the bit in your electric drill. Be sure to use low speed and moderate pressure on the drill so that you don't overload the motor as you drill through the wood.

You could use ½-inch threaded steel rod to make your bolts instead of cutting down concrete-setting bolts, but the concrete bolts will be cheaper than rod if you buy them by the bag complete with washers and nuts.

⤸ HOW TO USE A JACKING POST

Tools and supplies needed:

Screwdriver
Level
Drill and bits
Jacking post
Wood screws about 1–1½ inches

Procedure:

Jacking posts are the basic tool for making structural repairs to an old house. They can raise a sagging joist, temporarily support a porch or floor while repairs are made, or be installed and left permanently in place as part of a structural modification.

Assemble the post and adjust it to within 3 inches of the ceiling height. Use the holes and steel pins on the post to make this rough adjustment. Place the bottom plate on the floor or footing. Attach the top plate to the joist or framing member with screws. Set the jack on the bottom plate, and make another height adjustment with the adjusting holes and steel pins if necessary. Turn the screw jack until it makes contact with the top plate. Check the post with a level to make sure that it's absolutely straight. Draw the jack up snug with the top plate and recheck the post with the level. Make a one-quarter turn each day with the jack to lift the framing member into place.

In Brief:

1. Assemble the post and adjust it to within 3 inches of ceiling height.

2. Set the bottom plate on the floor or footing. Attach the top plate to the joist or framing member with screws.

3. Set the jack post on the bottom plate and make another height adjustment if necessary.

4. Turn the screw jack until it makes contact with the top plate.

5. Check the post with a level to make sure that it's straight.

6. Draw the jack up snug with the top plate and recheck the post with the

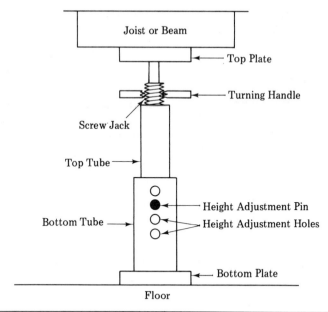

Components of a Jacking Post.

level. Turn the jack one-quarter each day to lift the framing member into place.

Tips:

The jack post must be on a firm footing. If your basement has a dirt floor or a thin (less than 3 inches) slab, you will have to dig and pour a footing for the post. Dig a hole 16 inches square and 24 inches deep. Fill the hole with gravel-mix concrete. Level the surface of the footing with the surrounding floor, and let it cure for 2 weeks.

If the jack posts are to be only temporary, you can spread their weight over a weak floor by using ¼-inch steel plates about 18 inches square under the bottom plates of the temporary posts. You can also use 3-foot-lengths of 4 x 4-inch hardwood timber to distribute the load over a weak surface.

If you are using a jack post to replace a sinking or deteriorated wood post in the basement, you must get the weight off the post by installing 2 jack posts under the joist, 3 feet on either side of the post. Remove the post, pour a footing, and erect another jack post under the joist. Turn the post until it takes the weight of the joist. Lower the temporary posts a one-quarter turn a day until you can remove them.

To jack up a floor sag that can't be shimmed or otherwise repaired, set a post in place on a footing and use it to support a 4 x 6-inch hardwood beam that pushes against four or more joists. Center the post under the beam and raise the jack a one-quarter turn each day until the sag evens out.

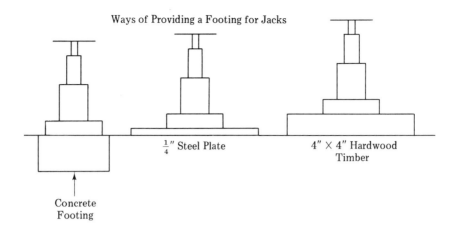

Ways of Providing a Footing for Jacks

$\frac{1}{4}''$ Steel Plate

4″ × 4″ Hardwood Timber

Concrete Footing

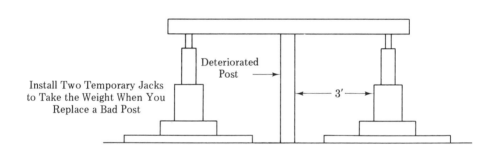

Install Two Temporary Jacks to Take the Weight When You Replace a Bad Post

Deteriorated Post

3′

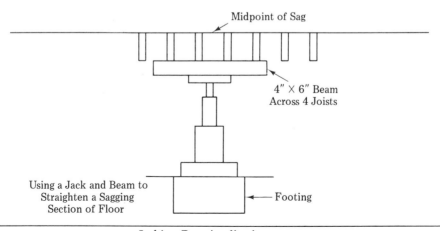

Midpoint of Sag

4″ × 6″ Beam Across 4 Joists

Using a Jack and Beam to Straighten a Sagging Section of Floor

Footing

Jacking Post Applications.

A jacking post is a powerful lifting device, and you must resist the temptation to crank it up all at once to correct sagging structural members. A one-quarter turn on the post every 24 hours is the most that you should attempt. This gradual lifting gives the house time to adjust slowly to the lifting. If you go any faster with the jack, you can cause plaster to crack, floors to bow, wood to crack, and doors and windows to get out of line.

⤶ HOW TO HANG GUTTERS

Tools and supplies needed:

Tin snips
Hacksaw
Hammer
Tape measure
Level
Half-round or square aluminum or galvanized gutter
Half-round or square aluminum or galvanized downspout
Elbows, end caps, and slip-joint connectors
Gutter hangers and downspout straps

Procedure:

Gutters conduct rainwater off a roof and send it down a length of pipe called a *downspout,* which connects to a storm drain or empties onto a lawn or pavement. A gutter system performs an important function by keeping rainwater off the house walls and windows and conducting it away from the house foundation where it can cause damage.

Gutter systems are available in many different materials. Just about every material but aluminum or galvanized steel has a serious drawback. Vinyl or fiberglass can crack in severe weather, and such materials may detract from the appearance of an old house. Copper gutters are strong and attractive but are extremely expensive. Wood gutters are perhaps best of all from an appearance standpoint, but they require almost constant maintenance to keep them from rotting and splitting.

For considerations of economy and performance, galvanized steel or aluminum with a baked enamel finish are the two best choices. You should select the material that will complement your house. Aluminum is generally available with a white or brown finish. If you don't like those colors, you will have to go to a galvanized-steel system which can be primed and painted any color you wish.

The two basic styles of gutter are square and half round. Follow the style that is presently installed on the house. The two popular sizes of gutter are 3 and 4 inches in diameter. Gutters and downspouts are supplied in ten-foot lengths, and you should figure a 10–20 percent wastage when installing. A gutter system assembles very quickly and easily. The difficult aspects are drawing up a parts list and hanging the system with the proper slope.

For each 35 feet of gutter you will need one downspout. If the run of gutter is over 35 feet you will need two downspouts. For a single gutter system, you will need enough gutter and downspout to cover the roof and reach to the ground—one downspout connector, two elbows, two end caps, and one slip-joint connector for each joint in the system, excluding the ends. You will also need one gutter hanger for each 3 feet of gutter. Downspout is fastened to the wall with one U-shaped strap for each 3 feet of downspout.

Cut gutter and downspout with a hacksaw and tin snips. The ends of the gutter fit together with slip joints, which are simply pressed into place, hand-tight. Select an end of the gutter for the downspout connector and install it with a slip joint at one end and an end cap at the other. Install an end cap at the other end of the gutter.

Gutters are hung so that they slope $1/16$ inch per foot from the high end to the low end, where the downspout connector is. Drive a nail into the mounting surface 2 inches below the roof line. Place the nail at the high point of your gutter run. At the other end of the run drive another nail into the mounting surface one inch lower than the first nail for every 16 feet of gutter. If the gutter run is 16 feet exactly, the second nail should be 3 inches below the roof line. Use these two nails to guide your gutter as you install it with hangers. When the gutter is hung you can remove the guide nails.

The easiest way to hang the gutter is to install a two-piece bracket hanger every 3 feet along the gutter run. These hangers have a series of adjustment holes that allow you to achieve the proper slope after the gutter is supported. Another style of hanger, the *spike and ferrule,* nails through the gutter and into the mounting surface; so you must wire or hold the gutter in the proper position while you nail the gutter in place.

After the gutter is mounted, you must connect the downspout to it. You want the downspout to lie flat against the wall to be supported yet inconspicuous. Fit two downspout elbows together to form the letter S. Fit the elbows to the outlet on the downspout connector and turn them so that one end lies flat on the wall. Mark the place where the bottom edge of the assembly falls against the wall.

Place a length of downspout against the wall. Position the top edge of the downspout 2 inches above the mark on the wall. The downspout should extend 4 inches into an existing drain pipe, unless it is to terminate in an elbow. If this is the case, place the elbow on the ground and mark where the top edge falls on the wall. Mark your cut line on the downspout 2 inches below the mark on the wall.

Cut the downspout with a hacksaw. Fit the bottom end into the drain pipe or elbow. Fit the top end into the elbow assembly. Attach the downspout to the wall with straps every 3 feet along its length. Anchor the straps to the wall with $1/2$-inch masonry anchors or nails.

In Brief:

1. Measure the length of gutter and downspout needed. Order one downspout connector, two elbows, two end caps, and one slip joint connector for each joint in the system excluding ends. Order one gutter hanger and one downspout strap for each 3 feet of gutter and downspout.

2. Cut gutter and downspout with a hacksaw and tin snips. Fit gutter together with slip joints, hand-tight. Install the downspout connector with a slip joint. End caps install by themselves at each end of the gutter system.

3. Drive a guide nail 2 inches from the roof line into the mounting surface at the high end of the run. Drive a second nail at the low end of the run. Install this nail 1 inch lower than the first nail for each 16 feet of gutter.

4. Install a two-piece bracket hanger every 3 feet along the run. Place the gutter in the brackets and adjust them to slope the gutter. If you use

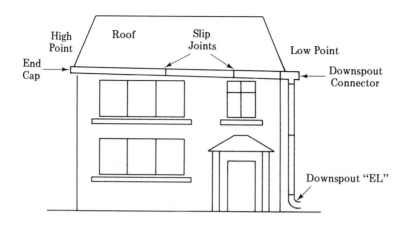

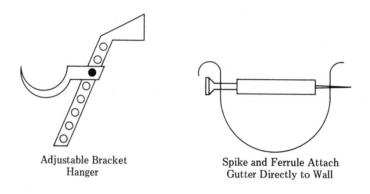

Adjustable Bracket
Hanger

Spike and Ferrule Attach
Gutter Directly to Wall

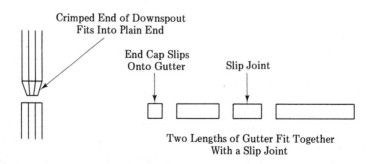

Crimped End of Downspout
Fits Into Plain End

End Cap Slips
Onto Gutter

Slip Joint

Two Lengths of Gutter Fit Together
With a Slip Joint

Drainage Techniques.

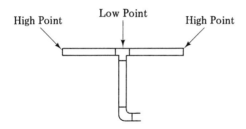

System for Draining Gutters from the Middle fo the Run

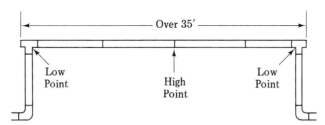

Twin Downspout System for a Roof Over 35 Feet Long

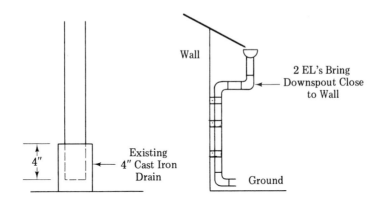

Drainage Techniques.

spikes and ferrules to install the gutter, you must hang the gutter to the proper slope with wire or have it held by a helper while you nail.

5. Fit two downspout elbows together to form the letter S. Fit the elbows to the downspout connector and turn

them so that one end lies flat against the wall. Mark the place where the bottom edge of the assembly falls against the wall.

6. Place a length of downspout against the wall. Position the top edge of the downspout 2 inches above the mark

on the wall. Mark the bottom of the downspout for cutting so that it fits into an existing drain pipe or an elbow.

7. Cut the downspout and fit it to the drain pipe or elbow and the elbow assembly. Attach the downspout to the wall with clips every 3 feet along the run. Use masonry anchors or nails to secure the clips.

Tips:

If necessary, a gutter system can be set up so that the downspout occurs in the middle of the run. Simply hang the gutter so that the ends are the high points and the downspout connector is at the low point.

If a run of gutter is more than 35 feet, use a downspout at each end of the run. The midpoint of the gutter run will be the high point, and the two ends will be low points.

If you intend to prime and paint galvanized steel gutter and downspout, you should let the metal weather for at least 6 months to remove manufacturing oils

and deposits. When the metal is weathered, treat with a zinc-oxide or zinc-chromate primer especially created for galvanized metal. These primers will do most of the work in protecting the metal, and a color coat is strictly optional from a protection standpoint.

For flat roofs that have no gutters, the only things needed are a downspout and a gutter box. A gutter box looks a bit like a downspout connector except that only one end of the box is open. The preferred size for downspouts and gutter boxes for flat roofs is 4 inches in diameter. The new gutter box is installed at the low point of the flat roof where the old deteriorated box is. Simply remove the old box and nail the new box in place with roofing nails. Apply roofing cement to seal the nails and the edges of the box with the rest of the roof. The downspout connects with the outlet on the underside of the box. Attach the downspouts to the wall with U straps, and place the bottom edge of the downspout into an existing drain pipe or use an elbow to conduct the water away from the foundation of the house.

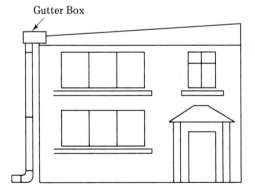

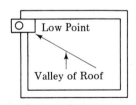

A Gutter Box Collects All of the Water from a Flat Roof and Sends It Down a Single Downspout

A Gutter Box Collects All of the Water from a Flat Roof and Sends It Down a Single Downspout.

↘ HOW TO FIGHT WATER IN THE BASEMENT

Tools and supplies needed:

Rental drain cleaner
Sump pump
Stucco and concrete tools
Stiff-bristled whitewash brush
Stucco and cement materials
Portland-cement-based paint

Procedure:

Water or excessive dampness in the basement is a very common problem. Many old houses are especially vulnerable because their basement walls are constructed of stone. Often this stone was mortared with a mixture of clay and lime, which over the years can become very porous.

The first step is to check the drainage system. Water from the roof and gutter system should be conducted to drains. If the drains are clogged with debris, water can find its way to the basement. Rent a rotary drain cleaner and run the cleaning head through the drains with plenty of water from a hose. You should clean all drains: yard, basement, and rainwater lines.

If this doesn't clear up the problem, you can assume that the drain lines are broken underground or that your basement walls are so porous that normal ground water can seep in. Short of having your drains dug up or your foundation rebuilt, there are several possibilities.

If your problem is dampness seeping through the basement walls, you can paint your walls with a portland-cement-based paint. This is more like a coating than a paint, and it comes in dry form to be mixed with water. It can only be applied over clean, unpainted masonry surfaces. Wet the walls down with a mist of water from a hose. Mix the powder with water to come up with a paint about the consistency of heavy whipping cream. Apply the paint to the walls with a stiff-bristled whitewash brush. At least two coats are needed to resist moisture, and three coats provide the best protection. These paints come in white and pastel colors and make an attractive, durable finish over masonry.

If your problem is heavy seepage of water through the walls, you should stucco the basement walls. Use the same formula and procedure for this stucco that you use for the exterior walls. If the walls are rough and unpainted, the stucco can be applied directly to the masonry. If the walls are smooth or painted, you should apply stucco over a wire lath. Apply the same three coats of stucco that are used in outside work, and observe the curing times and dampness requirements to obtain a strong, water-resistant bond.

For severe water problems that include a flood in the basement from time to time, the only inexpensive solution is to install a sump pump. Severe problems indicate poor design of the drainage and foundation system, or a high water table, or both. A sump pump will enable you to live with the situation by standing ready to pump out any water that enters your basement.

Install the pump at the lowest point in the basement, where all the water eventually flows. Dig a pit 28 inches deep and 28 inches in diameter. Pour gravel-mix concrete into the pit to make a 3-

inch-thick footing for the sump pump. The surface of the footing should be exactly 25 inches below the surface of the basement floor. Trowel the footing smooth and level, and let it cure for two days.

When the footing is firm, place a 20 x 20-inch piece of terra-cotta flue lining in the hole. Center the flue lining in the hole. Pour gravel-mix concrete around the flue lining to anchor it in place. Tamp the concrete with a piece of wood and hold the flue lining in place as you tamp. Bring the concrete to the top of the flue lining. Prepare a small quantity of mortar, and apply it with a trowel to make a sloped coping between the top edge of the flue lining and the surface of the basement floor.

Let the concrete and mortar cure for about a week. Set a pedestal-type sump pump in the pit you have created, and lead the outlet hose to the house sewer pipe or let the hose drain into a laundry tub. Adjust the float switch on the pump to turn on at 6 inches of water, and plug the pump into house current.

In Brief:

1. First check the drainage system. Rent a rotary drain cleaner and run it down all the drain lines with plenty of water from a hose.

2. If dampness seeps through the walls, paint the walls with two or three coats of portland-cement-based paint. Wet the walls, mix the paint to a heavy whipping cream consistency, and brush it on with a stiff brush.

3. Heavy seepage calls for the standard three coats of stucco. Apply the stucco directly to unpainted rough textured walls. Apply stucco over lath if the walls are smooth or painted.

4. Severe water seepage and occasional floods need the installation of a sump pump. Dig a hole 28 inches deep and 28 inches in diameter in the lowest spot in the basement. Pour a 3-inch footing of gravel-mix concrete and let it cure for two days. Place a 20 x 20-inch piece of terra-cotta flue lining in the hole and pour gravel-mix con-

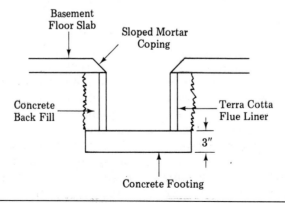

Basement Floor Slab

Sloped Mortar Coping

Concrete Back Fill

Terra Cotta Flue Liner

3"

Concrete Footing

Sump Pump Pit.

crete around it to anchor it. Apply a sloped coping of mortar to the edge of the terra cotta and the basement floor. Set a pedestal-type sump pump in the pit, and connect the drain line to the house sewer or a laundry tub.

Tips:

If you plan to stucco your basement walls using wire lath, you can provide an extra measure of waterproofing under the stucco. Before applying lath, cover the walls with an asphalt waterproofing compound designed for the outside of basement walls. This compound is very much like roof coating and can be brushed on with a whitewash brush. After the walls are covered with compound, apply lath and proceed to stucco.

There is another alternative to a pedestal-type sump pump. You can install a submersible sump pump. This pump will operate under water and needs only a shallow pit of a foot or less. The drawback to this pump is that it may need more maintenance than a conventional pump (because of complicated seals) and generally has a less powerful motor than the pedestal pump.

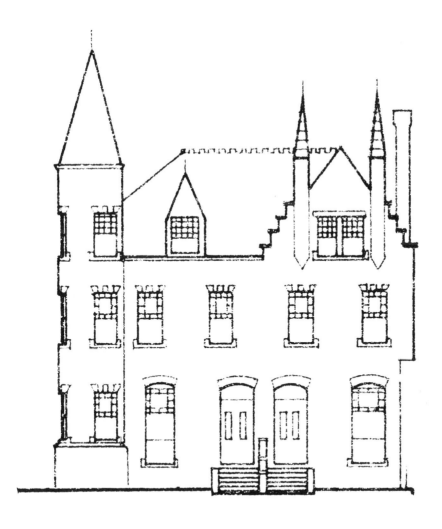

15

Maintenance and Miscellaneous Projects

⤷ HOW TO CAULK

Tools and supplies needed:

Caulking gun
Putty knife
Wire brush
Tubes of caulk (oil, latex, or butyl rubber)

Procedure:

Caulking is necessary to prevent outside air from entering your house and robbing you of heat. Caulking is as important as insulation and storm windows in the effort to increase the energy efficiency of your house. Air infiltration through uncaulked gaps in an old house can account for as much as 17 percent of the house's energy loss. Caulking also prevents water and insects from entering the house and causing damage to wood and masonry.

You want caulk to stay pliable for many years, expanding and contracting with the temperature changes. Oil-based caulks are inexpensive but tend to dry out and crack after a short time. They are best suited for interior work. Latex caulks are a bit more expensive than oil but last a good deal longer. Butyl-rubber and silicone caulks are expensive but can last up to twenty years.

Caulk around doorframes, window frames, basement windows and frames, vents, fans, air conditioners, roof flashing, pipe flashing, between the foundation and upper walls, in any cracks in wood siding, brick, or stucco, and any places where two different materials come together.

Begin to caulk by cleaning out any joints of old, flaking material. Use a putty knife and a wire brush to clean the surface. Slip a caulk cartridge into the gun and push the plunger into the end of the cartridge. Engage the notches on the plunger rod with the gun's handle.

Snip the plastic nozzle of the cartridge off at a 45-degree angle. Notice that the nozzle is tapered so that by cutting it at different places along its length you can get a different size of bead. Pierce the inner seal of the caulk by shoving a long nail or stiff piece of wire down the nozzle. Squeeze the handle of the gun and caulk will come out of the nozzle.

Start caulking at the top of a vertical joint and on either end of a horizontal joint. Hold the gun at a 45-degree angle to the surface and move the gun slowly along the joint, squeezing the handle to apply a smooth and seamless bead of caulk. The caulk should fill the joint completely and overlap the sides of the joint by about ¼ inch. This overlap will allow the caulk to shrink into place as it cures.

In Brief:

1. Select a caulk that will perform well in your situation. Inspect the exterior of your home and identify places that need treatment. Look closely at all areas where two different materials or kinds of construction come together.

2. Prepare the joint to be caulked. Clean any loose or flaking material out of the joint with a putty knife and wire brush.

3. Slip a caulk cartridge into the gun and push the plunger into the cartridge. Engage the notches on the plunger rod with the gun's handle.

4. Snip the plastic nozzle of the cartridge off at a 45-degree angle. Select the size of the caulk bead needed and cut along the length of the nozzle to get the proper size. Pierce the inner seal of the caulk with a long nail or stiff wire. Squeeze the handle of the gun to produce caulk.

5. Start caulking at the top of a vertical joint and at either end of a horizontal joint. Hold the gun at a 45-degree angle to the surface and move the gun slowly along the joint as you squeeze the handle. Make a smooth and seamless bead that fills the joint and overlaps the sides by about ¼ inch.

Tips:

If you are having a hard time making a smooth joint right out of the gun, try smoothing the caulk with your finger or a flat stick. If the caulk sticks and pulls, try wetting your finger or the stick in linseed oil or water.

If you have a deep and wide joint that is impossible to bridge with caulk alone, stuff the joint with newspapers or rags. When you have built the joint up to within ¼ inch of the surface, you can lay a bead of caulk. Deep and wide joints can also be sealed with polyurethane foam caulk. This material comes out of a spray can and expands to more than twice its original volume before curing. Use urethane foam only for special situations, because it is expensive.

Oil and latex caulks can, as a general rule, be painted over once they have cured for a few days. Silicone rubber can't be painted, and so you must select a color that you can live with. Some butyl-rubber caulks can be painted and some can't, so you must check the label on the product carefully.

Caulk labeled "acrylic latex" will be superior to that marked simply "latex."

HOW TO WEATHERSTRIP

Tools and supplies needed:

Hammer

Shears

Felt or sponge-rubber weatherstrip

Box of ½-inch tacks

Procedure:

Weatherstripping doors and windows is part of your program to reduce air infiltration in your house. Tight-fitting storm windows will often seal window spaces, but you may still want to install weatherstripping on the joints in the original windows. You should certainly weatherstrip exterior doors since most people don't want to install modern-looking storm doors on an old house. Weatherstripping, along with caulking, insulation, and storm windows, can significantly reduce the amount of heat lost from your house.

There are so many different kinds of weatherstripping materials available that it is impossible to cover them all. Most of the low-cost, easy-to-install weatherstrips consist of foam or felt tapes with an adhesive backing that are pressed in place in the window or door jamb. The drawback here is that the material may last for one season or less, and it often comes loose and binds in the window or door.

On the high-cost end of weatherstrips there are spring-metal and metal-interlocking weatherstrips. The drawback here is expense and the need for very precise installation. The material is not forgiving, and you may waste a whole package or significantly reduce its effectiveness by not being expert in its installation.

A good compromise for expense, durability, and ease of installation is felt or sponge-rubber-gasket weatherstrips. Buy wool felt bonded to a stiff aluminum bead, or buy sponge-rubber gasket coated with neoprene rubber or plastic and with a metal and cord mounting edge.

The idea is to install felt or rubber so that it butts against the loose door or window and prevents drafts from entering. Install the weatherstripping with the door or window in the closed position. Begin with the top edge of the frame and work your way down the sides to the bottom edge. Weatherstrip doors from the outside and windows from the inside.

Cut the felt or rubber with a pair of shears. Cut each piece of weatherstrip so that it is continuous across each edge of the frame. Lay the weatherstrip so that its edge rests lightly against the door or window, and nail it into the stop molding with one tack about every 5 inches.

In Brief:

1. Select metal-backed felt or sponge-rubber weatherstrip. Close the window or door. Begin weatherstripping the top edge and work down the sides to the bottom edge. Weatherstrip doors from the outside and windows from the inside.

2. Cut the felt or rubber with a pair of shears. Cut each piece so that it is continuous across each edge.

3. Lay the weatherstrip so that its edge rests lightly against the door or window and nail it to the stop molding with one tack every 5 inches.

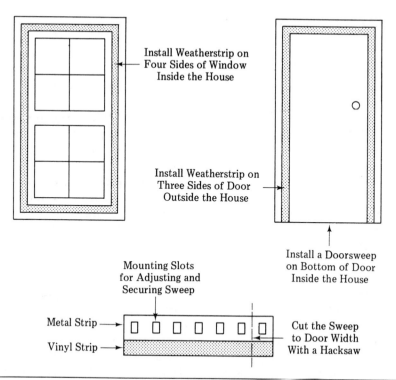

Install Weatherstrip on Four Sides of Window Inside the House

Install Weatherstrip on Three Sides of Door Outside the House

Install a Doorsweep on Bottom of Door Inside the House

Mounting Slots for Adjusting and Securing Sweep

Metal Strip

Vinyl Strip

Cut the Sweep to Door Width With a Hacksaw

Weatherstripping Techniques.

Tips:

About the only place where felt or rubber can't be used is at the bottom edge of a door. The simple solution here is to use a *door sweep.* This is a metal strip which is screwed to the bottom of the door. Attached to the metal strip is a flap of vinyl which brushes along the floor and seals the bottom of the door. Sweeps are installed on the inside of the door. Cut the sweep to the proper length, screw the sweep to the bottom of the door, and use the adjustment holes to make the edge of the vinyl rest lightly against the threshold piece of the door.

For double doors with a gap in the space between them, you can weather-strip the top and outside edges as you would normally. The space between the doors can be weatherstripped with round sponge-rubber gasket. Simply install the gasket on both inside edges of the doors so that the two gaskets just touch each other.

There is one other option for weatherstripping doors. You can buy a rigid gasket which looks something like a door sweep. The weatherstrip consists of a metal mounting strip bonded to a flap of vinyl or neoprene rubber. The weatherstrip is screwed to the door stops just as you would mount felt or sponge rubber. The mounting strips are highly visible but do provide a very durable and adjustable seal for the door. This kind of

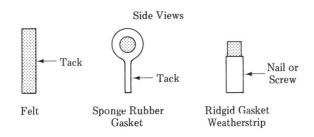

Side Views

Felt — Tack

Sponge Rubber Gasket — Tack

Ridgid Gasket Weatherstrip — Nail or Screw

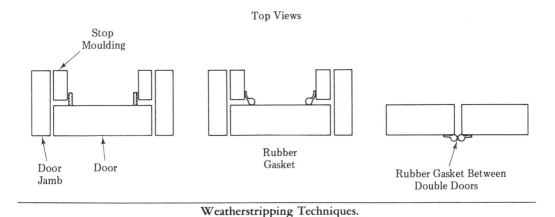

Top Views

Stop Moulding

Door Jamb   Door

Rubber Gasket

Rubber Gasket Between Double Doors

Weatherstripping Techniques.

weatherstrip offers performance near to spring- or interlocking-metal weatherstrips with much less critical installation.

⤳ HOW TO WRAP PIPES IN INSULATION

Tools and supplies needed:

Heavy shears
Tape measure
Gloves and respirator
3½-inch-thick fiberglass insulation
Roll of foil vapor barrier
Twine and duct tape

Procedure:

You can reduce heat loss from heating and hot-water supply pipes by wrapping them in insulation. Hot-water pipes should be wrapped from the water heater all the way to the fixtures they supply. Insulated hot-water pipes will allow you to run your heater at the lowest setting and still enjoy very hot water at the fixtures.

Heating pipes can also benefit from insulation. If you don't mind a chilly basement, you can wrap the supply and return lines in insulation from the furnace to where they branch off to supply the upstairs radiators. If any heating

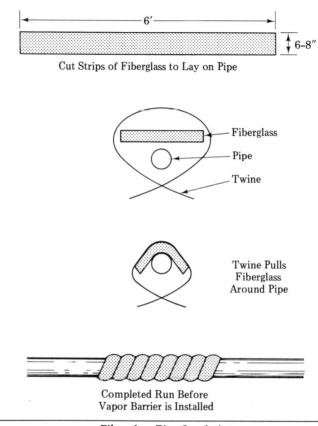

6'

6-8"

Cut Strips of Fiberglass to Lay on Pipe

Fiberglass

Pipe

Twine

Twine Pulls
Fiberglass
Around Pipe

Completed Run Before
Vapor Barrier is Installed

Fiberglass Pipe Insulation.

lines run through a garage or unheated space, they should definitely be wrapped in insulation to prevent heat loss.

Commercial pipe wraps are available, but they are expensive for the amount of insulation they provide. You can cut your own pipe wraps from rolls of fiberglass and save money while providing better insulation.

Cut fiberglass into 5-foot lengths. Cut the lengths into strips that will cover the diameter of pipe you are working with. Cut a test strip before doing the rest. Lay the strips on the pipe, vapor barrier out. Use twine to secure the insulation to the pipe, and wrap it around the insulation to draw it over the pipe. Don't wrap *too* tight, as this will compress the insulation and reduce its efficiency.

After the insulation is secured to the pipe, use foil vapor barrier to protect the insulation from moisture. Cut the vapor barrier into strips that will cover the insulation and overlap about 1½ inches. Secure the overlapped edges of the vapor barrier with strips of 2-inch-wide duct tape.

In Brief:

1. Cut roll fiberglass into 5-foot lengths, and cut these into strips that will cover the diameter of the pipe. Cut a test strip and check for fit. Lay the strips on the pipe, vapor barrier out.

2. Wrap the insulation with twine to draw it around the pipe. Don't wrap too tight or you will reduce the insulation effect.

3. When insulation is secure to the pipe, cut foil vapor barrier into strips and overlap the edges around the fiberglass by 1½ inches. Secure the edges of the vapor barrier with strips of duct tape.

Tips:

Always use a respirator and gloves to reduce your contact with the fiberglass.

Duct tape is a very useful product that was originally developed to seal the seams in air ducts. It is a very tough, tenacious tape with a silver coating. Use long strips of duct tape to seal the seams in the foil vapor barrier. Simply lay the duct tape over the center of the vapor-barrier seam and press it in place.

↰ HOW TO USE REPLACEMENT WINDOW CHANNELS

Tools and supplies needed:

Hammer
Screwdriver
Electric drill and bits
Two replacement window channels for each window
Screws and finishing nails

Procedure:

Replacement window channels can make repairing deteriorated and leaky windows easy. These spring-loaded channels replace the rope-and-pulley system in double-hung sash windows and also eliminate the need for weather-stripping the window. They are a good choice for windows that have loose, faulty frames but sound wooden sashes.

Measure the height of the window frame and the thickness of the sashes, and buy two channels for each window. Several companies make replacement channels and you should check carefully that the brand you buy fits the thickness of your sashes and comes in your exact window frame height (or is able to be cut down with a hacksaw).

Carefully remove the stop molding from around the window frame. Remove the sashes and the parting strips from the window frame, and cut the cords or chains that hold the weights. Let the weights and cord fall into the interior of the window frame. Clean up the edges of the sashes, and paint them if desired.

Unscrew the four pulleys from the top of the window frame and remove them. Clean up the inside edges of the window frame. Place the replacement channels along the inside edges of the window frame and check for proper fit. Remove the channels from the window, and place them on the sashes. Hold the channels on the sashes and replace them into the window frame.

Drill and screw the channels to the window frame. Check the movement of the top sash frequently while installing to make sure that the channels are straight. Replace the stop molding and nail it in place with finishing nails. Check the movement of the bottom sash frequently to make sure that you are installing the stop molding correctly.

The replacement channels will hold the sashes in any position because of the spring loading and will also tightly weatherstrip the sashes along the vertical surfaces.

In Brief:

1. Measure the height of the window frame and the thickness of the window sash, and buy the proper window channels. Buy two channels for each window.

2. Carefully remove the stop molding from around the window frame. Remove the sashes and parting strips, and cut the chain or cord that holds the weights.

3. Unscrew the four pulleys from the top of the window frame and remove. Clean up the inside edges of the window frame.

4. Place the channels on the sashes. Hold the channels on the sashes and place them in the window frame.

5. Drill and screw the channels to the window frame. Replace the stop molding, and nail it in position with finishing nails.

⌐ HOW TO INCREASE THE EFFICIENCY OF RADIATORS

Tools and supplies needed:

Heavy shears
Measuring tape
Gloves and respirator

Thin flat stick about 3 feet long
3½-inch-thick fiberglass insulation
Roll of foil vapor barrier

Procedure:

To help radiators throw out more heat into the living space, construct insulation packets. These packets are stuffed behind the radiators and reflect heat out into the room and prevent the radiator from heating the wall behind it.

Measure the radiator outline and cut 3½-inch insulation to the same size. For thin spaces behind radiators you may have to pull the fiberglass apart to come up with an acceptable thickness. Cut two pieces of foil vapor barrier big enough so that you can fold all four edges together around the insulation to form a packet.

Place one piece of vapor barrier on the floor, foil side down. Place the insulation on top of the vapor barrier, centered within the dimensions. Place a second piece of vapor barrier on top of the insulation, foil side up. Fold all the edges of the two pieces of vapor barrier together to form a packet around the insulation. You can staple the edges of the packet with an ordinary hand stapler.

Insert the completed packet behind the radiator. Use a stick to guide the packet around any obstructions. Fold any excess vapor barrier back from the outlines of the radiator.

In Brief:

1. Measure the radiator outline and cut insulation to the same size. If the insulation is too thick for the space behind the radiator, pull it apart.

2. Cut two pieces of foil vapor barrier

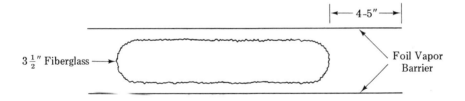

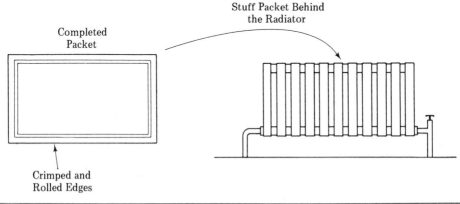

Radiator Insulation.

big enough to fold all four edges together around the insulation.

3. Place one piece of vapor barrier on the floor, foil down. Center the insulation on top of that piece. Place a second piece of vapor barrier on top of the insulation, foil up. Fold all the edges of the vapor barrier together to make a packet.

4. Insert the completed packet behind the radiator. Use a stick to guide it into place. Fold any excess vapor barrier back from the outlines of the radiator.

↰ HOW TO BLEED RADIATORS

Tools and supplies needed:

Radiator key
Saucepan

Procedure:

When you fill a heating system after repair or replacement of the furnace and distribution system, you must systematically bleed the radiators of air as the water level rises.

You need two people to bleed radiators. One person is stationed in the basement at the water-supply valve to the furnace. The other person moves through the house with a radiator key, opening and closing the bleed valves on the radiators.

Open all the bleed valves on the radiators in the house, and return to the first floor. Signal your helper to turn on the water supply to the furnace. (Use two hits on a pipe to signal water, one hit to stop water.) As the water fills the lower radiators it will spurt out the bleed valves. Shut off each valve as it spurts water. Use a saucepan to catch water from the valve as you close it.

When you reach the top floor, signal your helper to shut off the water before you close each bleed valve. After you close a bleed valve, have him turn it on for the next valve, and so on. This stop-start routine is necessary to avoid putting excessive pressure on the system which might cause the relief valve on the furnace to open, spilling water all over the basement.

In Brief:

1. Station one person at the water-supply valve to the furnace. The other person should then open all the bleed valves on the radiators.

2. Return to the first floor, and signal the helper to turn on water to the furnace. As water fills the lower radiators, it will spurt out the bleed valves. Close each valve as it spurts water.

3. When you reach the top floor, signal your helper to shut off the water before you close each bleed valve. After you close a valve, signal for water for the next valve, and so on until you have filled the last radiator on that floor.

Tips:

When bleeding air out of an operating system, turn off the furnace and circulator and use a helper to turn the water on and off for each radiator. In an operating system, air will generally collect in the top-floor radiators only.

To determine quickly if a radiator needs bleeding, feel the top and bottom of it when the system is operating. If the top is cooler than the bottom, the radiator probably needs bleeding.

⌐ HOW TO BUILD A POT GRID FROM OLD IRON FENCE

Tools and supplies needed:

Electric drill and bits
Hacksaw
Wire brush
Tape measure
Length of salvaged iron fence
Four 4-inch screw hooks
Twenty 3-inch S hooks
Can of enamel spray paint

Procedure:

If you have decided to follow the open plan for your kitchen, the central system for storage and display can be an overhead grid. Professional-kitchen-supply houses and gourmet specialty stores sell prefabricated pot grids, but you can make your own from a length of iron fence for less money. Your pot grid will save you from having to build or buy storage cabinets and it will also increase efficiency in the kitchen by having every pot and tool in easy reach.

Buy or salvage an old piece of iron fence. A straight bar and cross-piece design will be more efficient than an ornate one. A piece of fence about 3 x 5 feet will do nicely. You can cut the fence down with a hacksaw to fit your kitchen space.

Decide what area in the kitchen is best for the grid. The best place would be directly over a countertop food-preparation area; the next best would be over the sink or range; and the least ideal is over a traffic lane. Measure the area and decide how long you want your grid to be. Cut the grid to size with a hacksaw. Clean the grid with a wire brush, and paint it with two coats of enamel from a spray can to prevent rusting.

Get up near the ceiling and tap around to find the joists under the plaster. Mark the position of the joists with a pencil. You are going to screw four hooks to the ceiling joists so that the grid can be hung from them by S hooks. Experiment with the tape measure until you find the right joist spacing and position to mount the four hooks so that they will support the grid at the four outside corners of the bars. You don't have to be super exact with the hooks, because the S hooks will take up some slack. Drill pilot holes into the joists, and screw the hooks firmly into the ceiling until no threads show on the hooks.

Have a helper hold the grid near the ceiling while you attach four S hooks to the grid corners and then to the ceiling hooks. Let the grid hang from the ceiling, and adjust the position of the S hooks to get the best hold on the grid. The combination of the ceiling hooks and the S hooks will allow the grid to hang about 4½ inches from the ceiling.

Use the rest of the 3-inch S hooks to hang pots, pans, and kitchen tools from all points of the iron grid. For handles with small-diameter hanging holes, you can use 2-inch S hooks made of thin-diameter wire. For a kitchen with an 8-foot ceiling, the pot grid hanging 4½ inches from the ceiling is about right for most people's reach. For kitchens with higher ceilings, the pot grid can be dropped down from the ceiling with lengths of 1-inch link chain connecting the hooks and the S hooks on the grid corners.

In Brief:

1. Cut the grid to size with a hacksaw. Clean the grid with a wire brush, and paint it with two coats of enamel from a spray can.

2. Tap around the ceiling to find the joists under the plaster. Mark the position of the joists.

3. Use a tape measure to determine the proper place to install the four screw hooks into the joists so that the grid will hang in the proper area. Drill four pilot holes through the plaster and into the joists. Screw the hooks into the holes until no threads show.

4. Have a helper hold the grid near the ceiling while you attach four S hooks to the grid corners and then to the ceiling hooks. Let the grid hang, and adjust the S hooks if necessary.

5. Use the rest of the S hooks to hang pots and kitchen tools from the grid. If the grid is too high for reaching the utensils, lower it with lengths of 1-inch chain from the ceiling hooks to the S hooks on the grid corners.

Glossary

Balusters. The upright pieces of wood that support a stair railing. The railing itself is called a *balustrade*. In most old houses you will deal with balusters only when stripping them of paint, for which you will need a wire brush and steel wool to get at the carving. If a baluster is broken or missing, you can have one reproduced for you by a mill yard. Simply remove a good baluster and present it to the yard as a sample. New balusters are turned on a lathe and can sometimes be molded of plastic materials if you intend to paint them.

Baseboards. The wooden trim that covers the base of interior walls to protect them against damage and scuffing. In old houses the baseboard is quite wide (6–12 inches) and has a carved base-cap molding at the top edge and a shoe molding at the bottom edge. It is worth restoring the original baseboards, because modern baseboards are thinner

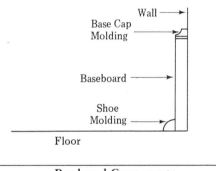

Baseboard Components.

and less ornate. If you must replace baseboards, you might use 1 x 6-inch (or wider) white pine and buy quarter-round molding for the shoe molding and concave molding for the base-cap molding.

Basin Wrench. This is a special plumbing tool that allows you to remove and install faucets and other plumbing units in tight places. It consists of a pipe-wrench head on a long rod. At the base of the rod is a sliding handle. The tool can be used in situations where you can't maneuver a pipe wrench or an adjustable wrench.

Bead. In caulking, a bead is a smooth, seamless, slightly raised strip of material laid in a joint. Laying a good bead is the basic skill in caulking all kinds of joints. Bead is also used to describe a thin metal strip called a *corner bead*. This bead is used on outside corners of plaster and drywall construction. The bead provides an even corner to guide the wall finisher, and the raised metal edge protects the plaster or drywall from damage.

BTU. Short for British Thermal Unit. This is the basic rating system for air conditioning and heating equipment. A BTU is the amount of heat required to raise the temperature of one pound of water one degree Fahrenheit.

Chalk Line. An inexpensive tool used to mark straight lines. Line, coated with chalk, is stretched between two points and then snapped so that the line deposits chalk on the surface to be marked. Snapping a chalk line is very useful in tile work, rough carpentry, masonry and any other job that requires a straight line over long distances (5–20 feet).

Coping. In mortar work, a coping is a sloped application of mortar designed to guide water into or away from an element of masonry. A flue liner should have a coping of mortar to shed water away from the chimney. A sump-pump pit should have a coping of mortar to guide water into the pit. Coping is also the name of a U-shaped strip of metal that is often used to protect electrical and telephone wires that run on the exterior surface of a building. The metal coping is applied from ground level up to 10 feet high to protect the wires from damage and tampering.

Cutting In. The basic preparation for painting large areas. A small brush (about 2 inches) is used to paint all the edges, corners, and tight places before the main area is painted. Professional painters cut in their work before doing the bulk of the area for reasons of efficiency and accuracy. It is highly recommended that you cut in all of your work before using a roller, sprayer, or large brush.

Door Components. A solid wood door is composed of two vertical pieces called *stiles*. On the lock and doorknob side of the door, the stile is called the *lock stile*. On the hinge side of the door, it's called the *hinge stile*. At the top edge of the door is a horizontal solid piece called the *top rail*. In the center of the door is the *lock rail,* and at the bottom of the door is the *bottom rail*. The two stiles and the three rails support the balance of the door which, depending on the door's complexity, is composed of two or more panels of wood.

Doorway Components. Doorways consist of casing which performs the same function as baseboard and is often

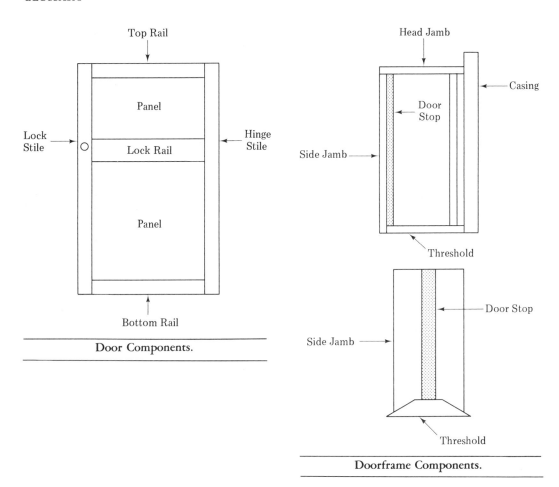

Door Components.

Doorframe Components.

wide and ornate in old houses. The *side jambs* and *head jamb* are the surfaces which bridge the thickness of the doorway. Hinges attach to the *hinge jamb,* and a lock engages with the *lock jamb.* Running through the center of the side jambs and the head jamb is a strip of wood called the *doorstop.* This piece stops the door and makes it sit flush with the edges of the side jambs and the head jamb. Running across the base of the doorway, bridging the thickness of the doorway, is a *threshold piece.* This

threshold piece is often omitted in the original design of interior doorways in some old houses. It is never absent in exterior doorways.

Drywall. The common name for gypsum and paper building material. In some areas of the country drywall is known as *gypsum board* or *sheetrock.* Because this material can be installed dry and finished with tape and prepared compound, it is superior to plaster over lath and other interior finishing methods from a cost and time standpoint. If drywall is installed in ⅜-inch thicknesses or greater and in double layers, it can perform as well or better than plaster over lath in soundproofing rooms.

Duplex Outlet. The standard wall outlet for lighting, appliances, and other electrical equipment. It consists of two sockets ganged into a single device which can be wired to a branch electrical circuit and housed in a single outlet box mounted in the wall. Duplex outlets now incorporate a U-shaped hole in each socket for the ground blade of three-pronged plugs. This grounded duplex outlet provides an extra measure of safety against electrical shock.

Finish Flooring. In an old house finish flooring can be strip hardwood, marble, ceramic tile, wood block, or slate. These materials were applied in a thin layer to the subflooring to provide a high-quality surface. Because these materials don't contribute significantly to the structure, they can be stripped and sanded repeatedly to bring up their natural beauty. Finish flooring can also be applied to raw subflooring or damaged finish flooring to provide a new surface. Some of the inexpensive finish flooring options available include 1 x 6-inch roofing boards, chipboard tiles, quarry tiles, and composition tiles.

Flange. A lip of metal or other rigid material used for mounting and positioning. The common flanges around an old house are in plumbing—a sewer-pipe flange sits at floor level and positions the toilet and provides a mount for the closet bolts. In a sink trap, a flange occurs on the bent end of the downtube to position the rubber washer and mount the threaded nut.

Flashing. A sheet of metal, plastic, rubber, or asphalt-soaked felt used to shed water from joints that are likely to leak. Metal flashing of copper or aluminum is used to shed water from chimneys and from the edges of buildings. Stucco that is applied to the whole exterior surface of a masonry building needs a flashing to prevent water from entering behind it. Installing a flashing is precise and skilled work and should be contracted to a professional. Vent pipes and plumbing pipes that exit through the roof need plastic or rubber collars to shed water away from the joint between the pipe and the roof.

Footing. A thick, solid slab of concrete which is required to support foundation walls and structural posts. Footings must be laid below the local frost line to prevent heaving and buckling from the action of frozen water. Local codes usually govern the size of footings for different applications. You are likely to need footings for new posts in the basement, for posts that support porches and terrace roofs, and for new brick and concrete block walls. Footings for small projects are commonly poured with pre-mixed gravel-mix concrete. For large jobs, a ready-mix concrete delivered by truck is needed.

Glazing. Any sheet material used to cover windows and skylights. Glazing could be glass, plexiglass, formed plastic, fiberglass, or plastic sheeting. Glazing is also the process of cutting, fitting, and securing these materials to a frame.

Joists. The principal wooden structural members of an old masonry house. Joists are installed horizontally and anchored at their ends to the masonry walls of the house. In most houses, joists support the floor on their top edges and the ceiling on their bottom edges. Joists are generally about 3 x 12 inches and spaced 12–16 inches from each other. A *beam* is a different structural member. It is a very heavy timber, at least 5 x 7 inches, and it runs between posts, columns, or walls to support the joists above it.

Key. The mechanical bond that is necessary when using mortar, stucco, concrete, or plaster. A key is the undercut around the edges of a crack or hole that will tend to hold the patching material in place. Wire and wood lath provides a key for stucco and plaster. The small gaps in the lath allow material to curl behind the wood or metal. When the material dries, the lath and finish become one unit. When laying brick or concrete block over old material, use a chisel to cut out inverted Vs in the surface of the old material to provide a key for the mortar in the first course of brick or block.

Mastic. The generic name for any heavy, paste-like adhesive or cement. Mastic is often used to set quarry and ceramic tile, secure drywall sheets and thin wood paneling, install furring strips, and secure floor tiles of all kinds. Always select the mastic that specifically states that it can be used for the material you wish to secure. Adhesive manufacturers provide thorough information on their products, and you can expect good results if you read and follow the label information carefully.

Muriatic Acid. Another name for hydrochloric acid. This acid is used to clean masonry of stains and to remove efflorescence. It is dangerous and should be handled with rubber gloves, eye and face protection, and the utmost care to follow the package directions for proper use.

Newel Post. The large, usually ornate, post at the start and finish of a run of stairs. There are often smaller newel posts stationed at sharp turns in the stairway.

Plastic Laminates. These are sheets of extremely durable plastic material in thicknesses of $1/32$ inch (for walls) and $1/16$ inch (for counters) and available in 4 x 8-foot panels. Laminates are useful for covering bathroom and kitchen cabinets, countertops, and walls in wet locations. The laminates must be glued to a rigid and stable surface (chipboard is recommended) in an unbroken surface. The edges are rounded off after gluing, or the rough edges are bound with molding.

Plumb Bob. A simple and inexpensive tool which is very useful in carpentry and masonry. A pointed weight hangs from a line and always describes a straight line from where it is hung. Use it to position the sole plate exactly in line with the top plate in wall framing, and use it to guide straight corners when building masonry walls.

Ream. When cutting copper pipe, there are often burrs and rough edges left on the cut end of the pipe. The pipe must be reamed with a triangular tool (often part of the pipe cutter) to remove these irregularities. For extra precise reaming of copper and brass tubing you can buy a reamer that will accept pipe up to $1\frac{1}{2}$ inches. This large tool is especially useful for reaming trap tubes and copper branch sewage line.

Router. Many of the details in old houses were machine-carved into wood. Balusters, door carving, porch gingerbread, baseboard, and molding pieces are all examples of machine-carved wood. The modern machine used for this carving is called a *router*. If you wish to duplicate some of the original details of your house into new wood, you must do it by routing. A good router will have a 1 hp motor, a ¼-inch chuck, and an easy-to-use depth-of-cut adjustment. To get the full use of a router, you will have to stock at least ten different bits, each of which makes a distinctive cut in the wood. Make an inventory of the size and type of cuts that are typical in your house's woodwork, and stock these bits for cutting new wood into matching pieces.

Settlement. Structural settlement is a natural phenomenon in houses sixty years or older. The natural pull of gravity, changes in the water table of the ground, the action of the elements, and even increased traffic on the street can all contribute to a loosening of an old structure. Settlement usually appears in jagged cracks near window and door openings, as cracks and bulges in foundation walls, and as skewed doorways and window frames in the house's interior. You can accept a bit of settlement in an old house but you need the opinion and advice of a structural engineer to guide you when you detect large bowing of walls, severely skewed framing, and large cracks (¼ inch and larger) in the foundation and exterior walls.

Shim. Since most old houses have uneven surfaces and out-of-square lines, you must compensate for this when installing cabinets and framing by shim-

ming. Shimming involves placing wedges of wood behind and under new construction to make the new element level and square. The best shims are made from cedar shingles. These shingles are sold in bundles at the lumber yard. They are wedge-shaped and can be driven into tight places easily.

Shoe Molding. This is the strip of wood that occurs at the bottom of most baseboards in old houses. It covers the gap between the baseboard and the floor. You will often take up shoe molding for the purpose of getting close to the baseboard for sanding and tiling. It is difficult to pry up the old molding without damaging it. Unless the old shoe molding is especially ornate, you can replace it with new quarter-round wood molding which can be painted or finished to match the floor or baseboard.

Splice Box. This is the basic device for making connections between electrical cable. Any time you need to splice into an electrical cable, or take a new branch circuit from an existing circuit, you should use a splice box. The most common splice box is known as a 4-inch round box for plastic cable. This box has built-in clamps which accept and hold plastic cable. The cable is secured to the box, the ends are stripped, wires are connected with wire nuts, and the box is closed with a metal cover and secured with screws.

SPST. Short for single-pole, single-throw. This describes the most common kind of electrical switch. Single-pole means that the switch only controls one pole of a two-pole circuit. SPST switches are installed to interrupt only one wire of a two-wire circuit. Single-throw means that the switch has only one option for movement; it can move from off to on or from on to off. Most of the switches around a house are SPST switches. Light switches, time switches, and doorbell switches are all SPST switches.

Subfloor. In most old houses the flooring that lies directly on top of the joists is composed of 1 x 4-inch or 1 x 6-inch tongue-and-groove boards. If a finish floor is in place on top of these boards, they are known as the subfloor. Generally the finish floor is installed crosswise or on a diagonal to the subfloor. In some old houses, the 1-inch-thick subflooring constitutes the only floor. In this case you must be careful not to remove too much thickness with floor-sanding equipment, or risk weakening the floor. In general, a raw subfloor can be sanded a maximum of two times in its life before it becomes dangerously thin. The best course may be to install a finish floor of tile, wood blocks, or 1 x 6-inch roofing boards.

Toenail. This is one of the basic techniques of wood framing. Nails are driven into the sides or edges of lumber at a 45-degree angle to tie two pieces of lumber together. Toenailing is fine for rough framing but may not be precise enough for cabinetry. Metal corner braces that are nailed or screwed to the wood provide a precise and strong joint which even some professional carpenters prefer to toenailing.

Window Components. Standard double-hung windows (the type most often found in old houses) are composed of two *sashes* which ride up and down in a window frame. The elements of each sash are two *stiles* at each side and two *rails* at the top and bottom of the sash. If there is more than one pane of glass in

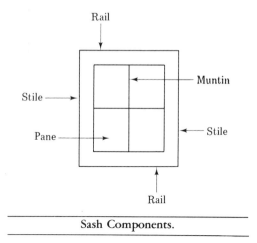

Sash Components.

the sash, the dividing strips which hold the individual panes are called *muntins.*

Window Frame Components. The frame for double-hung windows is composed of an inside and outside casing which serves the same function as baseboards. The pieces which bridge the thickness of the window frame are called the *head jamb* (stretches across the top of the frame), the *side jambs* (at the two sides of the frame), and the *sill* (which runs across the bottom of the frame and which may be extended a bit on the exterior side). There are also three pieces of molding that hold and guide the two sashes within the frame. On the exterior side of the upper sash is the *outside stop molding;* in the middle between the upper and lower sash is the *parting strip;* and on the interior side of the lower sash is the *inside stop molding.* Part of the frame also are four window weights with a separate chain and pulley for each weight. These weights run up and down channels just inside the two side jamb pieces. (An illustration of window frame components follows.)

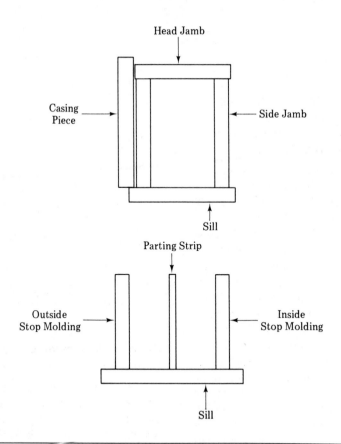

Window Frame Components.

Construction and Renovation Lore

⤺ CUTTING TILE

Thin (⅛-inch) ceramic and earthenware tiles can be cut and snapped using a common glass cutter with the same procedure described for glass cutting. Do not try this method for thick tiles, slates, quarry tiles, or milk glass. A commercial tile cutter is recommended for accuracy in cutting any tile. This unit uses a glass cutter mounted on a track to score the tile. The tile is then snapped with a bar that holds the tile against a piece of rubber mat.

When laying stiff composition floor tiles (asphalt-asbestos or solid-vinyl tiles for instance) you can use your hand propane torch with a medium-flame fitting to soften the tiles for easy cutting. Place the torch on a solid surface and hold the underside of the tile over the tip of the flame. Move the tile constantly over the flame, tracing the path of the cut lines.

After about four or five passes over the flame, cut the tile with a utility knife or shears; the heat-softened tile will cut easily.

Your propane torch can also be used to remove a damaged tile from the floor. Pass the flame over the whole surface of the tile until it begins to curl and soften. Work a putty knife under the tile, and keep heating the tile until you can lift it off the floor.

⤺ CUTTING WITH THE CIRCULAR SAW

To avoid binding the blade, veering off the cut line, and overloading the motor, always set the depth-of-cut adjustment on your circular saw before cutting. The proper depth of cut will be one blade tooth extending below the bottom surface of the wood. Set the saw on your

243

lumber and adjust the blade until one tooth shows below.

⤣ FINDING HIDDEN NAILING SURFACES

There will be many times when you need to know the location of the original studs or furring behind lath and plaster or drywall surfaces. You must know where to nail or screw fixtures, drywall sheets, and cabinets or shelves. Unfortunately, in old houses there is very little regularity about studs and furring. They were often placed according to the individual carpenter's taste and the plasterer's requirements.

You can determine the location of hidden nailing surfaces by tapping on the plaster with your hammer. Spaces between nailing surfaces will have a lower tone than spaces on top of nailing surfaces. It takes practice and a good ear to use this method. Another option is to use a magnetic stud finder. This is an inexpensive tool that detects the presence of nails behind plaster and wood lath. Where nails are, studs and furring should also be. A stud finder will not work if a wall contains metal lath under the plaster (usually only found on houses built between 1920 and 1950). You must move the stud finder in the general area of a nailing surface. Use a circular search pattern to blunder over a hidden nail. When the finder hits a nail, the pointer will move perpendicular to the wall.

You can always count on nailing surfaces at all corners of a room and at the edges of windows and doorways (al-though the casing pieces of windows and doors will often cover the entire hidden nailing surface). In the ceiling, your nailing surfaces will be the joists that support the floor or roof above. Go into your basement and check the exposed joists there to see which direction they run and to measure the typical spacing between them. Armed with this information and your hammer and stud finder, you should be able to find and mark all of the hidden nailing surfaces available to you on the ceiling.

⤣ INSTALLING HINGES

You will notice that hinges are recessed into the surface of the door edge and the doorjamb. This recess is called a *mortise,* and it allows the door to mate tightly with the doorjamb. If you replace or add hinges to a door or install a new door, you will have to make mortises in the door and doorjamb.

Professional door carpenters use an inexpensive tool called a *butt gauge* to make precise marks in the door edge and doorjamb to guide the chiseling of mortises. Buy a butt gauge sized for the hinges you plan to install (common sizes are 3½ or 4 inches).

Lay the butt gauge against the door or doorjamb in the position of the hinge. Drive the butt gauge into the wood with a hammer—it will go about $\frac{1}{16}$ inch into the wood. Tap the underside of the butt gauge with a hammer to remove it. The gauge will leave cuts in the wood, outlining the proper mortise. Simply chisel out the wood from the outlines, and you have your mortise.

NAILING

Professional carpenters agree that the chance of injuring your fingers when nailing is reduced if you hold the nail with only two fingers (thumb and index) and place them high on the shank of the nail. The closer your fingers are to the head of the nail, the more conscious you are of them, and you will apply more concentration to hitting the head of the nail squarely.

When nailing flooring and stair treads, you will achieve better holding power with common nails if you angle the nail slightly as you drive it. The proper angle is about 10 degrees off vertical.

If you are having trouble with wood splitting as you drive nails, try blunting the end of the nail. Place the head of the nail on a secure surface and pound the point of the nail blunt with your hammer. The blunt nail will chew through the wood instead of parting it and will tend to reduce splitting. With some hardwood and thick softwood lumber, you may have to drill pilot holes in the wood to drive thick nails without splitting the wood.

When using masonry nails, always try to drive into mortar joints and not into solid brick or stone. If you must drive into solid masonry, drill pilot holes with a masonry drill or use lead masonry anchors.

PAINTING WITH FIVE-GALLON BUCKETS

Professional painters buy interior latex paint in 5-gallon plastic buckets for economy and ease of handling. You can roll your paint directly from these buckets without using roller pans. Simply buy several plastic or metal roller grids from your paint supplier. These grids fit into the 5-gallon buckets and secure to the lips. The grids let you pick up paint on your roller from the bucket and trim off any excess by moving the roller on the grid. Using buckets and grids is a very economical and effective paint-rolling system.

PRYING OFF WOODWORK

If you must remove woodwork (such as baseboards, shoe and cap molding, window and door casing) and you wish to recycle it, you need to pry it off carefully to reduce the chance of damaging it. Break the paint seal between pieces of woodwork with a utility knife or razor blade. Run the knife along the joint between the wall and woodwork, between the woodwork and any framing pieces, and between separate pieces of woodwork (such as baseboard, cap molding, and shoe molding). When you pry the woodwork off, the old paint usually won't stick, and this reduces the chances of cracking or splitting delicate pieces.

Use a wide-blade brick chisel to do the initial prying. Drive the chisel gently between the woodwork and the wall or framing. Once the chisel is in, use a 1-foot wrecking bar or your claw hammer to pull the piece out further. You may have to use the chisel and bar or hammer several places along the piece to pull it free. If you are concerned about marring the wall or woodwork, use pieces of cardboard, ⅛-inch paneling, or hardboard behind the chisel, bar, and hammer. Use pieces of 2 x 4 between your prying tools and the wall or floor to get extra leverage.

⤳ PUTTY IN NAIL HOLES

If you use a powdered-latex putty mix to fill small countersunk nail or screw holes in floors and cabinets, you can mix sawdust with the putty to make a match with the wood. Mix sawdust from your wood in equal parts with powdered-latex putty to make a matching putty for holes. The sawdust will color the putty a bit and will tend to take up any stain or urethane you use in the same way as the general wood surface.

⤳ THREADED FITTINGS

In America all standard nuts, screws, and threaded fittings (including plumbing hardware) tighten when turned clockwise and loosen when turned counterclockwise. This general rule also applies to plumbing valves, taps, shut-offs, and faucets—flow is started by turning clockwise and stopped by turning counterclockwise.

One notable exception to this general rule is in the use of a stud extractor. This tool is used to remove broken-off threaded fittings. The stud extractor tightens when turned counterclockwise so that the tool has a bite on the threaded stump as it backs out of the hole.

Index

HOW TO (Index to step-by-step procedures)

INDEX